Vue.js 2 and Bootstrap 4 Web Development

Build Responsive SPAs with Bootstrap 4, Vue.js 2, and Firebase

Olga Filipova

BIRMINGHAM - MUMBAI

Vue.js 2 and Bootstrap 4 Web Development

First published: September 2017

Production reference: 1250917

Published by Packt Publishing Ltd.
Livery Place
35 Livery Street
Birmingham B3 2PB, UK.

ISBN 978-1-78829-092-0

www.packtpub.com

Credits

Author
Olga Filipova

Project Coordinator
Ulhas Kambali

Reviewer
Jan-Christian Nikles

Proofreader
Safis Editing

Commissioning Editor
Kunal Chaudhari

Indexer
Rekha Nair

Acquisition Editor
Reshma Raman

Graphics
Abhinash Sahu

Content Development Editor
Nikhil Borkar

Production Coordinator
Melwyn Dsa

Technical Editor
Jijo Maliyekal

Cover Work
Melwyn Dsa

Copy Editor
Safis Editing

About the Author

Olga Filipova was born in Kyiv, in Ukraine. She grew up in a family of physicists, scientists, and professors. She studied system analysis in the National University of Ukraine Kyiv Polytechnic Institute. At the age of 20, she moved to Portugal, where she did her bachelors' and masters' degrees in computer science from the University of Coimbra. During her studies, she participated in the research and development of European projects and became an assistant teacher of operating systems and computer graphics subjects. After obtaining her masters' degree, she started working at Feedzai. At that time, it was a small team of four, starting the development of a product from scratch, and now, it is one of the most successful Portuguese start-ups. At some point, her main responsibility became to develop a library written in JavaScript whose purpose was to bring data from the engine to the web interface. This marked Olga's main direction in tech: web development. At the same time, she continued her teaching practice, giving a course of professional web development to the local professional education center in Coimbra.

In 2013, along with her brother and her husband, she started an educational project based in Ukraine. This project's name is EdEra and it has grown up from a small platform of online courses into a big player at the Ukrainian educational system scene. Currently, EdEra is moving towards an international direction and preparing an awesome online course about IT. Don't miss it!

In 2014, Olga, with her husband and daughter, moved from Portugal to Berlin, where she started working at Meetrics as a frontend engineer and, after a year, became the team lead of an amazing team of frontend software developers. Currently Olga works in a fintech company called OptioPay as a lead frontend engineer.

Olga is happily married to an awesome guy called Rui, who is also a software engineer. Rui studied with Olga at the university of Coimbra and worked with her at Feedzai. Olga has a smart and beautiful daughter, Taissa, a fluffy cat, Patusca, and two fluffiest chinchillas, Barabashka and Cheburashka.

Acknowledgments

I would like to thank the people and the teams that surround me.

First of all, a huge thank you goes to the Packt team. You are amazing in supporting this process and striving for quality and delivery. Thank you, Nikhil, for being with me all this time and providing me with all the necessary and just-in-time feedback.

My Meetrics team not only gave me an invaluable moral support but also helped me with the book's content. Safi did a UI/UX investigation and helped me with the initial mockups for the application. Jan Christian made a thorough technical review of the book. His deep technical understanding helped me improve the code and his attention to tiny details helped me improve my writing and my way of expressing and approaching some subjects. Thanks a lot!

My EdEra team has given me great help and support. My friends from EdEra Berlin, thank you for helping me with ideas, thank you for listening and brainstorming with me, and thank you for helping me with CSS. Oleg, Jenia, and Nadia, you are awesome!

How can you create a great application if you are a total noob in design? You can't! But if you have friends who can help you with design, you are the happiest person on Earth. Thank you, Vanessa, for helping me with the application design and thank you, Filipe for helping me with its implementation. Thank you, Carina, for the fantastic logo!

Thank you, Marina for your friendship and for being the first person who heard the idea of ProFitOro and encouraged me to go ahead.

Thank you, mom and dad, for being with me and believing in me. Thank you my wonderful brother, Ilia, for being an inspiring example for me. Thank you Ukraine, for being with me in my heart. Thank you Portugal, for being my second Ukraine. Thank you Berlin, for being such a great city that helps people in being creative.

Thank you, my little Taissa, for being the reason for me to work and try my best. I know that you are proud of me, and this is something that drives me.

Thank you, my beloved husband, Rui, for reviewing all my chapters. Thank you for your patience. Thank you for your love.

About the Reviewer

Jan-Christian Nikles had already started tinkering around with computers in his teenage years and had developed a strong passion for it. After graduating from high school, he first followed a different path and studied audio engineering, since music plays a big role in his life.

He worked in this business for several years, mostly in television production. But soon enough, he found his way back to his old passion.

Graduating in media computer science at the Beuth University of Applied Science, Berlin, in 2013, Jan worked in multiple companies—agency work, early-stage start-ups, and, most recently, at Meetrics. While coming from a fullstack background originally, he specialized in frontend development with cutting-edge technologies. The fast paced JavaScript ecosystem both overwhelmed and fascinated him, but his fascination lasted eventually. He saw the whole thing starting from Vanilla JS, over the big, messy jQuery era, leading to very sophisticated frameworks that make JavaScript development such a pleasure these days. Jan lives and works in Berlin, Germany, always looking for new and interesting projects.

www.PacktPub.com

eBooks, discount offers, and more

Did you know that Packt offers eBook versions of every book published, with PDF and ePub files available? You can upgrade to the eBook version at www.PacktPub.com and as a print book customer, you are entitled to a discount on the eBook copy. Get in touch with us at customercare@packtpub.com for more details.

At www.PacktPub.com, you can also read a collection of free technical articles, sign up for a range of free newsletters and receive exclusive discounts and offers on Packt books and eBooks.

https://www.packtpub.com/mapt

Get the most in-demand software skills with Mapt. Mapt gives you full access to all Packt books and video courses, as well as industry-leading tools to help you plan your personal development and advance your career.

Why subscribe?

- Fully searchable across every book published by Packt
- Copy and paste, print, and bookmark content
- On demand and accessible via a web browser

Customer Feedback

Thanks for purchasing this Packt book. At Packt, quality is at the heart of our editorial process. To help us improve, please leave us an honest review on this book's Amazon page at https://www.amazon.com/dp/1788290925.

If you'd like to join our team of regular reviewers, you can e-mail us at customerreviews@packtpub.com. We award our regular reviewers with free eBooks and videos in exchange for their valuable feedback. Help us be relentless in improving our products!

I dedicate this book to my daughter, Taissa.

Table of Contents

Preface   **v**

Chapter 1: Please Introduce Yourself – Tutorial   **1**

Hello, user   **1**

Creating a project in the Firebase console   **2**

Adding a first entry to the Firebase application database   3

Scaffolding a Vue.js application   **4**

Connecting the Vue.js application to the Firebase project   6

Adding a Bootstrap-powered markup   **10**

Adding a form using Bootstrap   13

Making things functional with Vue.js   **14**

Adding utility functions to make things look nicer   17

Exercise   19

Extracting message cards to their own component   19

Exercise   21

Deploying your application   **22**

Extra mile – connecting your Firebase project to a custom domain   **24**

Summary   **25**

Chapter 2: Under the Hood – Tutorial Explained   **27**

Vue.js   **28**

Vue project – getting started   31

Including directly in script   31

CDN   31

NPM   31

Vue-cli   31

Vue directives   32

Conditional rendering   33

Text versus HTML   34

Loops   37

Binding data   38
Handling events   41
Vue components   46
Exercise   52
Vue router   53
Vuex state management architecture   57
Bootstrap   **66**
Bootstrap components   67
Bootstrap utilities   70
Bootstrap layout   70
Combining Vue.js and Bootstrap   **71**
Exercise   73
Combining Vue.js and Bootstrap continued   74
What is Firebase?   **75**
Summary   **78**
Chapter 3: Let's Get Started   **79**
Stating the problem   **80**
Gathering requirements   **81**
Personas   **82**
User stories   **84**
Retrieving nouns and verbs   **85**
Nouns   86
Verbs   86
Mockups   **88**
The first page – login and register   90
The main page displaying the Pomodoro timer   91
Workout during the break   92
Settings   93
Statistics   94
Workouts   95
Logo   96
Summary   **97**
Chapter 4: Let It Pomodoro!   **99**
Scaffolding the application   **99**
Defining ProFitOro components   **101**
Exercise   106
Implementing the Pomodoro timer   **106**
SVG and trigonometry   107
Exercise   116
Implementing the countdown timer component   117

Responsiveness and adaptiveness of the countdown
timer using Bootstrap   119
Countdown timer component – let's count down time!   122
Exercise   128
Pomodoro timer   128
Exercise   131
Introducing workouts   **133**
Summary   **135**

Chapter 5: Configuring Your Pomodoro   **137**
Setting up a Vuex store   **137**
Defining actions and mutations   **145**
Setting up a Firebase project   **149**
Connecting the Vuex store to the Firebase database   **150**
Exercise   **155**
Summary   **155**

Chapter 6: Please Authenticate!   **157**
AAA explained   **157**
How does authentication work with Firebase?   **158**
**How to connect the Firebase authentication API to a web
application**   **161**
Authenticating to the ProFitOro application   **162**
Making the authentication UI great again   **168**
Managing the anonymous user   **171**
Personalizing the Pomodoro timer   **173**
Updating a user's profile   **177**
Summary   **182**

**Chapter 7: Adding a Menu and Routing Functionality Using
vue-router and Nuxt.js**   **183**
Adding navigation using vue-router   **185**
Exercise - restrict the navigation according to the authentication   188
Using Bootstrap navbar for navigation links   **189**
Code splitting or lazy loading   **194**
Server-side rendering   **196**
Nuxt.js   **196**
Adding links with nuxt-link   200
Exercise – making the menu button work   203
Nuxt.js and Vuex store   203
Nuxt.js middleware   204
Exercise – finish 'em all!   205
Summary   **206**

Chapter 8: Let's Collaborate – Adding New Workouts Using Firebase Data Storage and Vue.js **207**
Creating layouts using Bootstrap classes **208**
Making the footer nice **210**
Storing new workouts using the Firebase real-time database **211**
Storing images using the Firebase data storage **216**
Let's search! 220
Using a Bootstrap modal to show each workout **223**
Exercise 227
It's time to apply some style **227**
Summary **231**
Chapter 9: Test Test and Test **233**
Why is testing important? **235**
What is Jest? **236**
Getting started with Jest **236**
Coverage 239
Testing utility functions **240**
Mocking with Jest 242
Testing Vuex store with Jest **246**
Testing mutations 247
Asynchronous testing with Jest – testing actions 248
Making Jest work with Vuex, Nuxt.js, Firebase, and Vue components **254**
Testing Vue components using Jest **256**
Snapshot testing with Jest **259**
Summary **263**
Chapter 10: Deploying Using Firebase **265**
Deploying from your local machine **265**
Setting up CI/CD using CircleCI **268**
Setting up staging and production environments **276**
What have we achieved? **279**
Summary **280**
Index **283**

Preface

This book is about web development using Vue.js, Bootstrap, and Firebase. We will start with a simple tutorial, followed by the detailed explanation of it, and then, we will create a fully functional application from scratch. The application itself is a simple Pomodoro timer with integrated office workouts during the Pomodoro breaks. Throughout the book, you will go through the whole software development process, starting from the definition of requirements, user stories, and mockups, proceeding to the basic scaffolding, and followed by enriching the application with complex features such as authentication, routing, collaborative content, and finishing thorough testing and deployment. You will learn how to use Firebase to implement the authentication and storage for your Vue application and, in the end, how to deploy it. You will enjoy using Bootstrap along with your Vue application in order to easily implement complex components and achieve their responsiveness. You will revisit your trigonometry knowledge by having fun in using it with SVG and Vue.js to build a reactive timer component. So, technology-wise, we will cover as the following topics:

- Vue.js data binding and single file components
- Routing using vue-router
- Server-side rendering and code splitting using nuxt.js
- Testing with jest
- Real-time databases with Firebase
- Authentication using Firebase Authentication
- Deployment using Firebase
- Combining SVG, trigonometry, and Vue.js in reactive components

In the end, you will have your fully functional and fun Pomodoro application ready to use on a daily basis and to keep you fit at your workplace.

What this book covers

Chapter 1, Please Introduce Yourself, covers a tutorial that implements a "Hello, I am <name>" page. It uses Vue.js, combined with Bootstrap, for the basic form and Firebase for basic storage.

Chapter 2, Under the Hood - Tutorial Explained, explains the technologies used in the first chapter — Vue.js, Bootstrap, and Firebase. Not only does it cover each framework or service but it also explains how these tools can work together.

Chapter 3, Let's Get Started, describes what is going to be implemented during the course of the book. It describes the application and its requirements. It contains some user stories and defines the functionality of the application.

Chapter 4, Let it Pomodoro!, covers the bootstrapping phase of the Vue.js application using the Webpack loader. It adds the basic functionality to the Pomodoro timer. It also explains how to use Bootstrap's grid along with basic Vue.js directives.

Chapter 5, Configuring Your Pomodoro, enriches the application with configuration and personalization. It also covers data storage and retrieval mechanisms using the Firebase database and the Vuex state management architecture. It covers the usage of Bootstrap modals and forms along with the component system of Vue.js.

Chapter 6, Please Authenticate!, adds the authentication based on the Firebase auth API to the application. On the visualization layer, it explains how to build forms powered by Bootstrap.

Chapter 7, Adding a Menu and Routing Functionality Using vue-router and Nuxt.js, explains how to embed the navigation menu into the application using Bootstrap's elements and a routing functionality with the Vue router. It also describes how to use nuxt.js in order to achieve server-side rendering, code splitting, and routing in Vue applications.

Chapter 8, Let's Collaborate - Adding New Workouts Using Firebase Data Storage and Vue.js, adds collaborative content to the application. Again, it uses Bootstrap-powered forms, Vue.js to add reactivity to these forms, and Firebase to store the collaborative content.

Chapter 9, Test Test and Test, describes how to add unit and end-to-end tests to the Vue.js application.

Chapter 10, Deploying Using Firebase, covers the process of deployment of the application using the Firebase hosting solution.

What you need for this book

The requirements for this book are as follows:

- A computer with an active internet connection
- Text editor/IDE
- Node.js

Who this book is for

This book is for web developers or for someone who wants to become one. You will build a full-stack web application from scratch until its deployment. Even if you are an experienced programmer, you will probably find something new for yourself. If you are working with Vue.js, you will find out how to connect a Vue.js application to the Google Firebase backend. If you work with Bootstrap, you will learn how nicely it plays along with a Vue.js application. If you already work with Vue.js, Bootstrap, and Firebase, you will find out how to leverage the power of these three things to easily build complex applications. If you already use these technologies together, you will have fun building yet another application during the course of this book.

Conventions

In this book, you will find a number of text styles that distinguish between different kinds of information. Here are some examples of these styles and an explanation of their meaning.

Code words in text, database table names, folder names, filenames, file extensions, pathnames, dummy URLs, user input, and Twitter handles are shown as follows: " Now run `npm install` inside the newly created directory "

A block of code is set as follows:

```
//LandingPage.vue
export default {
  components: {
    Logo,
    Authentication,
    GoToAppLink,
    Tagline
  }
}
```

When we wish to draw your attention to a particular part of a code block, the relevant lines or items are set in bold:

```
//LandingPage.vue
export default {
  components: {
    Logo,
    Authentication,
    GoToAppLink,
    Tagline
  }
}
```

Any command-line input or output is written as follows:

```
# npm install sass-loader node-sass --save-dev
```

New terms and **important words** are shown in bold. Words that you see on the screen, for example, in menus or dialog boxes, appear in the text like this: "Clicking the **Next** button moves you to the next screen."

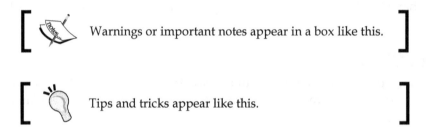

> Warnings or important notes appear in a box like this.

> Tips and tricks appear like this.

Reader feedback

Feedback from our readers is always welcome. Let us know what you think about this book—what you liked or disliked. Reader feedback is important for us as it helps us develop titles that you will really get the most out of.

To send us general feedback, simply e-mail feedback@packtpub.com, and mention the book's title in the subject of your message.

If there is a topic that you have expertise in and you are interested in either writing or contributing to a book, see our author guide at www.packtpub.com/authors.

Customer support

Now that you are the proud owner of a Packt book, we have a number of things to help you to get the most from your purchase.

Downloading the example code

You can download the example code files for this book from your account at http://www.packtpub.com. If you purchased this book elsewhere, you can visit http://www.packtpub.com/support and register to have the files e-mailed directly to you.

You can download the code files by following these steps:

1. Log in or register to our website using your e-mail address and password.
2. Hover the mouse pointer on the **SUPPORT** tab at the top.
3. Click on **Code Downloads & Errata**.
4. Enter the name of the book in the **Search** box.
5. Select the book for which you're looking to download the code files.
6. Choose from the drop-down menu where you purchased this book from.
7. Click on **Code Download**.

You can also download the code files by clicking on the **Code Files** button on the book's webpage at the Packt Publishing website. This page can be accessed by entering the book's name in the **Search** box. Please note that you need to be logged in to your Packt account.

Once the file is downloaded, please make sure that you unzip or extract the folder using the latest version of:

* WinRAR / 7-Zip for Windows
* Zipeg / iZip / UnRarX for Mac
* 7-Zip / PeaZip for Linux

The code bundle for the book is also hosted on GitHub at https://github.com/PacktPublishing/Vue.js-2-and-Bootstrap-4-Web-Development. We also have other code bundles from our rich catalog of books and videos available at https://github.com/PacktPublishing/. Check them out!

Downloading the color images of this book

We also provide you with a PDF file that has color images of the screenshots/ diagrams used in this book. The color images will help you better understand the changes in the output. You can download this file from `https://www.packtpub. com/sites/default/files/downloads/Vuejs2andBootstrap4WebDevelopment_ ColorImages.pdf`.

Errata

Although we have taken every care to ensure the accuracy of our content, mistakes do happen. If you find a mistake in one of our books—maybe a mistake in the text or the code—we would be grateful if you could report this to us. By doing so, you can save other readers from frustration and help us improve subsequent versions of this book. If you find any errata, please report them by visiting `http://www.packtpub. com/submit-errata`, selecting your book, clicking on the **Errata Submission Form** link, and entering the details of your errata. Once your errata are verified, your submission will be accepted and the errata will be uploaded to our website or added to any list of existing errata under the Errata section of that title.

To view the previously submitted errata, go to `https://www.packtpub.com/books/ content/support` and enter the name of the book in the search field. The required information will appear under the **Errata** section.

Piracy

Piracy of copyrighted material on the Internet is an ongoing problem across all media. At Packt, we take the protection of our copyright and licenses very seriously. If you come across any illegal copies of our works in any form on the Internet, please provide us with the location address or website name immediately so that we can pursue a remedy.

Please contact us at `copyright@packtpub.com` with a link to the suspected pirated material.

We appreciate your help in protecting our authors and our ability to bring you valuable content.

Questions

If you have a problem with any aspect of this book, you can contact us at `questions@packtpub.com`, and we will do our best to address the problem.

1
Please Introduce Yourself – Tutorial

Hello, user

Hello dear reader, my name is Olga. Would you like to introduce yourself as well? Open `https://pleaseintroduceyourself.xyz/` and leave a message for me and the other readers.

The page itself doesn't look like anything special. It's just a web page that allows users to write a message, and then, this message is immediately displayed along with the other users' messages in a reverse chronological order:

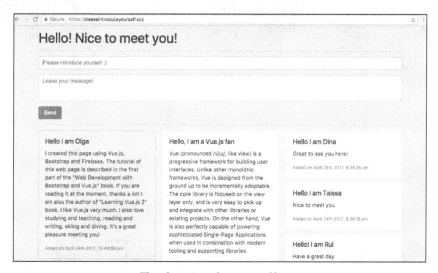

The please introduce yourself page

Do you want to know how long it took me to create this page? It took me around half an hour, and I am not only talking about writing the HTML markup or reversing the order of the messages but also about the database setup, deployment, and hosting.

You probably noticed that the very first message never changes, and it's actually my message where I wrote that I love to learn and teach. This is indeed true. That's why I will devote this chapter to teaching you how to create the exact same page in just 15 minutes. Are you ready? Let's go!

Creating a project in the Firebase console

If you still don't have a Google account but you really want to continue with this tutorial, then well, I am really sorry, but you will have to create one this time. Firebase is a service powered by Google, so a Google account is more than required.

If you already have your account, log in to the Firebase console:

`https://console.firebase.google.com/.`

Let's start by creating your new Firebase project. Click on the **Add project** button. Give it a meaningful name and select your country from the list. Once you are done, click on **CREATE PROJECT**:

Create a project using the Firebase console

You're done! Now, you can use the Firebase-powered backend for your application, including a real-time database, authentication mechanism, hosting, and analytics.

Adding a first entry to the Firebase application database

Let's add the first database entry. Click on the **Database** tab on the left-hand side. You should see a dashboard similar to this one:

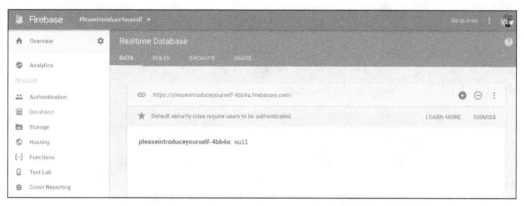

Real-time database on the Firebase project dashboard

Let's add an entry called `messages` and the very first message as a key-value object containing `title`, `text`, and `timestamp` by clicking on the plus sign:

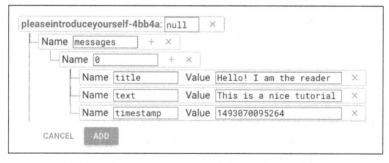

Adding the first value to the Firebase real-time database

Click on the **ADD** button, and your database will persist the added entry. Add as many message entries as you wish or leave it like that. Now, for the sake of simplicity, let's change the rules of our database and make it readable and writable for everyone. Beware! Never do this for something in production for public usage. In this example, we just want to test some Firebase features, but your future applications must be smart and secure. Click on the **RULES** tab and type the following rules in the opened text area:

```
{
  "rules": {
    ".read": true,
    ".write": true
  }
}
```

So, your **RULES** tab now looks like this:

Rules tab after changing the rules

Click on the **PUBLISH** button and you're done! Now, it would be interesting to start using this data within our application. However, first we have to create this application and connect it to our project.

Scaffolding a Vue.js application

In this section, we will create a *Vue.js* application and connect it to the Firebase project that we created in the previous step. Make sure you have *Node.js* installed on your system.

You must also install Vue.js. Check out the instructions page from the official Vue documentation at `https://vuejs.org/v2/guide/installation.html`. Alternatively, simply run the `npm install` command:

```
$ npm install -g vue-cli
```

Now, everything is ready to start scaffolding our application. Go to the folder where you want your application to reside and type the following line of code:

```
vue init webpack please-introduce-yourself
```

It will ask you several questions. Just choose the default answer and hit *Enter* for each of them. After the initialization, you are ready to install and run your application:

```
cd please-introduce-yourself
```

```
npm install
```

```
npm run dev
```

If everything is fine, the following page will automatically open in your default browser:

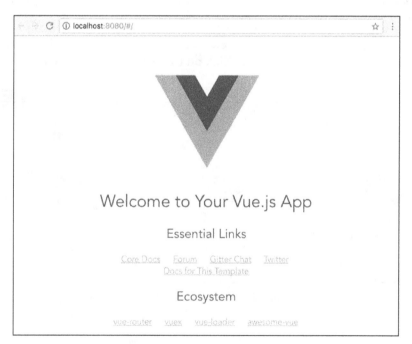

Default Vue.js application after installing and running

If not, check the Vue.js official installation page again.

Connecting the Vue.js application to the Firebase project

To be able to connect your application to the Firebase project, you must install *Firebase* and *VueFire*. Run the npm install command while being in the root directory of your new application:

```
cd please-introduce-yourself
npm install firebase vuefire --save
```

Now, you can use Firebase's powerful features inside your application. Let's check if it worked! We just have to do the following:

- Import Firebase
- Create a config object containing the Firebase app ID, project domain, database domain, and some other stuff needed to connect it to our project
- Write the code that will use the Firebase API and the created config file to connect to the Firebase project.
- Use it

Where do we get the necessary information for the configuration of our Firebase instance? Go to the Firebase console, click on the cog to the right of the **Overview** tab, and select **Project Settings**. Now, click on the **Add Firebase to your web app** button:

Click on the Add Firebase to your web app button

A popup with all the information we need will open:

All the information needed for the config object is here

OK, now, just leave this popup open, go to your Vue application, and open the `main.js` file that resides in the `src` directory of your application. Here, we need to tell our Vue application that it will use VueFire. In this way, we will be able to use all the features provided by Firebase inside our application. Add the following lines to the import section of the `main.js` file:

```
//main.js
import VueFire from 'vuefire'
Vue.use(VueFire)
```

Great! Now, open the `App.vue` file. Here, we will import Firebase and initialize our Firebase application inside the Vue application. Add the following lines of code inside the `<script>` tags:

```
//App.vue
<script>
  import Firebase from 'firebase'

  let config = {
    apiKey: 'YOUR_API_KEY',
    authDomain: 'YOUR_AUTH_DOMAIN',
    databaseURL: 'YOUR_DATABASE_URL',
    projectId: 'YOUR_PROJECT_ID',
    storageBucket: 'YOUR_STORAGE_BUCKET',
    messagingSenderId: 'YOUR_MESSAGING_SENDER_ID'
  }

  let app = Firebase.initializeApp(config)
</script>
```

Copy what's needed for the `config` object information from the popup that we opened in the previous step.

Now, we will obtain the reference to our messages database object. It is pretty simple using the Firebase API:

```
//App.vue
<script>
  <...>
  let db = app.database()
  let messagesRef = db.ref('messages')
</script>
```

We're almost done. Now, we just have to export the `messages` object in the Vue data object so that we are able to use it inside the template section. So, inside the `export` section, add an entry with the `firebase` key and point `messages` to `messagesRef`:

```
export default {
  firebase: {
    messages: messagesRef
  },
}
```

Now, inside the `<template>` tag, we will use a `v-for` directive to iterate through the `messages` array and print all the information about each message. Remember that each message is composed of `title`, `text`, and `timestamp`. So, add the following `<div>` to the template:

```
//App.vue
<div v-for="message in messages">
  <h4>{{ message.title }}</h4>
  <p>{{ message.text }}</p>
  <p>{{ message.timestamp }}</p>
</div>
```

In the end, your `App.vue` component will look like this:

```
//App.vue
<template>
  <div id="app">
    <div v-for="message in messages">
      <h4>{{ message.title }}</h4>
      <p>{{ message.text }}</p>
      <p>{{ message.timestamp }}</p>
    </div>
  </div>
```

```
  </template>

  <script>
    import Firebase from 'firebase'

    let config = {
      apiKey: 'YOUR_API_KEY',
      authDomain: 'YOUR_AUTH_DOMAIN',
      databaseURL: 'YOUR_DATABASE_URL',
      projectId: 'YOUR_PROJECT_ID',
      storageBucket: 'YOUR_STORAGE_BUCKET',
      messagingSenderId: 'YOUR_MESSAGING_SENDER_ID'
    }

    let app = Firebase.initializeApp(config)
    let db = app.database()
    let messagesRef = db.ref('messages')
    export default {
      name: 'app',
      firebase: {
        messages: messagesRef
      }
    }
  </script>
```

If you had chosen the default linter settings on the app initialization, the code that you will copy from Firebase and paste into your application will not pass linter. That's because the default linter settings of Vue-cli initialization would require the use of single quotes and no use of semicolon at the end of the line. By the way, *Evan You* is particularly proud of this no semicolon rule. So, bring him this pleasure; remove all the semicolons from the copied code and replace the double quotes with single quotes.

Aren't you curious to check out the page? If you are not running your application already, switch inside the application folder and run it:

```
cd please-introduce-yourself
npm run dev
```

I am pretty sure that you are seeing the following screenshot:

Hello! I am the reader

This is a nice tutorial

1493070095264

The Vue.js web application displaying the information from the Firebase database

Congratulations! You have successfully completed the first part of our tutorial, connecting the Vue.js application to the Firebase real-time database.

Adding a Bootstrap-powered markup

Let's add basic styling to our application by adding Bootstrap and using its classes.

First of all, let's include Bootstrap's CSS and JS files from Bootstrap's CDN. We will use the upcoming version 4, which is still in alpha. Open the `index.html` file and add the necessary `link` and `script` tags inside the `<head>` section:

```
//index.html
<link
rel="stylesheet"
href="https://maxcdn.bootstrapcdn.com/bootstrap/4.0.0-alpha.6/css/
bootstrap.min.css"crossorigin="anonymous">
<script src="https://code.jquery.com/jquery-3.2.1.min.
js"crossorigin="anonymous"></script>
<script src="https://npmcdn.com/tether@1.2.4/dist/js/tether.min.js">
</script>
<script src="https://maxcdn.bootstrapcdn.com/bootstrap/4.0.0-alpha.6/
js/bootstrap.min.js"crossorigin="anonymous">
</script>
```

You've probably noticed that I added *jQuery* and *Tether* dependencies as well; this is because Bootstrap depends on them.

Now, we can use Bootstrap classes and components in our application. Let's start by adding a bit of styling using Bootstrap's classes.

I will wrap the whole app `div` tag into the `jumbotron` class, and then, I will wrap the content of it into the `container` class. So, the template will look a bit different:

```
//App.vue
<template>
  <div id="app" class="jumbotron">
    <div class="container">
      <h1>Hello! Nice to meet you!</h1>
    <hr />
    <div v-for="message in messages">
    <...>
    </div>
  </div>
</div>
</template>
```

Check out the page; doesn't it look different? Now, I would like to wrap up the content of each message into the `card` class. Cards seem to be an appropriate container for this kind of things. Check out the official Bootstrap documentation regarding cards at `https://v4-alpha.getbootstrap.com/components/card/`. I will add `div` tag with a `card-group` class and put all the cards with messages inside this container. Thus, I don't need to be worried about the positioning and layout. Everything becomes responsive just by itself! So, the markup for the messages will look like this:

```
//App.vue
<template>
<...>
  <div class="card-group">
    <div class="card" v-for="message in messages">
      <div class="card-block">
        <h5 class="card-title">{{ message.title }}</h5>
        <p class="card-text">{{ message.text }}</p>
        <p class="card-text"><small class="text-muted">Added on
        {{ message.timestamp }}</small></p>
      </div>
    </div>
  </div>
</template>
```

Check out the page. It's almost looking nice! In a few steps, we were able to nicely display the messages that are stored in our Firebase database. Try to add another message using the Firebase real-time database dashboard. Keep the web page open! Fill in the Firebase database fields:

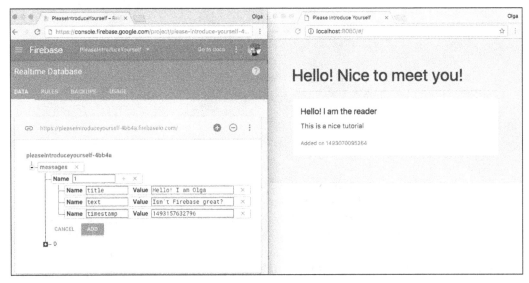

Adding an entry to the Firebase database

Now, click on the **ADD** button. The new message automatically appears on your web page:

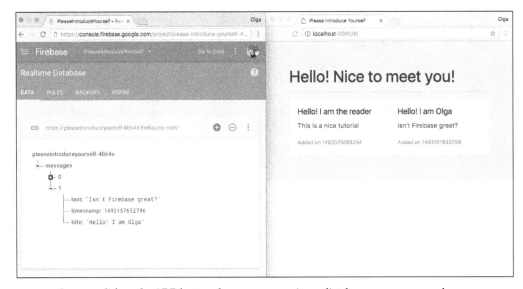

Once we click on the ADD button, the new message immediately appears on our web page

Isn't it great? Now, we can add as many messages as we want. We can also delete them and manipulate them, and all changes will be automatically propagated to our web page. This is pretty nice, but do we really want to keep playing with our backend database to see something changing on the web page? Of course, not! We want the users of our page to be able to add their messages using our page and not our database dashboard. Let's go back to our Vue.js application and add a form that will allow us to add new messages.

Adding a form using Bootstrap

Let's add a simple form to our application that will enable us to add new messages to our message board. Check Bootstrap's documentation regarding forms at `https://v4-alpha.getbootstrap.com/components/forms/`.

Let's add a form just before the list of messages. This form will contain the input for the title, the text area for the message, and the submit button. It will look like this:

```
//App.vue
<template>
  <div id="app" class="jumbotron">
    <div class="container">
      <h1>Hello! Nice to meet you!</h1>
      <hr />
      <form>
        <div>
          <input maxlength="40" autofocus placeholder=
          "Please introduce yourself :)" />
        </div>
        <div>
          <textarea placeholder="Leave your message!"  rows="3">
          </textarea>
        </div>
        <button type="submit">Send</button>
      </form>
      <hr />
      <...>
    </div>
  </div>
</template>
```

Look at the page. Doesn't look that beautiful, does it?

Our form doesn't look so beautiful

In fact, let's be honest, it just looks ugly! However, with Bootstrap classes, it is really easy to fix it. If we add the `form-control` class to the `input` and `textarea` elements, the `form-group` class to each `div` tag that surrounds these elements, and probably the `btn btn-primary` class to the `submit` button…well, we will have something nicer!

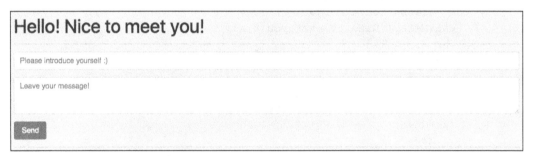

The form looks really nice with the Bootstrap classes

OK, so now we have a nice-looking form, but if we try to fill it out, nothing will happen. We have to make it functional, and for that, we will use the power of Vue.js.

Making things functional with Vue.js

So, what do we want to achieve with our form? We want the new message to be created. This message has to be composed of title, text, and the timestamp. We also want to add this message to our messages reference array.

Let's call this new message `newMessage` and add it to the `data` attributes of `App.vue`:

```
//App.vue
<script>
  <...>
  export default {
    data () {
      return {
        newMessage: {
          title: '',
          text: '',
          timestamp: null
        }
      }
    },
  <...>
  }
</script>
```

Now, let's bind the title and the text of this `newMessage` object to `input` and `textarea` of our form. Let's also bind a method called `addMessage` to the submit handler of our form so that the whole form's markup looks like this:

```
<template>
<...>
  <form @submit="addMessage">
    <div class="form-group">
      <input class="form-control
      "v-model="newMessage.title"maxlength="40"
      autofocus  placeholder="Please introduce yourself :)" />
    </div>
    <div class="form-group">
      <textarea class="form-control"v-model="newMessage.text"
      placeholder="Leave your message!"  rows="3"></textarea>
    </div>
    <button class="btnbtn-primary" type="submit">Send</button>
  </form>
  <...>
</template>
```

Well, we have bound the `"addMessage"` method to the `submit` callback of the form, but we haven't defined this method yet! So, let's define it. Add the `methods` object to our `App.vue` export section and define the `addMessage` method inside it. This method will receive the event attribute from our form and will just grab the `newMessage` object and push it into the `messagesRef` array. Doesn't it sound easy?

```
//App.vue
<script>
  export default {
  <...>
    methods: {
      addMessage (e) {
        e.preventDefault()
        this.newMessage.timestamp = Date.now()
        messagesRef.push(this.newMessage)
      }
    }
  }
</script>
```

Now, open the page, fill in the form, and hit the **Send** button. You'll see your message immediately appearing on the list of messages:

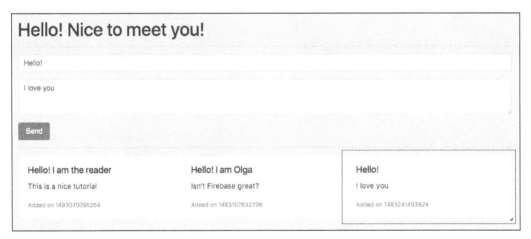

The message we introduce in the form is immediately propagated to the messages list

There is still something we need to fix. We don't want the values we fill the form with to remain there after our message is added to the messages list. So, we need to clear it inside the `addMessage` method. Probably, some basic check, at least for the title, would also be nice. So, rewrite the method as follows:

```
//App.vue
addMessage (e) {
  e.preventDefault()
  if (this.newMessage.title === '') {
    return
  }
  this.newMessage.timestamp = Date.now()
  messagesRef.push(this.newMessage)
  this.newMessage.text = ''
  this.newMessage.title = ''
  this.newMessage.timestamp = null
}
```

Now, if you start adding more messages, things look a bit weird. The way we're displaying the messages is probably not the best way for our case. Do you remember we wrapped up our message cards into `div` with the `card-group` class? Let's try to replace it with the `card-columns` class and check whether it looks better. In fact, it does. Let's keep it like that.

Adding utility functions to make things look nicer

We already have a fully functional single-page application, but it still lacks some awesomeness. For example, it's not really beautiful that the time appears as a timestamp. Let's write the utility function that will transform our timestamp into something beautiful.

We will use the *Moment.js* library (https://momentjs.com/). Install it in the application folder:

```
npm install moment --save
```

Create a folder and call it `utils`. Add a file called `utils.js` to this folder. Import `moment` and write the following function:

```
//utils.js
import moment from 'moment'

function dateToString (date) {
  if (date) {
    return moment(date).format('MMMM Do YYYY, h:mm:ss a')
```

```
    }
    return''
}
```

Export it in the end of the file:

```
//utils.js
<...>
export { dateToString }
```

Let's import this function to `App.vue` and use it to format our timestamp. Open the `App.vue` file and add the `import` statement at the beginning of the `script` section:

```
//App.vue
<script>
  import Firebase from 'firebase'
  import { dateToString } from './utils/utils'
  <...>
</script>
```

In order to be able to use this function within the Vue template, we have to export it in the `methods` section. Just add a new entry to the `methods` object:

```
//App.vue
<script>
  export default {
    <...>
    methods: {
      dateToString: dateToString,
      <...>
    }
</script>
```

Since we use ES6, we can just write the following lines of code:

```
methods: {
  dateToString
}
```

Now, we can use this method inside the template section. Just wrap the `message.timestamp` binding object in the `dataToString` method:

```
<p class="card-text"><small class="text-muted">Added on {{
dateToString(message.timestamp) }}</small></p>
```

Check out the page! Now, you can see beautiful dates instead of Unix timestamps.

Exercise

I have a small exercise for you. You saw how easy it was to add a utility function to transform the timestamp into the nicely formatted date. Now, create another utility function and call it `reverse`. This function should be used to display the array of messages in the reversed order, so the most recent messages should appear first. Check the code for this chapter in case you're in doubt.

Extracting message cards to their own component

You probably noticed that the first message of the demo application is always there. It's not moved by other, fresh message items. So, it seems that it's kind of a special message, and it's treated in a special way. In fact, it is. If you want to make a card sticky, just add it before the `card` element that iterates through other messages. You can also add some class to this card to show that it's really special. In my case, I added Bootstrap's `card-outline-success` class that outlines the element in a nice green color:

```
//App.vue
<div class="card-columns">
  <div class="card card-outline-success">
    <div class="card-block">
      <h5 class="card-title">Hello!</h5>
      <p class="card-text">This is our fixed card!</p>
      <p class="card-text"><small class="text-muted">
      Added on {{ dateToString(Date.now()) }}</small></p>
    </div>
  </div>
  <div class="card" v-for="message in messages">
    <div class="card-block">
      <h5 class="card-title">{{ message.title }}</h5>
      <p class="card-text">{{ message.text }}</p>
      <p class="card-text"><small class="text-muted">
      Added on {{ dateToString(message.timestamp) }}</small></p>
    </div>
  </div>
</div>
```

Now, you have a nice sticky card with a color that differs from other cards' color. But... don't you see any problem? We have the very same code repeated twice in our template. I'm pretty sure that you are aware of the rule of thumb of any developer: DRY — don't repeat yourself!

Let's extract the card to an individual component. It's really easy. Add a component called Card.vue to the components folder. The code for this component is really simple:

```
//Card.vue
<template>
  <div class="card">
    <div class="card-block">
      <h5 class="card-title">{{ title }}</h5>
      <p class="card-text">{{ text }}</p>
      <p class="card-text"><small class="text-muted">
      {{ footer }}</small></p>
    </div>
  </div>
</template>

<script>
  export default {
    props: ['title', 'text', 'footer']
  }
</script>
```

Now, let's invoke this component from App.vue with different values for title, text, and footer. First of all, it should be imported and exported in the Vue components object:

```
//App.vue
<script>
<...>
  import Card from './components/Card'
  <...>
  export default {
  <...>
    components: {
      Card
    }
  }
</script>
```

Now, we can use the `<card>` element within our template. We need to bind title, text, and footer. Footer is actually the text that says **Added on ...**. So, the markup for the first card will look like this:

```
//App.vue
<template>
  <div class="card-columns">
    <card class="card-outline-success":title="'Hello!'"
    :text="'This is our fixed card!'":footer="
    'Added on ' + dateToString(Date.now())"></card>
  </div>
</div>
</template>
```

The list of other messages will follow the same logic. For each message from the `messages` array, we will bind the corresponding message's entries (title, text, and timestamp). So, the markup for the list of message cards will look like this:

```
<div class="card-columns">
<...>
  <card v-for="message in messages"
  :title="message.title":text="message.text":footer="
  'Added on ' + dateToString(message.timestamp)"></card>
</div>
</div>
```

As you can see, we have replaced fourteen lines of code with only two lines! Of course, our component also contains some lines of code, but now, we can reuse it again and again.

Exercise

The way we've extracted the card code into its individual component is, without any doubt, great, but the way we are binding attributes for the first message is a bit ugly. What if at some point we need to change the message's text? First of all, it's not easy to find the text inside the markup. Also, it is pretty difficult to manage the text inside the markup attributes, because we have to be really careful not to mess up with double/single quotes. And, admit it, it's just ugly. Your task for this exercise is to extract title, text, and date for the first message into something nicer (for example, export it in the data object) and bind it the same way we bind other messages. If you have doubts regarding this exercise, check out this chapter's code.

Don't be confused by the v-bind directive in the provided code. We've been using it already, just its shortened version—the name of a bound property written after the semicolon. So, for example, v-bind:messages is the same as :messages.

Deploying your application

Well, now that we have a fully working application in our hands, it's time to make it public. In order to do this, we will deploy it to Firebase.

Start by installing Firebase tools:

```
npm install -g firebase-tools
```

Now, you have to tell your Firebase tools that you are actually a Firebase user who has an account. For this, you have to log in using Firebase tools. Run the following command:

```
firebase login
```

Follow the instructions to log in.

Now, you must initialize Firebase in your application. From the application root, call the following:

```
firebaseinit
```

You will be asked some questions. Select the third option for the first question:

```
? What Firebase CLI features do you want to setup for this directory?
 ◉ Database: Deploy Firebase Realtime Database Rules
 ◉ Functions: Configure and deploy Cloud Functions
❯◉ Hosting: Configure and deploy Firebase Hosting sites
```

Select the Hosting option for the first question

Select the PleaseIntroduceYourself project from the list of projects to associate to the application.

Initialization is over. Check whether the file called `firebase.json` has been created in the project's folder. This file can contain an innumerous number of configurations. Check out the official Firebase documentation in this regard at `https://firebase.google.com/docs/hosting/full-config`. For us, the very basic indication of the public directory to be deployed would be enough. The directory where `vue-cli` builds the production-ready assets is called `dist`; therefore, we will want the content of this directory to be deployed. So, add the following line of code to your `firebase.json` file:

```
{
  "hosting": {
    "public": "dist",
    "ignore": [
      "firebase.json",
      "**/.*",
      "**/node_modules/**"
    ]
  }
}
```

Do not forget to save your `firebase.json` file. Let's now build and deploy our application. Sounds like a big devops task, right? It's not really huge. Run `npm build` and then `firebase deploy`:

```
npm run build
firebase deploy
```

How difficult is it? After the successful deployment, Firebase will output the URL of your project. Now, you can start playing with it and send it to your friends. It's probably not the most beautiful URL in the world, right? Maybe you would like to connect it to your domain? Of course, it is possible!

Extra mile – connecting your Firebase project to a custom domain

It's fairly easy to connect the Firebase project to a custom domain. First of all, of course, you need to buy this domain. For this application, I bought the *pleaseintroduceyourself* domain with the cheapest top-level domain, .xyz. It cost me a bit more than a dollar per year on GoDaddy (https://godaddy.com). After you have your domain, it's really easy. Go to the Firebase web console of the project. Click on the **Hosting** tab on the left-hand side. Then, click on the **CONNECT DOMAIN** button:

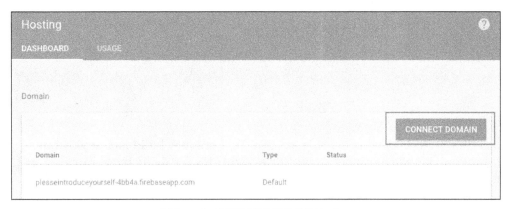

Click on the CONNECT DOMAIN button

In the popup, input your domain name:

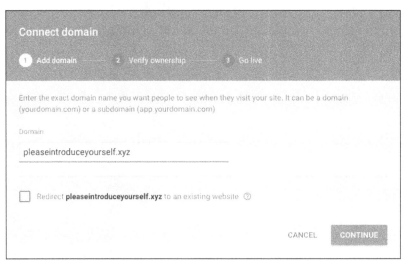

Input your domain name

It will suggest that you add a TXT DNS record to your domain. Just open your DNS provider page, select your domain, find out how to add DNS records, and add the record with the TXT type. In my case, with GoDaddy, the record adding section looks like this:

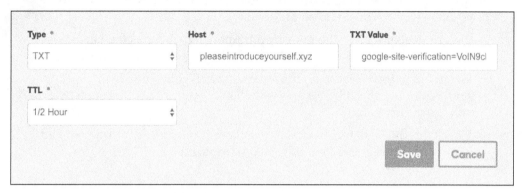

Adding the DNS TXT record to our domain

After the handshake is established (mind, it might take some time), Firebase will propose you the final step—adding the **A** record to your domain. Follow the exact same procedure as in the previous step; just instead of records of type TXT, add records of type **A**.

It will take some time until the changes are completely propagated. In my case, it took around an hour. After a while, you will be able to open your new page with the `https://<your domain>.<your top level domain>` address. In my case, as you already know, it's `https://pleaseintroduceyourself.xyz/`.

Summary

In this chapter, we followed a tutorial where we have developed a single-page application from scratch. We used the Vue.js framework to structure our application, the Bootstrap framework to apply style to it, and the Firebase platform to manage the application's persistence layer and hosting.

In spite of being able to achieve a considerable result (a fully functional deployed application), we did everything without a deep understanding of what is going on behind the scenes. The tutorial didn't explain what Vue.js, Bootstrap, or Firebase was. We just took it for granted.

In the next chapter, we will understand the underlying technologies in detail. We will do the following:

- Take a closer look at the Vue.js framework, starting from a basic understanding and then covering topics such as directives, data binding, components, routing, and so on

- Have a deeper look at the Bootstrap framework, and check what is possible to achieve using it and how to do it

- Get to know the Firebase platform better; we'll gain some basic understanding about it and go through more complex topics such as data storage or functions

- Check out different techniques to use these three different projects to add simplicity, power, and flexibility to our applications

2
Under the Hood – Tutorial Explained

In the previous chapter, we built a simple single-page application from scratch. We used Vue.js to implement the application's functionality, Bootstrap to make it beautiful, and Firebase to manage the backend part of the application.

In this chapter, we will get to know all these technologies in depth and see how and why they can work nicely together. We will mostly discuss Vue.js since this will be our number one framework to build our application. Then, we will touch on Bootstrap and Firebase to get a basic understanding of how powerful these technologies are. Having said that, in this chapter we will:

- Discuss the Vue.js framework, reactivity, and data binding. Not only will we cover Vue.js' basics, but we will also dig into topics such as directives, components, routing, and so on.

- Discuss the Bootstrap framework. We will see what is possible to achieve with it, discuss how it can be useful to lay out an application, and discuss how its components can enrich your application with useful self-contained functionality.

- Discuss the Firebase platform. We will see what it is, what functionalities it provides, and how to use its API to bring those functionalities to the application.

- Check how all the mentioned technologies can be combined together in order to achieve simplicity in the development of complex things.

Vue.js

The official Vue.js website suggests that Vue is a progressive JavaScript framework:

Screenshot from the official Vue.js website

What does that mean? In a very simplified way, I can describe Vue.js as a JavaScript framework that brings reactivity to web applications.

It's undeniable that each and every application has some data and some interface. Somehow, the interface is responsible for displaying data. Data might or might not change during runtime. The interface usually has to react somehow to those changes. The interface might or might not have some interactive elements that might or might not be used by the application's users. Data usually has to react to those interactions, and consequently, other interface elements have to react to the changes that have been done to the data. All of this sounds complex. Part of this complex architecture can be implemented on the backend side, closer to where data resides; the other part of it might be implemented on the frontend side, closer to the interface.

Vue.js allows us to simply bind data to the interface and relax. All the reactions that must happen between data and the interface will happen on their own. Let's look at a very simple example where we will bind a message to the page title. Start by defining a simple HTML structure:

```
<!DOCTYPE html>
<html>
  <head>
  <meta charset="UTF-8">
    <title>Vue.js - binding data</title>
  </head>
  <body>
    <div id="app">
      <h1>Hello, reader! Let's learn Vue.js</h1>
```

```
    </div>
  </body>
</html>
```

Now, let's initialize a **Vue.js** instance on this page and bind its data to the `<h1>` element. For this simple example, we will use a standalone `Vue.js` file. Download it from the Vue.js official page at `https://vuejs.org/js/vue.js`. Import it within the `<script>` tag. Let's now initialize a **Vue** instance. The minimum that a Vue.js instance needs is the **element** to be attached to and the `data` object. We want to attach our Vue instance to the main `<div>` tag with the `app` ID. Let's also create a data object containing an entry for the name:

```
var data = {name:'Olga'}
```

Let's create our Vue.js instance with this data:

```
new Vue({
  el: '#app',
  data
})
```

Let's now bind `data` to our HTML element. We will do this using double curly brackets (`{{}}`). Once the element has been attached to the `Vue` instance, everything that is inside of it becomes special—even the curly brackets. Everything that you put inside the double curly brackets will be interpreted and evaluated. So, if you put, for example, `2 + 2` inside the curly brackets, `4` will be rendered on the page. Just try it. Any expression, any statement will be compiled and calculated. Don't be too excited though; don't start writing chunks of JavaScript code inside those brackets. Let's leave the computation to the script logic that is written where script resides. Use the brackets to access the data that you pass to your `Vue` instance. So, in our case, if you insert `{{name}}` anywhere inside your HTML markup, you will see the name that we passed to the `Vue` instance within the data object. Let's, for example, replace the word `reader` inside the `<h1>` element by `{{name}}`:

```
<h1>Hello, {{name}}! Let's learn Vue.js</h1>
```

If you refresh the page, you will see that the name we passed to the Vue instance is rendered. Try to change the `data.name` attribute in the developer tools console. You will see the changes immediately propagated. What we see here is a **one-way data binding**—the changes that happen to data are reactively propagated to the element to which the data is bound. Vue.js also supports **two-way data binding**; so, the changes that happen to the element on the page are also propagated to the data to which the element is bound.

To achieve this, just bind the given piece of data to the element using the v-model attribute. Let's, for example, add a text input to the page and bind it to the data attribute name:

```
<input type="text"v-model="name">
```

Now, once you start typing in the text input, the change is immediately propagated to any other element bound to this piece of data:

The data changes are reactively propagated through all the bound elements

The complete code for the HTML markup and JavaScript code looks like this:

```
<body>
  <div id="app">
    <div>
      <label for="name">What's your name? </label>
      <input id="name" type="text" v-model="name">
    </div>
    <h1>Hello, <strong>{{name}}</strong>! Let's learn Vue.js</h1>
  </div>
  <script src="vue.js"></script>
  <script>
    var data = {name:'Olga'}

    new Vue({
      el: '#app',
      data
    })
  </script>
</body>
```

As you can see, there is nothing difficult at all. All you need is to pass data to the Vue instance and bind it to the elements of your page. The Vue framework does everything else. In the upcoming chapters, we will find out what else is possible using Vue.js and how to Bootstrap a Vue.js project.

Vue project – getting started

So, now that we know what Vue.js is for and what its main focus is, we would like to get our hands dirty and start a Vue.js project and explore all the Vue.js features with it. There are plenty of ways of including Vue into the project. Let's explore all of them.

Including directly in script

You can use Vue.js by just downloading it and including it within the `<script>` tag. Actually, we've done it in the previous section. So, if you have a project already running and want to use some Vue.js features, you can simply include the `vue.js` file and use it.

CDN

If you don't want to bother downloading and managing Vue versions yourself, you can simply use the CDN version. Just include `https://unpkg.com/vue` script in your project and you are good to go! It will always be in sync with the latest Vue version:

```
<script src="https://unpkg.com/vue"></script>
```

NPM

If you are all into the Node.js development, you can simply add an `npm` dependency to your `package.json` file. Just run `npm install` on your project's root:

```
npm install vue --save
```

Vue-cli

Vue provides a nice and clean command-line interface that is perfect for bootstrapping new projects. First of all, you must install **vue-cli**:

```
npm install --global vue-cli
```

Now, you can start a fresh new project using the Vue command-line interface. Check out the *vue-cli* repository for the detailed documentation at `https://github.com/vuejs/vue-cli`.

As you can see, it is possible to setup a project using different templates — starting from a simple single HTML page project and going to a complex webpack project setup. The command that should be used for scaffolding a Vue project is as follows:

```
vue init <template-name><project-name>
```

The following templates are available:

- **webpack**: This is a full-featured webpack setup with `vue-loader`. It supports hot reload, linting, testing, all kind of pre-processors, and so on.
- **webpack-simple**: This is a simple webpack setup that is useful for quick prototyping.
- **browserify**: This is a full-featured browserify setup with vueify that also supports hot reload, linting, and unit testing.
- **browserify-simple**: This is a simple browserify setup with vueify that can be used for quick prototyping.
- **simple**: This generates a simple HTML page that includes Vue.js. It is perfect for quick feature exploration.

It is also possible to create custom templates. Check out the documentation at `https://github.com/vuejs/vue-cli#custom-templates` and try it.

In this book, we will use the `webpack` template. We will include some loaders, and we will use linters, unit, and end-to-end testing techniques. To bootstrap a project using the `webpack` template, simply run the following line of code:

```
vue init webpack my-project
```

Now that we know how to scaffold a project with *vue-cli*, let's check what Vue offers besides what we already explored in the previous section.

Vue directives

Vue directives are no more than just **attributes** attached to your HTML elements. These directives provide some extra functionality to your template.

All these directives start with the prefix `v-`. Why? Because it's *Vue*! You have already used some of them in the previous section. Now, we will see what directives exist and what you can do with them.

Conditional rendering

Open our Hello page and remove user's input. Something not really beautiful is happening:

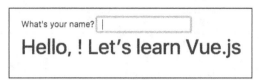

"Hello,!"

It would be interesting to render the **Hello,** name message conditionally, depending on the user input. If there is a name, render it; if there's no name, don't render.

For example, only render the **Hello,** name message if there's a name. Directives v-show and v-if are used exactly for the conditional render. Open the index.html file of this example and let's change it. Wrap the Hello, {{name}}! part into span and add a v-show attribute with the name value:

```
<h1><span v-show="name">Hello, <strong>{{name}}</strong>! </span>Let's
learn Vue.js</h1>
```

Now, if you refresh the page and remove the input completely, the message will only say **Let's learn Vue.js**:

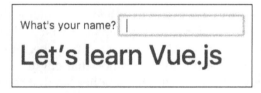

The v-show attribute allows conditional rendering

Try to replace the `v-show` directive with the `v-if` directive. The end result will be quite the same. Why do both exist then? Check out the developer tools' elements tab and try to add or remove the text in the input. You will see that in the case of `v-show`, the conditional span will just gain a `display:none` property if the condition does not verify. In the case of `v-if`, the element disappears completely:

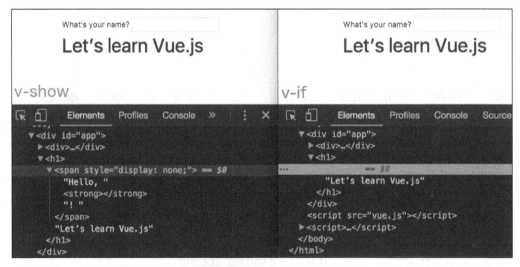

Using the v-show attribute manipulates the display CSS property, whereas using the v-if attribute adds/ removes an element completely

When do we use either attribute? If you have a lot of elements that should be visible depending on some data (this data is really dynamic, so it will happen a lot during the runtime), I would advise using the `v-show` attribute, because adding or removing elements in DOM is a rather expensive operation that might affect the application's performance and even the DOM itself. On the other hand, if the elements should be conditionally rendered only once, let's say, at the application startup, use the `v-if` attribute. If some elements should not appear, they will just not be rendered. Thus, the number of elements on the page will be reduced. Consequently, the computational cost of the application will be also reduced, as, now, it has fewer elements to go through and compute.

Text versus HTML

I am sure you know pretty well from the previous chapter how to bind some data using the mustache syntax {{ }}.

Since this is a technical book about programming, we have to have a cat here 😸!
A cat is pretty easy to render. Its Unicode is `U+1F638`; thus, we just have to add the
`&#x1f638;` code to our HTML:

```
<div>&#x1f638;</div>
```

And, surely, we will have a cat:

Emoji cat saying hello to us

It's nice, but if we want to replace the cat with a dog, we will have to use Google to
look for another Unicode representing a dog and replace it. If at some point we want
to replace it with a unicorn, we will have to run the same procedure. Moreover, just
by looking at our code, we will not be able to say what we are actually rendering
unless we know all emoji codes by `&hearts;`. It might be a good idea to map the
names of the emojis to their codes.

Let's add a map of some of them. Open your HTML file and add the following lines
of code to the `<script>` area:

```
//index.html
<script>
  const animalCodes = {
    dog: '&#x1f436;',
    cat: '&#x1f638;',
    monkey: '&#x1f435;',
    unicorn: '&#x1f984;'
  }
  const data = {
    animalCodes
  }

  new Vue({
    el: '#app',
    data
  })
</script>
```

Now, you can bind the values of this map to your HTML elements. Let's try to do it using the mustache annotation:

```
<div>{{animalCodes.cat}}</div>
```

Refresh the page. The result is not exactly the same as we expected, is it?

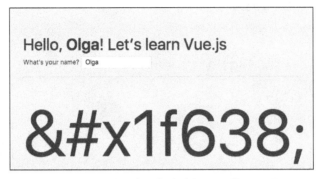

The code is rendered instead of the actual cat emoji

This is happening because mustache interpolation actually interpolates text. Using mustache interpolation is the same as using the `v-text` directive:

```
<div v-text="animalCodes.cat"></div>
```

What we actually want to render here is not the text; we want the value of the Unicode for the emoji being rendered as HTML! This is also possible with Vue.js. Just replace a `v-text` directive with the `v-html` directive:

```
<div v-html="animalCodes.cat"></div>
```

Now, we will get our cat back, and we know exactly what we are rendering when we are looking at the code.

So, remember to use the `v-text` directive or mustache annotation for text interpolation and the `v-html` directive for interpolating pure HTML.

Loops

In the previous section, we put a cat on our page. In this section, I would like to have a whole zoo! Imagine that our zoo has a cat 😺, a dog 🐶 , a monkey 🐵 , and, of course, a unicorn 🦄.We would like to display our zoo in an ordered list. Of course, you can write a simple markup that will look like this:

```
<ol>
  <li>&#x1f638;</li>
  <li>&#x1f436;</li>
  <li>&#x1f435;</li>
  <li>&#x1f984;</li>
</ol>
```

However, this makes your code unreadable, and if you want to add more animals to your zoo or remove one of them, you would have to know all these codes by heart. In the previous section, we added a map for emoji animals Unicode. Let's use it in our markup. You already learned that we must use a v-html directive so that the codes are interpolated as HTML. Hence, our markup will look like this:

```
<div id="app">
  <ol>
    <li v-html="animalCodes.cat"></li>
    <li v-html="animalCodes.dog"></li>
    <li v-html="animalCodes.monkey"></li>
    <li v-html="animalCodes.unicorn"></li>
  </ol>
</div>
```

It looks better, but still there's something we could improve. Imagine if you want to render all the animals from the emoji world! There are plenty of them. For each animal, you will have to repeat the code of the list item. Every time you would like to reorder the list, remove some elements, or add new ones, you will have to deal with this markup. Wouldn't it be nice if we just had an array of animals that we want to render and then somehow iterate over it and render what's inside of it? Of course, it would! It is possible using the v-for directive. Create an array of animals using the following lines of code:

```
const animals = ['dog', 'cat', 'monkey', 'unicorn']
```

Export it in the `vue data` object:

```
var data = {
  name:'Olga',
  animals,
  animalCodes
}
```

Now, you can use this array in the `v-for` directive and replace multiple `<li>` elements by only one:

```
<ol>
<h2><span>{{name}}! </span>Here's your Zoo</h2>
    <li v-for="animal in animals" v-html="animalCodes[animal]"></li>
</ol>
```

The result will be quite nice:

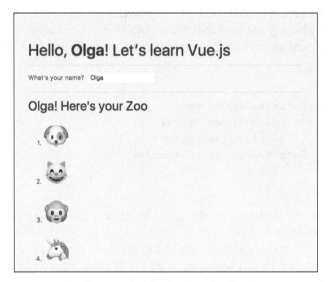

Emoji zoo rendered using the v-for directive

Binding data

We dealt a lot with rendering different data using Vue.js in the previous section; so now, you are already familiar with different ways of binding it. You know how to interpolate data as *text* and as *HTML*, and you know how to iterate over arrays of data.

We've also seen that two-way data binding is achieved using the v-model directive. We used it to bind a name to the input element:

```
<input id="name" type="text" v-model="name">
```

The v-model directive can only be used with the input, select, and textarea elements. It also accepts some modifiers to be used with. Modifiers are special keywords that affect the input in some way. There are three modifiers that can be used with this directive:

- .lazy: This will only update the data on a change event (try it with our input and you'll see that changes in the input will only affect other parts where the name is used when the *Enter* button is pressed and not on each key press)
- .number: This will cast your input to number
- .trim: This will trim the user's input

It is also possible to chain the modifiers:

```
<input id="name" type="text"v-model.lazy.trim="name">
```

So now, we know nearly everything about binding data to the elements. What if we want to bind some data to the elements' properties? Imagine, for example, the dynamic value for the image's source property or class property depending on some data value. How could we do that?

For this, Vue provides a v-bind directive. With this directive, you can bind whatever you want!

As an example, let's show a sad picture when the name is not defined and a glad picture when the name is defined. For this, I've created two pictures, glad.png and sad.png, and put them into the images folder of my application. I will also export their paths into the data object:

```
//index.html
var data = {
  name:'Olga',
  animals,
  animalCodes,
  sadSrc: 'images/sad.png',
  gladSrc: 'images/glad.png'
}
```

Now, I can create an image and bind its source using `v-bind:src`, and I'll provide a JavaScript expression as the value. This expression will check the value of the name. If it's defined, the `glad` image will be applied, and if not, the `sad` image will be applied instead:

```
<img width="100%" v-bind:src="name ? gladSrc : sadSrc">
```

The shortcut for the `v-bind` directive is `:`, so we can just write the following line of code:

```
<img width="100%" :src="name ? gladSrc : sadSrc">
```

Here is how our page looks when the value of `name` is defined:

Happy face image appears when the name is defined

If you remove the name from the input field, the image will automatically change! Open the page and try to remove the text from the input field and add it again. Continue removing and adding, and you will see how fast the image is changed to the corresponding one. This is how the page looks when the name is undefined:

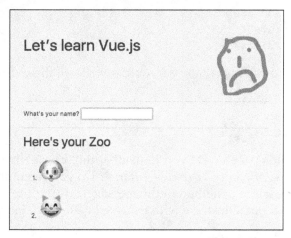

Once the input is cleaned, the image source is immediately changed

Basically, you can do exactly the same with any property binding, for example, class:

```
<label for="name" v-bind:class="{green: name, red: !name}">What's your
name? </label>
```

You can also bind properties to pass to the children components. We will see how to do it in the section about components.

Handling events

Besides the direct form of data binding to the elements, we want to handle some events because this is what our users do on the page — trigger some events so that they happen. They click, they hover, they submit forms — and all these events must be handled somehow by us. Vue provides a very nice way of attaching listeners to events on any DOM element and provides methods that can handle those events. The good thing about these methods is that they have direct access to Vue data using the `this` keyword. In this way, we can use methods to manipulate data, and since this data is reactive, all the changes will be immediately propagated to the elements to which this data is bound.

In order to create a method, you just have to add a `methods` object to the export section of your Vue application. In order to attach this method to any event listener, use the `v-on` directive with the corresponding event after the colon. Here is an example:

```
v-on:sumbit="handleSubmit"
v-on:click="handleClick"
v-on:hover="handleHover"
```

The shortcut for this directive is `@`, so we could rewrite all these directives as follows:

```
@sumbit="handleSubmit"
@click="handleClick"
@hover="handleHover"
```

It should sound familiar to you. Do you remember the tutorial that we followed in the *Chapter 1, Please Introduce Yourself – Tutorial*? Do you remember that we were listening on the `submit` method of the message, adding `form` and calling `addMessage`? Check it out. Our form with its `submit` directive looked like this:

```
//please-introduce-yourself/src/App.vue
<template>
  <form @submit="addMessage">
  <...>
  </form>
</template>
```

Then, inside the `methods` section, we actually had the `addMessage` method defined:

```
//please-introduce-yourself/src/App.vue
<script>
  <...>
  export default {
  <...>
    methods: {
      addMessage (e) {
      <...>
      },
    },
  }
</script>
```

Does it start to make more sense now?

Just to understand it better, let's add some methods to our zoo page! Wouldn't it be nice if you could compose your own zoo? Let's add a multiple select element that will contain all possible options, and your zoo will be populated from something that you actually choose! So, let's do the following:

- Add more animals to our `animalCodes` map
- Add another array called `animalsForZoo`
- Use this new array in our ordered list that displays the zoo
- Add a multiple `select` box composed of the keys of the `animalCodes` map
- Attach a `@change` listener to this select box that will call the `populateAnimalsForZoo` method
- Create a `populateAnimalsForZoo` method that will populate the `animalsForZoo` array with the selected options from our multiple select element

Doesn't it sound easy? Of course, it does! Let's get started. So, at first, add more animals to our `animalCodes` map:

```
var animalCodes = {
    dog      : '&#x1f436;',
    cat      : '&#x1f638;',
    monkey   : '&#x1f435;',
    unicorn  : '&#x1f984;',
    tiger    : '&#x1f42f;',
    mouse    : '&#x1f42d;',
    rabbit   : '&#x1f430;',
    cow      : '&#x1f42e;',
    whale    : '&#x1f433;',
    horse    : '&#x1f434;',
    pig      : '&#x1f437;',
    frog     : '&#x1f438;',
    koala    : '&#x1f43c;'
}
```

Let's also rethink our `animals` array and generate it out of our map. In this way, every time we need to add some new animal, we just add its key-value name-unicode to the mapping object instead of maintaining both object and array. So, our `animals` array will look like this:

```
var animals = Object.keys(animalCodes)
```

Now, we need another empty array. Let's call it `animalsForZoo`, and let's populate our zoo from this new array. Since it is empty, our zoo will also be empty. However, we are about to create a method that will populate this array. So, creating an array is easy, and don't forget to export it in a data object:

```
<script>
<...>
  var animalsForZoo = []
  var data = {
    name:'Olga',
    animals,
    animalCodes,
    animalsForZoo,
    sadSrc: 'images/sad.png',
    gladSrc: 'images/glad.png'
  }
  new Vue({
    el: '#app',
    data
  })
</script>
```

Don't forget to replace the usage of the `animals` array in our zoo display with the new `animalsForZoo` array:

```
<ol>
  <li v-for="animal in animalsForZoo"><span class="animal"
  v-html="animalCodes[animal]"></span></li>
</ol>
```

I know that now you are worried that your zoo on the page is empty, but give us a couple of minutes and we will take care of that!

First of all, let's create a multiple `select` element that will be populated based on the `animals` array:

```
<select multiple="multiple" name="animals" id="animals">
  <option v-for="animal in animals"
  :value="animal">{{animal}}</option>
</select>
```

Now, finally, we will attach an event listener to our select box. Let's attach a listener to the change event. Let's tell it to call the `populateAnimalsForZoo` method. Our directive will look like this:

```
@change="populateAnimalsForZoo"
```

The whole `select` element will obtain a new attribute:

```
<select @change="populateAnimalsForZoo" multiple="multiple"
name="animals" id="animals">
  <option v-for="animal in animals"
  :value="animal">{{animal}}</option>
</select>
```

Great! But there's no such method as `populateAnimalsForZoo`. But there's us!
Let's create it. This method will just iterate through the checked options of the
animals selected as input and push them into the `animalsForZoo` array:

```
new Vue({
  el: '#app',
  data,
  methods: {
    populateAnimalsForZoo(ev) {
      this.animalsForZoo = []
      const selected = document.querySelectorAll('#animals
      option:checked')
      for (var i = 0; i < selected.length; i++) {
        this.animalsForZoo.push(selected[i].value)
      }
    }
  }
})
```

Check out how the whole HTML and JavaScript code look after all these changes in
the `chapter2/example1-vue-intro/index.html` file. This is how our testing page
looks after the changes:

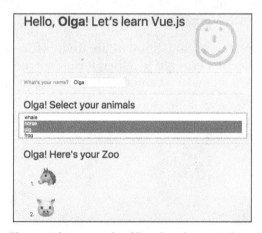

The zoo is being populated based on the user's choice

The page is messy, right? However, look how many things you have already learned just by using this page. And, admit it, it's a fun learning process! And we are not done with it yet.

Now that you have learned how to add methods and event listeners, I will teach you how we could have done the exact same thing without this method and `v-bind:change`. Remove all the code we just added and just add `v-model` to our `select` element with the `animalsForZoo` value:

```
<select v-model="animalsForZoo" multiple="multiple" name="animals"
id="animals">
  <option v-for="animal in animals"
  :value="animal">{{animal}}</option>
</select>
```

Now, everything we have just done inside the method is handled automatically by Vue! Isn't it great?

Vue components

We came to this chapter having a midsize HTML page in our hands that contains a lot of different parts. We could have thought of more things, for example, adding interactivity to each animal of our zoo, adding the possibility of feeding animals, or having some interesting facts about each animal showing up every time you hover over the animal's icon. At some point, let's face it, the HTML file along with its JavaScript will become unmaintainable.

Can you also see that our visualization layer (HTML) works along with our logical layer (JavaScript)? So, they kind of form blocks, items, bricks... For example, we have a piece of code that is responsible for the **Hello** name section. We have another block that contains our zoo. Each animal in the zoo is another item.

Call these things whatever you want, but they are undeniably separated pieces of structure and logic that, when brought together, form the whole puzzle. If you build a wall from a unique piece of material and decide to change some parts of the wall, it will not be the easiest task.

So, imagine, you build this wall and incorporate some yellow stars, blue polygons, red squares, and so on into it. Then, you decide that your yellow stars should be black. You have to change all your stars. Then, you decide that your green ellipsis should be a smiling face instead. What now? Change all ellipses, but first you have to find all the places in the wall that contain those ellipses. This is your wall, try to find all ellipses in it:

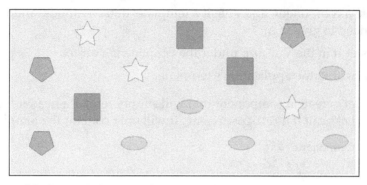

The wall built as a whole piece with incorporated parts of different colors and forms

Now, imagine that each piece actually resides on its individual brick. You can change them, add them, and remove them as much as you want. If you want to change the appearance of some of the wall elements, you just change this one brick and all the wall pieces containing this brick will change, because *all in all, it's just another brick in the wall*. So, instead of having the wall full of incorporated strange pieces, you have four bricks, and you change them whenever you need to change the piece of wall that relies on that brick:

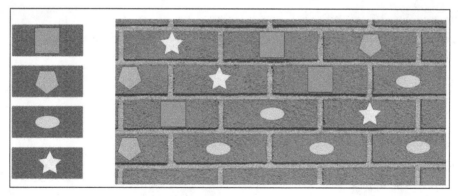

If you need to change the appearance of an element in the wall, you just change the corresponding brick

The wall is composed of bricks. These bricks are our components. What if we could also have components built with HTML, CSS, and JavaScript and our application could be built of those components? Did I just say "what if"? There's no "what if." We already have it. Vue.js supports component-based application structure. It's really easy to create components with Vue.js. The only three things you have to do are as follows:

1. Create a component, and give it a template, data, methods, and whatever you need to give to it.
2. Register it in the Vue app under the `components` object.
3. Use it within the application's template.

For example, let's create a component that will simply render a header element saying **Hello**. Let's call it `HelloComponent`. It will only contain the template string:

```
var HelloComponent = {
  template: '<h1>Hello!</h1>'
}
```

Now, we can register this component inside our Vue application initialization code:

```
new Vue({
  el: '#app',
  components: {

    HelloComponent

  }
})
```

Now, this component can actually be used inside the HTML section of the Vue application's element:

```
<div id="app">
  <hello-component></hello-component>
</div>
```

So, the whole section will look something like this:

```
<body>
  <div id="app">
    <hello-component></hello-component>
  </div>
  <script src="vue.js"></script>
  <script>
    var HelloComponent = {
```

```
      template: '<h1>Hello!</h1>'
    }
    new Vue({
      el: '#app',
      components: {
        HelloComponent
      }
    })
  </script>
</body>
```

Someone might ask, "What's so powerful in these components?" The amount of written code is actually the same as if I would have just written a piece of HTML that does the same. What's the point? Yes, sure, but in this example, our component had just one template inside. A template composed of one line only. We could have a huge template in there, and we could have some methods in this component and also its own data! Let's, for example, add an input for the name to this component and the name to its data object:

```
var HelloComponent = {
  template: '<div>' +
  '<input v-model="name" />' +
  '<h1>Hello! <strong>{{name}}</strong></h1>' +
  '</div>',
  data() {
    return {
      name: ''
    }
  }
}
```

If you need to reuse this component, you can do it as many times as you want:

```
<div id="app">
  <hello-component></hello-component>
  <hello-component></hello-component>
  <hello-component></hello-component>
</div>
```

Then, you will end up with three independent components on your page:

Using components helps avoid repeated code

These components are very nice, but there's still a big amount of code written within the same JavaScript code block. We declare components all in one place, and if there are too many of them, the application will become unmanageable again. Besides that, this HTML code within the template string is also not the most maintainable thing ever.

Well, if you are thinking so, I have some good news for you. Each component can be stored in its own file with its own HTML, JavaScript, and CSS code. These are special files with the `.vue` extension. Inside each file, there's a `<script>` section for the JavaScript code, a `<style>` section for the CSS code, and a `<template>` section for the HTML code. Isn't it convenient? Such components are called single-file components. Have a look at the first chapter's code — there's a main component called `App.vue` and there's also the `MessageCard.vue` component created by us. Isn't it nice?

If you want to use single-file components in your application, you must scaffold this application using some modular bundler, for example, `webpack`. We already talked about `vue-cli` and how easy it is to bootstrap a Vue application using the `webpack` template. Let's port the messy page with zoo to the `webpack` bundled application. Run the initialization and installation scripts:

```
vue init webpack zoo
cd zoo
npm install
npm run dev
```

Now, open the `App.vue` file and let's fill it up with our messy zoo application. The `<script>` section looks like this:

```
<script>
  <...>
  var data = {
    name: 'Olga',
    animals,
    animalCodes,
    animalsForZoo,
    sadSrc: '../static/images/sad.png',
    gladSrc: '../static/images/glad.png'
  }
  export default {
    name: 'app',
    data () {
      return data
    }
  }
</script>
```

Note the highlighted areas. I've copied the images into the `static` folder. Another important thing is that the data inside the component should be used as a function that returns an object and not as an object itself. Since the data object will still be one single instance across multiple components, the whole data object with its properties must be assembled in a dedicated function.

The rest of the script is completely the same.

The template area of the component is pretty much the same as the HTML structure from the previous example. Check out the code in the `chapter2/example3-components-started` folder.

Let's extract some of the functionality into the individual component. What do you think if we extract the zoo to its individual component? Create a `Zoo.vue` file in the `components` folder. Copy the template for the animals list to this component's `<template>` area:

```
//Zoo.vue
<template>
  <div v-if="animals.length > 0">
    <h2><span v-if="name">{{name}}! </span>Here's your Zoo</h2>
    <ol>
      <li v-for="animal in animals"><span class="animal"
      v-html="animalCodes[animal]"></span></li>
    </ol>
  </div>
</template>
```

Now, we should tell this component that it will receive `animals`, `name`, and `animalCodes` properties from the parent component that will call the following component:

```
//Zoo.vue
<script>
  export default {
    props: ['animals', 'animalCodes', 'name']
  }
</script>
```

Now, open the main `App.vue` component, import the `Zoo` component, and export it in the `components` object:

```
//App.vue
<script>
  import Zoo from './components/Zoo'
  <...>
  export default {
    name: 'app',
    components: {
      Zoo
    }
  }
</script>
```

Now, we can use this component inside the template! So, replace the whole `div` tag that contains our zoo with just the following code:

```
//App.vue
<template>
  <...>
  <zoo :animals="animalsForZoo"
  :animalCodes="animalCodes":name="name"></zoo>
  <...>
</template>
```

Check out the page! Everything works as it did earlier!

Exercise

Extract an animal to the individual component and call it inside the zoo within the `v-for` directive. Each animal has to have a small functionality that will display a small description when clicking its face (on `click`). I am pretty sure you will easily solve this exercise. If you need help, check out this chapter's code inside the `example4-components/zoo` directory.

Vue router

Single Page Applications (SPA) are great. They came to make our life easier. And it definitely is. With a bit of JavaScript code, you can achieve all the functionality that had to be done on the server side before, and the whole page should have been replaced just to display the result of that functionality. It is a golden era for web developers now. However, there is a problem that SPAs are trying to solve—*navigation*. History API and the `pushState` method (`https://developer.mozilla.org/en-US/docs/Web/API/History_API`) are already solving it, but it has been a long process until it became an established technology.

Our users are used to controlling their *where I am and where I want to be* using browsers' navigation buttons. If the whole functionality is located on the same page, how will these buttons help with the navigation? How do you use Google analytics to check which page (that, in fact, is the same) is being accessed more by your users? The whole concept is totally different. Of course, these kinds of applications are a lot faster because the number of requests is significantly reduced, and of course, our users are grateful for that, but they are not changing their web surfing habits just because we changed the way we implement things. They still want to go *back*. They expect that if they refresh the page, the page will open on exactly the same place where they were right before hitting the refresh button. They expect that they will understand where they are just by looking at the page's URL and checking what's behind the slash. For example, if it's `http://mySite/store` then it's a store; if it's `http://mySite/settings`, then most likely I'm somewhere where I can check my current settings and change them.

There are a lot of ways to achieve navigation without having to transform single-page applications into multiple-page applications. You can include an extra layer of logic on your application and change `window.location.href` every time a different URL is required—this will cause the page to refresh, which is not nice. You can also use HTML5 `history` API. It would not be the simplest thing to maintain, but it might work.

We all know that good developers are lazy, right? Being lazy means not solving problems that are already solved by someone else. This problem of navigation is being solved by many frameworks and libraries. Not only can you use some third-party libraries that help you deal with the routing in your application, but you can also use the mechanisms provided by the framework of your choice. Vue.js is one of the frameworks that offers a way of dealing with routing. You just map the URL path to your components and everything just works! Check out the official documentation of `vue-router` library at `https://router.vuejs.org/en/`.

In order to be able to use `vue-router`, you must install it for your project:

```
npm install vue-router -save
```

Optionally, `vue-router` usage can be selected on the Vue project initialization with `vue init`.

Now, you can use Vue router in your application. Just tell Vue to use it:

```
//main.js
import Vue from 'vue'
import VueRouter from 'vue-router'


Vue.use(VueRouter)
```

Let's create a simple routing example. We will have three components, one of which we consider as the Home component, meaning that it should be shown when someone navigates to the root route /. Let's call the second one `Hello` component and the third one `Bye` component. Open the `example5-router-started` code files from *Chapter 2, Under the Hood – Tutorial Explained*. You will find all the described components in the `components` directory:

The structure of the example application where we are going to try Vue router

Now, we must create a `router` instance. The constructor receives the `options` object as a parameter. This object can contain different configurable values. The most important one is the array of `routes`. Each entry of this array should consist of an object that indicates the `path` of the route and its corresponding `component`.

First, we will import all the needed components, and then, our `router` instance will look like this:

```
//main.js
import Home from '@/components/Home'
import Hello from '@/components/Hello'
import Bye from '@/components/Bye'
<...>
var router = new Router({
  mode: 'history',
  routes: [
    {
      name: 'home',
      component: Home,
      path: '/'
    },
    {
      name: 'hello',
      component: Hello,
      path: '/hello'
    },
    {
      name: 'bye',
      component: Bye,
      path: '/bye'
    }
  ]
})
```

If you want to understand better what the `mode: history` option is, check out the documentation page at `https://router.vuejs.org/en/essentials/history-mode.html` that explains it in a really nice manner. Now, we have to pass the router option to our Vue application. This option will point to our new `router` instance:

```
//main.js
new Vue({
  el: '#app',
  template: '<App/>',
  components: { App },
  router
})
```

Now, the whole application knows that we use this router. One more important step: we need to include the router component into the main component's template. For this, it is enough to just include the `<router-view>` tag in the `App.vue` component's template:

```
//App.vue
<template>
  <div id="app">
    <img src="./assets/logo.png">
    <router-view></router-view>
  </div>
</template>
```

Check out in more detail the `router-view` component at `https://router.vuejs.org/en/api/router-view.html`.

Voilà! Run the application if you haven't done so already:

npm run dev

Open the page at `http://localhost:8080` and check that it is displaying our home page component. Then, type `http://localhost:8080/hello` and `http://localhost:8080/bye` in the browser's address bar. Check that the content of the page actually changes according to the URL path:

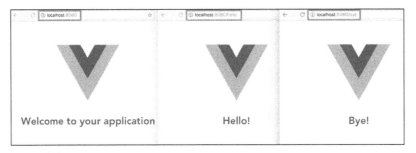

Basic routing with vue-router

Of course, you are already thinking about how to create a simple menu, pointing an anchor `<a>` element to your defined paths in the router. Don't think too much. Just use a `<router-link>` component with the `to` attribute pointing to the path of your choice. For example, to display a simple navigational menu for our router example application, we could write something like this:

```
//App.vue
<template>
  <div id="app">
    <router-link to="/">Home</router-link>
```

```
    <router-link to="hello">Hello</router-link>
    <router-link to="bye">Bye</router-link>
    <router-view></router-view>
  </div>
</template>
```

Alternatively, if you don't want to write your paths all over again, you can reference your routes by name and use the `v-bind:to` directive or simply use `:to`:

```
//App.vue
<template>
  <div id="app">
    <router-link :to="{name: 'home'}">Home</router-link>
    <router-link :to="{name: 'hello'}">Hello</router-link>
    <router-link :to="{name: 'bye'}">Bye</router-link>
    <router-view></router-view>
  </div>
</template>
```

Check how the code looks in the `example6-router` folder.

Open the page and check whether all the links actually work! Click on them several times and check whether you will actually go back if you click on the browser's go back button. Isn't it fantastic?

Vuex state management architecture

Do you remember our example with the `Zoo` and `animal` components? There was some data that had to be propagated from the main component to the child component of the child component. If this grandchild component had the possibility of somehow changing data, this change would have to be propagated from the child component to its parent component and so on until data reaches the main component. Don't think that you would do it simply with a `v-model` binding attribute. Vue has some restrictions regarding binding data to the children components via `props`. It is strictly one way. So, if the parent component changes the data, the child component's bindings will be affected, but it will never happen the other way around. Check out Vue's official documentation in regarding this at `https://vuejs.org/v2/guide/components.html#One-Way-Data-Flow`.

If you don't believe me, let's try it. Imagine that in our zoo page example, we would extract the introduction part to the separate component. I am talking about this part of our messy zoo page:

What if we'd like to extract this part to the separate component?

It seems easy. We have to declare a component, let's say `Introduction`, tell it that it will receive the `name` property, and just copy-paste HTML from `App.vue` to this new component. Inside `App.vue`, we will import this new component and export it inside the `components` object of the Vue instance. Of course, we will replace the HTML that we already copied to the new component with the `<introduction>` tag and bind the `name` property to it. Isn't it easy? Our `Introduction.vue` file will look like this:

```
//Introduction.vue
<template>
  <div>
    <label for="name" :class="{green: name, red: !name}">
    What's your name? </label>
    <input id="name" type="text" v-model.trim="name">
  </div>
</template>
<script>
  export default {
    props: ['name']
  }
</script>
```

Our `App.vue` file will import, export, and call:

```
//App.vue
<template>
  <div id="app" class="jumbotron">
    <...>
    <introduction :name="name"></introduction>
    <...>
  </div>
</template>

<script>
  <...>
```

```
import Introduction from './components/Introduction'

<...>
export default {
  components: {
    Zoo,
    Introduction
  }
  <...>
}
</script>
```

Check out this code in the code bundle of the *Chapter 2, Under the Hood – Tutorial Explained* in the `example7-events-started/zoo` folder. Run `npm install` and `npm run` inside this folder:

```
cd example7-events-started/zoo

npm install

npm run dev
```

Check out the page. It looks like it did before. Try to change the name inside the input. First of all, it doesn't change in other places where it should change, and second, our dev tools console is full of warnings and errors:

The name is not updated where it should have been updated, and the console is full of errors

It seems the documentation is right: we can't change the value of data passed as property to the child component. What can we do then? We can emit events and attach event listeners to the component, and change the data on the event. How do we do this? It's simple. First of all, let's call the property being passed by something that is not name, for example, `initialName`. Then, open the `Introduction` component and create a `data` function that will bind this component's `name` object to `initialValueprops`. In this way, we are at least telling Vue that it is not our intention to try to change parent's data from the child. So, `script` of the `Introduction.vue` component will look like this:

```
//Introduction.vue
<script>
  export default {
    props: ['initialName'],
    data () {
      return {
        name: this.initialName
      }
    }
  }
</script>
```

We also have to change the way we bind name to the component inside `App.vue`:

```
//App.vue
<introduction :initialName="name"></introduction>
```

Now, if you check the page, you will at least see that Vue doesn't complain anymore about something illegal that we try to do. However, still, if we try to change the name, the changes are not propagated to the parent, which is quite understandable; these changes only affect the data of the component itself. Now, we have to attach the `event` to the `input` element. This event will call a method that will finally emit the event to the parent component:

```
//Introduction.vue
<template>
  <div>
    <...>
    <input id="name" type="text"
    v-model.trim="name"@input="onInput">
  </div>
</template>
<script>
  export default {
    <...>
```

```
    methods: {
      onInput () {
        this.$emit('nameChanged', this.name)
      }
    }
  }
</script>
```

Now, the only thing we have to do is to bind the `nameChanged` event listener to the `<introduction>` component and call the method that will change the name of the `App.vue` data object:

```
//App.vue
<template>
<...>
<introduction @nameChanged="onNameChanged" :initialName="name"></
introduction>
<...>
</template>
<script>
  export default {
<...>
    methods: {
      onNameChanged (newName) {
        this.name = newName
      }
    }
  }
</script>
```

Check the page. Now, everything works as before! Check the code for this solution inside the `example7-events/zoo` code folder for this chapter.

Well, it was not very difficult, but do we want to emit all these events every time we need to update the state? And what if we have components inside the components? And what if we have other components inside those components? Will it be the events handling hell? And if we have to change something, will we have to go to all those components? Argh! Wouldn't it be great to have the application's data in some kind of centralized storage that would provide a simple API for its management and then we could just call this storage's methods in order to retrieve and update the data? Well, this is exactly what Vuex is for! Vuex is a centralized state management inspired by Redux. Check out its official documentation at `http://vuex.vuejs.org/en/`.

Now, in a nutshell, the three most important parts of a Vuex store are state, getters, and mutations:

- **State**: This is an initial state of the application, basically the data of the application
- **Getters**: These are exactly what you think, functions that return data from the store
- **Mutations**: These are functions that can mutate data on the store

A store can also have actions. These things are like wrappers for mutations with a bit more capacity. If you want to check what are they about, refer to the official documentation at http://vuex.vuejs.org/en/mutations.html.

Let's add the Vuex store to our Zoo application to check how it works. First of all, we need to install vuex. Open the code for *Chapter 2, Under the Hood – Tutorial Explained* from the example8-store-started/zoo folder and run npm install:

```
cd example8-store-started/zoo
npm install vuex --save
```

Let's create our store. Start by creating a folder named store with the index.js file inside. We will put all our store data inside this file. Before doing this, tell Vue that we will use Vuex:

```
//store/index.js
import Vue from 'vue'
import Vuex from 'vuex'
Vue.use(Vuex)
```

Now, we can create a new Vuex instance. It should receive state, getters, and mutations. Let's define them:

```
//store/index.js
import Vue from 'vue'
import Vuex from 'vuex'

Vue.use(Vuex)

const state = {
}

const getters = {
}

const mutations = {
```

```
}
export default new Vuex.Store({
  state,
  getters,
  mutations
})
```

Nice! Now, let's add all the data that resides in our application to the state:

```
//store/index.js
const animalCodes = {
  dog: '&#x1f436;',
  <...>
  koala: '&#x1f43c;'
}
const animalsDescriptions = {
  dog: 'I am a dog, I bark',
  <...>
  koala: 'I am a koala, I love eucalyptus!'
}
const animals = Object.keys(animalCodes)
const state = {
  name: 'Olga',
  animals,
  animalCodes,
  animalsDescriptions,
  animalsForZoo: [],
  sadSrc: '../static/images/sad.png',
  gladSrc: '../static/images/glad.png'
}
```

Now, if you inject the store on the Vue application initialization, all the components and their children will have access to the `this.$store` instance. Let's inject it:

```
//main.js
import Vue from 'vue'
import App from './App'
import store from './store'

new Vue({
  el: '#app',
  template: '<App/>',
  components: { App },
  store
})
```

Now, if we replace all the data with computed properties from the store in App.vue (except animalsForZoo, which is bound as a property for our zoo), the application will look quite the same:

```
//App.vue
<script>
  import Zoo from './components/Zoo'
  import Introduction from './components/Introduction'

  export default {
    name: 'app',
    components: {
      Zoo,
      Introduction
    },
    data () {
      return {
        animalsForZoo: []
      }
    },
    computed: {
      name () {
        return this.$store.state.name
      },
      animals () {
        return this.$store.state.animals
      },
      animalCodes () {
        return this.$store.state.animalCodes
      },
      sadSrc () {
        return this.$store.state.sadSrc
      },
      gladSrc () {
        return this.$store.state.gladSrc
      }
    },
    methods: {
      onNameChanged (newName) {
        this.name = newName
      }
    }
  }
</script>
```

If you open the page, nothing has changed. However, our changing name interaction doesn't work again!

Let's add `mutation` to change the name. Mutations are just methods that receive a state as first argument and anything you call them with as other parameters. So, let's call our mutation `updateName` and pass `newName` to it as a second argument:

```
//store/index.js
const mutations = {
  updateName (state, newName) {
    state.name = newName
  }
}
```

Now, we can use this mutation to access the `this.$store.mutation` property inside the component responsible for updating the name—`Introduction.vue`. We have to just change the `onInput` method:

```
//Introduction.vue
methods: {
  onInput (ev) {
    this.$store.commit('updateName', ev.currentTarget.value)
  }
}
```

By the way, we can also remove the properties and pass the name directly from the store, just like we did in the `App.vue` component. Then, you can remove the `name` binding to the `introduction` component inside the `App.vue` component's template. Now, you can replace the properties that are bound to the Zoo component by computed properties coming from the store. See how elegant the code becomes! For example, look at this line of code:

```
<introduction></introduction>
```

Doesn't it look better than the following line of code:

```
<introduction @nameChanged="onNameChanged" :initialName="name"></
introduction>
```

Check out the final code for this chapter in the `example8-store/zoo` code folder for *Chapter 2*, *Under the Hood – Tutorial Explained*. Note that we have used a very simplified version. We have not even used any getters. For a more sophisticated use, we would create `getters` and `actions`, and they would have been located in their own `actions.js` and `getters.js` files. We would also use `mapGetters` and `mapActions` helpers. However, for basic understanding, what we have done is enough. Refer to the official documentation to find out more about Vuex store and how to use it.

Bootstrap

Now that we know almost everything about Vue.js, let's talk about Bootstrap.
Check out the official Bootstrap page at `https://v4-alpha.getbootstrap.com/`.

Bootstrap — framework for responsive projects

In a nutshell, Bootstrap gives you a broad set of classes that allow building nearly
everything with any layout in an easy and effortless way.

Bootstrap provides with you four most important things:

- Easy layouts building at `https://v4-alpha.getbootstrap.com/layout/overview/`

- Broad range of classes to style nearly any web element at `https://v4-alpha.getbootstrap.com/content/`

- Self-contained components such as alerts, budges, modals, and so on at `https://v4-alpha.getbootstrap.com/components/`

- Some utilities for styling images, figures, for positioning, styling, and adding borders at `https://v4-alpha.getbootstrap.com/utilities/`

How to install Bootstrap? It can be installed from the CDN:

```
<link rel="stylesheet" href="https://maxcdn.bootstrapcdn.com/
bootstrap/4.0.0-alpha.6/css/bootstrap.min.css" integrity="sha384-
rwoIResjU2yc3z8GV/NPeZWAv56rSmLldC3R/AZzGRnGxQQKnKkoFVhFQhNUwEyJ"
crossorigin="anonymous">
<script src="https://code.jquery.com/jquery-3.1.1.slim.min.
js" integrity="sha384-A7FZj7v+d/sdmMqp/nOQwliLvUsJfDHW+k9Omg/a/
EheAdgtzNs3hpfag6Ed950n" crossorigin="anonymous"></script>
<script src="https://cdnjs.cloudflare.com/ajax/libs/tether/1.4.0/js/
tether.min.js" integrity="sha384-DztdAPBWPRXSA/3eYEEUWrWCy7G5KFbe8fFjk
5JAIxUYHKkDx6Qin1DkWx51bBrb" crossorigin="anonymous"></script>
<script src="https://maxcdn.bootstrapcdn.com/bootstrap/4.0.0-alpha.6/
js/bootstrap.min.js" integrity="sha384-vBWWzlZJ8ea9aCX4pEW3rVHjgjt7zpk
NpZk+02D9phzyeVkE+joOieGizqPLForn" crossorigin="anonymous"></script>
```

This is, actually, exactly what we have in the `PleaseIntroduceYourself` application from *Chapter 1*, *Please Introduce Yourself – Tutorial*, and in the messy zoo application from this chapter.

Bootstrap components

Bootstrap has a lot of components that can be used just out of the box.

I will not talk about all of them in this chapter, because we will have several opportunities to discover them during the course of the book. Let's look at some of them just to have an idea.

Let's look at the alert components. As you might know, alerts are nice elements that appear on the page when you have successfully filled in some form. Alerts are also those angry red elements that tell you that you've done something wrong. What would you need to create an alert element on the page that would disappear after some time or give the possibility to the user to close it by clicking on the **x** button? You would probably create a `div`, add some class to it, and add a bit of JavaScript that would remove the element from the DOM tree after a grace period. Using Bootstrap, you just add `alert` class to your `div` and add another class such as `alert-warning` or `alert-info` to specify which kind of alert it is:

```
<div class="alert alert-success" role="alert">
  <strong>Hello!</strong> You have successfully opened this page!
</div>
<div class="alert alert-info" role="alert">
  <strong>Hey!</strong> Important information - this alert cannot
  be closed.
</div>
<div class="alert alert-warning" role="alert">
  <strong>Warning!</strong> It might be raining tonight, take your
  umbrella!
</div>
<div class="alert alert-danger alert-dismissible fade show"
role="alert">
  <button type="button" class="close" data-dismiss="alert"
  aria-label="Close">
    <span aria-hidden="true">&times;</span>
  </button>
  <strong>Failure!</strong> Since you don't like this
  failure alert you can simply close it.
</div>
```

This code will produce nice alert boxes that look like this:

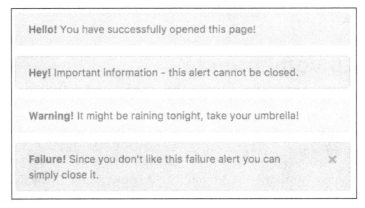

Bootstrap alerts — success, info, warning, and danger

Even a simple element like a button can be styled in hundreds of different ways using Bootstrap. Again, you can have buttons indicating success, danger zone, being informative, or just gray. There's a possibility of grouping buttons and making them look like a link. The code is pretty easy:

```
<button type="button" class="btn btn-primary">Primary</button>
<button type="button" class="btn btn-secondary">Secondary</button>
<button type="button" class="btn btn-success">Success</button>
<button type="button" class="btn btn-info">Info</button>
<button type="button" class="btn btn-link">Link</button>
<button type="button" class="btn btn-primary btn-sm">Small button</button>
```

This code will produce buttons as shown here:

Bootstrap buttons

Check out more about Bootstrap's buttons on the official documentation page at `https://v4-alpha.getbootstrap.com/components/buttons/`.

One of my favorite things about Bootstrap is that you might have a trivial element, but then you add some of the Bootstrap's classes to it and it suddenly becomes clean and nice. For example, create a simple page with some `<h1>` and `<p>` elements:

```
<div>
   <h1>Jumbotron</h1>
   <p>
      Lorem ipsum dolor sit amet…
   </p>
</div>
```

It will look normal, simple. Now, add the `container` class to the parent `div`. Isn't it much nicer? Also, add the `jumbotron` class to it.

The page looked like this earlier:

Jumbotron

Lorem ipsum dolor sit amet, consectetur adipiscing elit. Duis semper erat ac est semper convallis. Nunc mauris dui, interdum sed ullamcorper a, hendrerit congue enim. Maecenas semper id velit in posuere. Suspendisse id convallis neque, vel rutrum massa. Curabitur suscipit est et lectus convallis, nec faucibus ipsum sagittis. Morbi et turpis eu quam aliquam facilisis at quis lectus. Integer ultricies justo vitae mauris sollicitudin molestie. Sed vitae suscipit ex. Sed rhoncus orci et mi congue, luctus fermentum purus vehicula. Morbi in suscipit eros, sit amet maximus libero. Praesent posuere sem bibendum lacus fringilla, eget bibendum massa auctor. Cras vulputate metus ante, vel lobortis magna hendrerit vel.

The content inside the div before adding Bootstrap classes

All of a sudden, the same page looks like this:

Jumbotron

Lorem ipsum dolor sit amet, consectetur adipiscing elit. Duis semper erat ac est semper convallis. Nunc mauris dui, interdum sed ullamcorper a, hendrerit congue enim. Maecenas semper id velit in posuere. Suspendisse id convallis neque, vel rutrum massa. Curabitur suscipit est et lectus convallis, nec faucibus ipsum sagittis. Morbi et turpis eu quam aliquam facilisis at quis lectus. Integer ultricies justo vitae mauris sollicitudin molestie. Sed vitae suscipit ex. Sed rhoncus orci et mi congue, luctus fermentum purus vehicula. Morbi in suscipit eros, sit amet maximus libero. Praesent posuere sem bibendum lacus fringilla, eget bibendum massa auctor. Cras vulputate metus ante, vel lobortis magna hendrerit vel.

The content inside the div after adding Bootstrap classes

Actually, if you check our `PleaseIntroduceYourself` example from *Chapter 1, Please Introduce Yourself – Tutorial* (`chapter1/please-introuce-yourself/src/App.vue`), you will see that this exact class was used for the parent element.

There are a lot of different components: popovers, tooltips, modals, and so on. We will use all of them during the course of the book.

Bootstrap utilities

Do you want to have responsive floats (elements that flow to the left or to the right)? Just add the `float-left` and `float-right` classes to your elements, and you don't have to be worried about it anymore:

```
<div class="float-left">Float left on all viewport sizes</div><br>
<div class="float-right">Float right on all viewport sizes</div><br>
<div class="float-none">Don't float on all viewport sizes</div><br>
```

Just insert this code into your HTML page (or simply check out the `index.html` file in the `example11-responsive-floats` folder), open it, and resize your window.

You can easily control the sizing and spacing with simple classes. Check out `https://v4-alpha.getbootstrap.com/utilities/sizing/` and `https://v4-alpha.getbootstrap.com/utilities/spacing/`.

You can even enable flex-box behavior just by adding the `d-flex` class to your container. The *d* comes from *display*. With more classes attached to your flex element, you can control alignment and direction of your flex-box. Check it out at `https://v4-alpha.getbootstrap.com/utilities/flexbox/`.

There are a lot more utilities to explore, and we will get into most of them during our journey.

Bootstrap layout

Using Bootstrap, it is easy to control the layout of your system:

> *Bootstrap includes several components and options for laying out your project, including wrapping containers, a powerful flexbox grid system, a flexible media object, and responsive utility classes.*

> \- From Bootstrap
> (`https://v4-alpha.getbootstrap.com/layout/overview/`)

Bootstrap's grid system is pretty powerful and easy to understand. It is just a row composed of columns. Everything is controlled by classes that have pretty self-descriptive names such as `row` and `col`. If you just give your columns `col` class, every column inside the `row` element will have the same size. If you want to have columns of different sizes, play with the fact that the row can be composed of 12 columns. So, if you want to make some columns, let's say half of your row, give it a class **col-6**:

```
<div class="row">
  <div class="col">this is a column with class col</div>
  <div class="col-6">this is a column with class col-6</div>
  <div class="col-2">this is a column with class col-2</div>
</div>
```

This code will produce results similar to this:

this is a column with class col	this is a column with class col-6	this is a column with class col-2

Grid layout system combining row and col classes

The interesting part is that if you resize your window, your layout will not break. It will resize accordingly. You don't have to implement any CSS black magic in order to achieve that! That is why Bootstrap is a big ♥.

Combining Vue.js and Bootstrap

When we were talking about Vue, we devoted a big section to its components. When we talked about Bootstrap, we also talked about components. Doesn't it ring the same bell? Maybe we could create Vue components out of Bootstrap components? Maybe we can! Actually, we have already done it! Open the code of the first chapter's `PleaseIntroduceYourself` application. Check what we have inside the `components` folder. There's something that we called `MessageCard.vue`. Actually, this is an implemented Vue component for Card Bootstrap's component (`https://v4-alpha.getbootstrap.com/components/card/`)!

Open the `example13-vue-bootstrap-components-started/components` folder. Let's use this project as a playground to create the Vue component based on the Bootstrap alert component. Run `npm install` and run:

```
cd example13-vue-bootstrap-components-started/components
npm install
npm run dev
```

Let's create a Vue component called `Alert`. This component will contain the necessary code to simulate Bootstrap's alert component behavior.

Create a file named `Alert.vue` inside the `components` folder and add `template` tags. Our alert will definitely have the `alert` class. However, its additional class (`alert-danger`, `alert-info`, etc.) should be something configurable. Also, its title and text should be something passed by bound properties from the parent component. Thus, the template for the alert component will look like this:

```
//Alert.vue
<template>
  <div class="alert" :class="additionalClass" role="alert">
    <strong>{{title}}</strong>{{text}}
  </div>
</template>
```

Let's implement the `additionalClass` property as a computed property that will be calculated based on the `type` property passed by the parent component. So, the script for the `Alert` component will look like this:

```
//Alert.vue
<script>
export default {
  props: ['type', 'title', 'text'],
  computed: {
    additionalClass () {
      if (!this.type) {
        return 'alert-success'
      }
      return 'alert-' + this.type
    }
  },
  name: 'alert'
}
</script>
```

Then, we can call it from our main `App.vue` component:

```
//App.vue
<template>
  <div id="app" class="container">
    <img src="./assets/logo.png">
    <alert :title="title" :text="text"></alert>
  </div>
```

```
  </template>

  <script>
    import Alert from './components/Alert'
    export default {
      data () {
        return {
          title: 'Vue Bootstrap Component',
          text: 'Isn\'t it easy?'
        }
      },
      name: 'app',
      components: {
        Alert
      }
    }
  </script>
```

You will end up with a nice alert on your page:

We just created our Alert Vue Bootstrap component

Exercise

Enable a default value for the title of the alert component. So, if the `title` is not passed, it will say **Success** by default. Also, bind the `type` property to the component on its creation inside the `App.vue` parent component. Export this property as a computed property depending on some arbitrary value. For example, based on some random number, if it's divisible by 3, the type should be **danger**; if it's divisible by 5, the type should be **info**; and so on.

Check it out yourself. Go to the `example13-vue-bootstrap-components/` `components` folder and have a look, in particular, at the `App.vue` and `components/` `Alert.vue` components.

Combining Vue.js and Bootstrap continued

So, we know how to create Vue components based on Bootstrap components. Doesn't it feel like now it would be great to create all the Bootstrap components as Vue components and just use them in our Vue applications without having to think about Bootstrap classes whatsoever? Imagine Vue components such as `<button-success></button-success>` or `<button :type="success"></button>`. We could even create a whole library of Vue components based on Bootstrap! The question is, should we do it if it already exists? Yes, someone has already done all the work for us. These are the people who have done the work:

Core team of bootstrap-vue

These nice people have developed something called Bootstrap-Vue and that's something that does exactly what you think—it contains a full set of Bootstrap components implemented as Vue.js components. Check it out at `https://bootstrap-vue.github.io/`.

Let's check, for example, how the alert component is implemented at `https://bootstrap-vue.github.io/docs/components/alert`. It's a little bit more detailed than our alert. The data is passed within the component's tags and not as properties, like in our case, which also makes it more flexible. We will use it a lot while developing our application throughout the book.

What is Firebase?

To understand what is Firebase let's open its website `https://firebase.google.com/`. This is what we see:

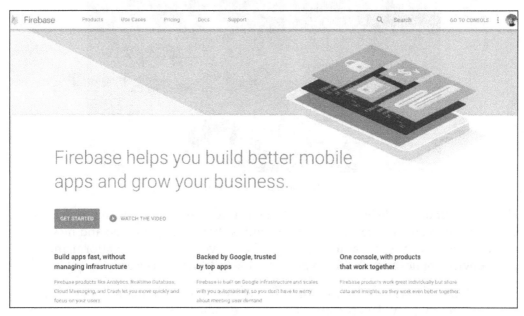

Google Firebase landing page

Firebase for Google is yet another cloud service, like AWS for Amazon or Azure for Microsoft, a bit simpler though, because Google already has Google Cloud Platform, which is huge.

If you feel like you want to choose between Firebase and AWS, do not forget that you will most likely Google it. In any case, someone has already done this for you so here you have this question on Quora at `https://www.quora.com/Which-is-better-cloud-server-Amazon-AWS-or-Firebase`.

I would say that it's more similar to Heroku — it allows you to easily deploy your applications and integrate them with analytics tools. If you have read the Learning Vue.js 2 book (`https://www.packtpub.com/web-development/learning-vuejs-2`), then you already know how much I love Heroku. I even have Heroku socks!

My beautiful Heroku socks

However, I find Google Firebase console also quite nice and simple to use. It also provides a backend as a service. This backend is shared for your web and mobile applications, which comes as a huge help when developing cross-platform and cross-device applications. Firebase provides the following services:

- **Authentication**: This uses Firebase API for authenticating users using different providers (Facebook, Google, e-mail, and so on).

- **Database**: This uses Firebase database API to store and retrieve your data. No need to choose between different database providers, and no need to establish connection. Just use the API out of the box.

- **Hosting**: This hosts and deploys your application using simple shell commands.

- **Storage**: This hosts static files using a simple API.

Again, if you think about how to integrate your Vue application with Firebase APIs, stop thinking about it because someone has already done the job for you. After creating your project using the Firebase console, you can simply use a `vuefire` wrapper for Firebase to connect to your database and fetch your data. Check it out at `https://github.com/vuejs/vuefire`. Actually, this is exactly what we did in our `PleaseIntroduceYourself` application from the first chapter. Check out the code that is located inside the `App.vue` component:

```
//PleaseIntroduceYourself/src/App.vue
<script>
import Firebase from 'firebase'

let config = {
  apiKey: '... ',
  ...
  messagingSenderId: '...'
}

let app = Firebase.initializeApp(config)
let db = app.database()
let messagesRef = db.ref('messages')

export default {
  ...
  firebase: {
    messages: messagesRef.limitToLast(100)
  }
}
</script>
```

Everything that is exported in the Firebase object becomes accessible via the `this` keyword, the same way as we access the `data` or `computed` properties. We will use `vuefire` in the application that we will develop throughout the book to better understand how it works.

Summary

In this chapter, we familiarized ourselves with Vue.js, Bootstrap and Firebase. We have also analyzed tools that integrate Vue.js with Bootstrap and Vue.js with Firebase.

Thus, now, we are familiar with Vue.js applications that are built using single-file components, Bootstrap's grid system, components, and CSS helpers to make our lives easier and to make Google Firebase console with its possibilities.

Also, we know how to initialize Vue.js project, and use Vue directives, components, store and routing.

You also learned how to leverage Bootstrap's grid system to achieve the responsibility of our application's layout.

And last but not least, you learned how to use the Firebase API within the Vue application using `vuefire` bindings.

With the end of this chapter, the first introduction part of our journey also comes to an end.

In the next chapter, we will actually dive deep inside the implementation. As a scuba diving tank, we will take everything that you have learned so far!

So, we will start developing the application that we will build during the whole book until it's ready for deployment. We will:

- Define what the application will do and its requirements
- Define whom we are building the application for
- Build basic mockups for the application
- Scaffold the application using Vue command-line interface

Are you as excited as much as I am? Then, let's go to the next chapter!

3
Let's Get Started

In the previous chapter, we discussed the three main technologies that we will use throughout this book to build our application. We explored a lot about Vue.js; we introduced some of the functionalities of Bootstrap, and we checked what we can achieve using the Google Firebase console. We know how to start an application from scratch using Vue.js. We know how to make it beautiful with the help of Bootstrap, and we know how to use Google Firebase to deploy it to live! What does that mean? It means that we are 100 percent ready to start developing our application!

Coding an application is a fun, challenging, and exciting process... only if we know what we are going to code, right? In order to know what we will code, we have to define the concept of the application, its requirements, and its target users. In this book, we will not go through the whole process of design building as for this, you have plenty of other books, because it's a big science.

In this book, particularly in this chapter, and before diving into the implementation, we will at least define a set of personas and user stories. Thus, in this chapter, we will do the following:

- State the problem we are going to solve with our application
- Define some personas and user stories
- Retrieve nouns and verbs from user stories
- Draw the mockups that will define the main screens and areas of our application

Stating the problem

There are many time-management techniques in the world. Several gurus and professionals have given a great amount of talks on how to effectively manage your time so that you are efficient and all your KPI values are above any possible benchmarks of productivity. Some of these talks are really amazing. When it comes to time-management talks, I always suggest Randy Pausch's talk at `https://youtu.be/oTugjssqOT0`.

Speaking of time-management techniques, there is one popular technique I particularly like, which I find very simple to use. It's called Pomodoro (`https://en.wikipedia.org/wiki/Pomodoro_Technique`). This technique consists of the following principles:

- You work during a certain period without any interruptions. This period can be 20 to 25 minutes and it's called Pomodoro

- After the working Pomodoro, you have a 5 minute break. During this break, you can do whatever you want—check e-mails, social networks, and so on

- After working four Pomodoros with short breaks, you have the right to a longer break that can last from 10 to 15 minutes

There are numerous implementations of the Pomodoro timer. Some of them allow you to configure the amount of time for working Pomodoros and for the short and long breaks. Some of them block social network pages during the working Pomodoros; some of them produce noises. In the book *Learning Vue.js 2*, we also built a simple Pomodoro timer that produced brown noise during the working period and showed random kittens during the short breaks.

If you are reading this book, then most likely you are a developer and you spend a big part of your day sitting or maybe standing because standing desks are quite popular nowadays. How often do you change your position during the working day (or night)? Do you have problems with your back? Do you go to the gym? Are you fond of jogging? How often do you work out at home? Being a developer requires a lot of concentration, and it's common for us to forget a bit about ourselves.

In this book, we will build a Pomodoro timer again. This time, it will not only try to solve a time-management problem, but also solve a fitness-management issue. Instead of allowing you to do whatever you want during the breaks or displaying some random kittens, it will tell you to do a simple workout. The workouts vary from very simple head-rotation exercises to push-ups and burpees. The users can choose a set of their favorite workouts depending on the kind of office they work in. The users can also add new workouts. Workouts can also be rated.

So, the main principles of the Pomodoro timer that we will implement are as follows:

- Work without interruptions. Concentrate on what you're doing.
- Exercise during the breaks.
- Collaborate and add new exciting exercises that can be used by you and by other users of the application.

Gathering requirements

Now that we know what we are going to build, let's define a list of requirements for the application. The application is all about displaying a timer and displaying workouts. So, let's define what it must be able to do. Here's my list of functional requirements:

- The application should display a countdown timer.
- The countdown timer can be from 25 to 0 minutes, from 5 to 0 minutes, or from 10 to 0 minutes.
- It shall be possible to start, pause, and stop the timer at any moment of the application's execution.
- The application shall produce some sounds when the time reaches 0 and the next period of break or the working Pomodoro starts.
- The application shall display a workout during the short and long breaks. It shall be possible to skip the current workout and switch to the next one. It shall also be possible to skip workouts completely during a break and just stare at kittens. It shall also be possible to mark the given workout as done.
- The application must offer an authentication mechanism. Authenticated users can configure the Pomodoro timer, add new workouts to the system, and visualize their statistics.
- Statistics for the authenticated users display the number of workouts performed daily, weekly, and monthly.
- Authenticated users are able to configure Pomodoro timers like the following:
  - Choose a value between 15 and 30 for the long working Pomodoro timer
  - Choose a value between 5 and 10 for the short break timer
  - Choose a value between 10 and 15 for the long break timer

- Authenticated users are able to configure their set of favorite workouts to display.

- Authenticated users are able to create new workouts and add them to the system.

- Each workout consists of four parts: title, description, image, and rating.

I also have a very basic list consisting of two items of non-functional requirements:

- The application should use persistent storage to store its data — Firebase's real-time database in our case

- The application shall be responsive and run on multiple platforms and devices

I guess that this is already enough for the functionality of our Pomodoro. Alternatively, since it's about fitness, maybe we can call it PoFIToro? Or, maybe, since we get some nice profit for our body, let's call it *ProFitOro*.

Personas

Usually, before developing an application we have to define its target users. For this, multiple questionnaires are conducted with the potential users of the application. The questionnaires usually include questions about the user's personal data, such as age, sex and so on. There should also be questions about the user's usage patterns — operating system, desktop or mobile, and so on. And of course, there should be questions about the application itself. For example, for the ProFitOro application, we could ask the following questions:

- How many hours per day do you spend in the office?
- For how long do you sit in the office during your working day?
- How often do you do sport activities such as jogging, fitness workouts, and so on?
- Do you work from the office or from home?
- Is there any area in your work place where you could do push-ups?
- Do you have problems with your back?

After all questionnaires are collected, the users are divided into categories by similar patterns and personal data. After that, each user's category forms one single persona. I will leave here four personas for the ProFitOro application.

Let's start with a fictitious character called Alex Bright:

Alex Bright

Age: 32 years old.

Sex: Male

Education: MSc

Occupation: Software engineer, full-time employment

Usage patterns: Works in an office, uses a laptop running Ubuntu and an iPhone.

Favorite browser: Google Chrome

Health and fitness: Once per month does 5 km jogging. Periodically feels back pain

Let's move on to our next fictitious persona — Anna Kuznetsova.

Anna Kuznetsova

Age: 22 years old.

Sex: Female

Education: BSc

Occupation: Student

Usage patterns: Works mostly from home using her desktop running Windows as well as an Android phone.

Favorite browser: Mozilla Firefox

Health and fitness: Goes to a fitness studio three times per week. Doesn't have any health issues

At the time of writing this book, a friend of mine had just entered our apartment for a visit. His name is Duarte, but we make fun of him calling him Dwart. Immediately after he showed up, the following persona was born (mind that our friend Duarte is very far from being 45):

Dwart Azevedo

Age: 45 years old

Sex: Male

Education: PhD

Occupation: VP engineer, full-time employment

Usage patterns: Works in an office, often from co-working spaces and from home sometimes. Uses a MacBook Pro and iPhone, and spends a lot of time sitting while working.

Health and fitness: Regularly does workouts at home. Sometimes feels pain in his back.

My husband Rui works for an online fitness company called Gymondo. There, they have a great fitness instructor called Steve. He pushes you to your very limits. Every time I do workouts with this guy, I can't even walk after. That's how the following persona was born:

Steve Wilson

Age: 35 years old

Sex: Male

Occupation: Fitness instructor, full-time employment

Usage patterns: Windows desktop at home

Health and fitness: Never feels pain, trains every day and every hour

We can see that a common thing for our users is that all of them spend some time in the same position (sitting), their work requires some concentration and probably time-management techniques, and they need to change their position sometimes in order to prevent problems with their backs.

User stories

After we've defined our users, let's write some user stories. When it comes to writing user stories, I just close my eyes and imagine that I am this person. Let's try out this mind exercise starting with Dwart Azevedo:

Dwart Azevedo

Dwart's working day consists of meetings, calls, video conferences, and paperwork. Today, he was really busy with interviews and meetings. Finally, he got a few hours for his paperwork that has been waiting for him for the whole week. Dwart wants to spend these hours in the most productive way. He opens the ProFitOro application, clicks on start, and starts working. After his paperwork is done, he clicks on stop, checks his statistics in ProFitOro, and feels happy. Even though his working time consisted of two hours only, he was able to finish everything he planned to finish.

Thus, we can come up with a formal user story like this:

As an authenticated user, I would like to check out my statistics page at ProFitOro in order to see the completeness of my working day.

Let's move on to our fitness instructor, Steve Wilson.

Steve Wilson

Steve is a fitness instructor. He knows everything about the human body, nutrition facts and how to do workouts correctly. He has a lot of friends — programmers that use the ProFitOro application. He comes home after his working day, logs in and opens the ProFitOro application, clicks on the Workouts section, and adds new exercises for the back.

Thus, a new formal user story can sound like this:

As a fitness instructor, I would like to easily add new exercises in order to enrich the ProFitOro application with more workouts.

Let's move on to our student Anna Kuznetsova.

Anna Kuznetsova

Anna is a student. Currently, she's going through her exam period. She needs to study for her exams every day. It's not an easy task — to concentrate on books when it's summer and all your friends are out having fun. Someone has told her about the ProFitOro application, so she starts using it without registration. After a while, she realizes that it actually helps her concentrate. After using it for some hours, she would like to check how much she has been working and how many exercises she has done. However, this information is not available to non-registered users. So, she clicks on the **Register** button on the first page of the application, registers with her e-mail, and now, she can access her statistical data.

Thus, another user story appears:

As a non-registered user, I would like to be able to register myself in order to be able to log in to the application and have access to my statistics data.

Retrieving nouns and verbs

Retrieving nouns and verbs from the user stories is a very fun task that helps you realize what parts your application consists of. For those who like **Unified Modeling Language (UML)**, after you retrieve the nouns and verbs from your user stories, you'll have the classes and entity-relationship diagrams almost done! Do not underestimate the number of nouns and verbs to retrieve. Write them all down — literally! You can remove the words that don't make sense after. So, let's do it.

Nouns

The nouns that I was able to retrieve out of my user stories are the following:

- Working day
- Meeting
- Call
- Interview
- Hour
- Day
- Week
- Application
- Statistics
- Working time
- Plan
- Fitness
- Instructor
- Human body
- Nutrition
- Workout
- Section
- Exercise
- E-mail
- Data
- Page
- Registration

Verbs

The verbs that I was able to retrieve from the user stories are the following:

- Consist
- Be busy
- Open
- Spend time
- Start

- Pause
- Stop
- Check
- Finish
- Plan
- Add
- Create
- Register
- Authenticate
- Login
- Concentrate

The fact that we have verbs such as **register**, **login**, and **authenticate** and nouns such as **e-mail,** and **registration** mean that the application will probably be used with and without registration. This means that the first page would probably contain the *login* and *registration* area, and somehow, it should also contain a link to the application that is possible to use without any authentication beforehand.

Then, we have verbs such as **start**, **pause,** and **stop**. These are the main actions that are applicable to our Pomodoro timer. We can start the application, we can pause it, and of course, we can stop it at any time of our working day. By the way, **working day** is one of our retrieved nouns. So, this means that the main page of our application will contain the countdown timer that will have the possibility of being started, paused, and stopped.

We have a lot of nouns related to fitness—**fitness** itself, **human body**, **exercise**, **workout,** and so on. This is actually what we are trying to achieve with this application—to train our *body* while we have a Pomodoro break. So, doing an exercise while taking a break from work. Note that there are also verbs such as **check** and **finish**. So, the exercise can be *finished* and something can be *checked*, indicating that the user has *finished* exercising. That's why, this Pomodoro interval representation should contain a *checkbox*. It should also contain a link that leads to the next exercise in case you spend less time on the current one. It might also have a skip button in case you are totally not into the exercise during this interval.

Check out the noun **statistics**. It doesn't mean that we have to talk about averages, sampling, population, and other stuff that you learned in school some years ago. The noun **statistics** in our context means that the user should be able to access their *statistical data* about the workouts performed during the *day, week,* or *month* (check out that there are actually **Day** and **Week** nouns in the nouns list). So, there will be another screen that will display the user's *statistics*.

Plan and **working time**. Something can be planned and probably configured. It makes sense—some users might feel that for them, the working time should be 30 minutes and not 25. Some might need smaller working intervals, such as 15 or 20 minutes. These values should be *configurable*. Thus, we come yet to another screen—*configuration*. In this screen, the users will be able to reset their passwords and configure their Pomodoro timers for working time, and short and long time breaks.

Check out the verbs **create** and **add** joined with the noun **workout**. We already discussed that workouts that appear during the Pomodoro breaks are a result of a collaborative work of the users of the application. So, there should be a *section* (check that the word **section** is also present in our list of nouns) that allows *visualizing* existing workouts and *creating* new ones.

So, as a result of the previous analysis, we will reach out to six important areas of the ProFitOro application:

- The first page where the user can register or login. This page also allows the user to start using the application without being authenticated.
- The main page where the Pomodoro timer resides.
- The main page with the timer of Pomodoro's break that displays a workout to be performed during this break.
- The area where it is possible to change the user settings such as username and profile picture, and configure the Pomodoro timer.
- The section where it is possible to observe the statistical data regarding the performed workouts during the day, week, or month.
- The section that displays all the existing workouts and allows the user to add a new workout.

Now that we already have an idea of how to outline our application, we can start thinking about creating some mockups to have a better feeling about it and anticipate possible issues as early as possible.

Mockups

Now that we have all our nouns and verbs, we can start making connections between all the sections of our application. We can actually start preparing some mockups. Sit down with someone, discuss, explain your idea, and collect feedback. Ask questions. Answer questions. Use a whiteboard, use post-its. Use paper: draw, discard, and redraw again.

I have a good friend called Safura. She is a working student currently studying computer science in Berlin, and we work together in the same team. She is interested in the UI/UX topic. Actually, she will write her master's thesis in the **Human-Computer Interaction (HCI)** area. So, we sat together, and I explained the idea of ProFitOro to her. You cannot imagine the number of questions she asked. Then, we started to draw. And to redraw. "And what if....?" redraw again.

This is how the first mockups on paper looked:

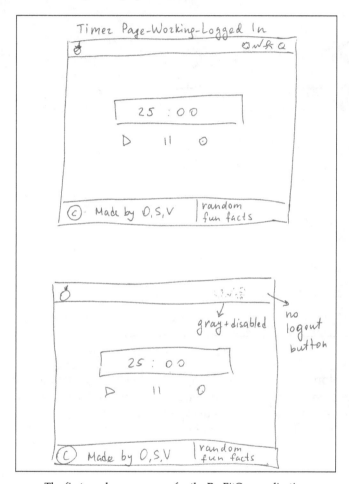

The first mockups on paper for the ProFitOro application

After all the brainstorming and drawing and redrawing, Safura prepared some nice mockups for me. She used *WireframeSketcher* for this purpose (http://wireframesketcher.com/).

The first page – login and register

The very first page that the user sees is the page that allows them to log in, register, or start using ProFitOro without any registration. This is how it looks:

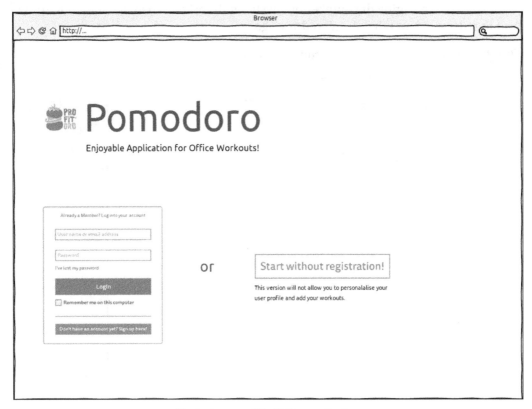

The login page of ProFitOro application

The wording, colors, and figures are not final yet. The most important part of your mockups is the positioning of the elements. You will still work with designers, and you will still have to implement this using your favorite programming language (which is JavaScript/HTML/CSS for us). Mockups help you remember the important details of your application.

The main page displaying the Pomodoro timer

The next mockup of the application shows when the Pomodoro timer is started:

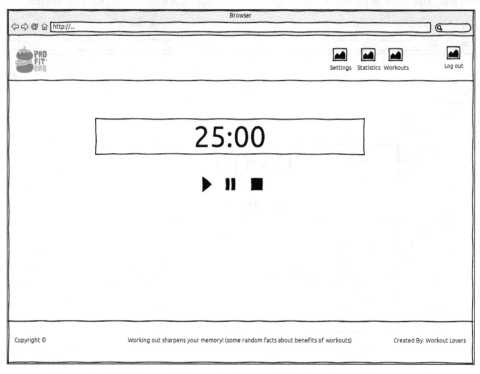

Main screen of the application – working timer is started

As you can see, we are aiming at having a simple and clean interface. There are four links in the header area. They are as follows:

- **Link to the settings page**: It will open the personal settings for the user. User can change personal data such as password, profile photo, and Pomodoro timer settings.

- **Link to the statistics page**: It will open the popup containing statistical user's data.

- **Link to the workouts**: This will open the page containing all the available workouts. This page will also provide the possibility to add new workouts.

- **Link to logout**

These links are only enabled for registered and authenticated users. For anonymous users, these links will be disabled.

Workout during the break

When the working Pomodoro is over, the small break of five minutes begins. During this break, the user is offered the possibility of doing a small simple workout:

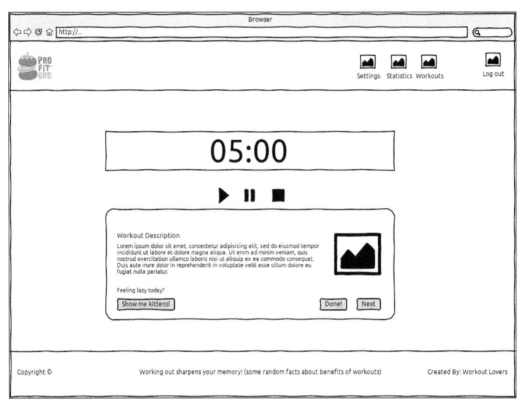

During the short break, the user is offered a possibility of doing a small workout

As you can see, the workout area offers the following:

- First of all, you can just finish your exercise and click on **Done!**. This action will store your workout to your statistical data.

- If, for some reason, you do not want to do the suggested exercise but you still want to do something, then you can click on **Next**. This will offer you a new randomly selected workout.

- If, for some reason, you feel tired and don't want to exercise at all, then you can click on the **Show me kittens!** button that will render the area with random kittens at which you can stare until the end of your break period.

Settings

If the user wants to change the configuration of their personal settings or their Pomodoro interval's time, the user has to proceed to the **Settings** area. This area looks like this:

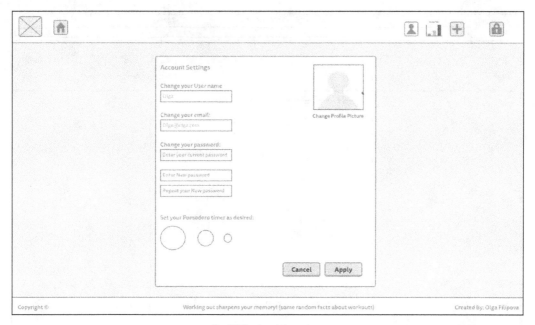

ProFitOro's settings area

As you can see, the **Settings** area allows us to change the user's personal data and to configure Pomodoro's timings.

Statistics

If the user wants to check their statistics and click on the **Statistic** menu button, a popup will open, with some charts showing what workouts have been done by the user daily, weekly, and monthly:

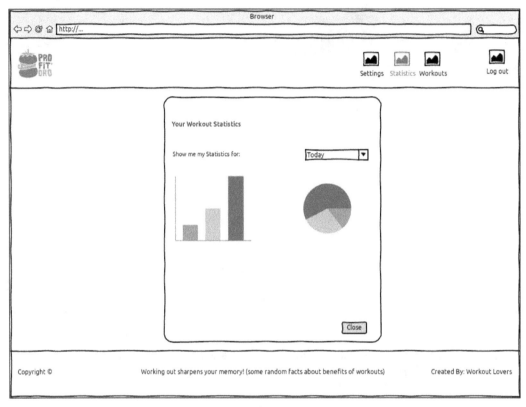

Statistic data popup

Workouts

Finally, if you feel that you might have an idea for a workout that is not present in the application, you can always open the **Workouts** section and add a new workout:

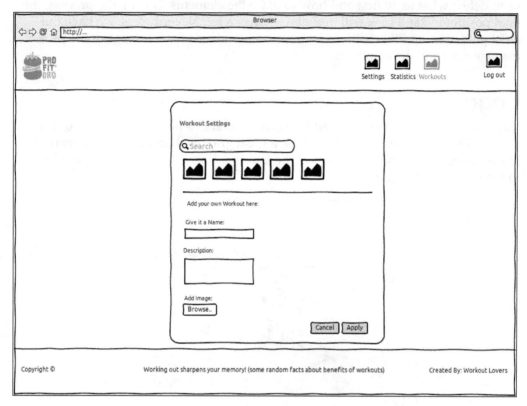

Workouts section

As you can see, in the **Workouts** section, users can visualize the whole list of workouts, search for them, and compile their own list of workouts. By default, all the workouts that are listed in the application will form your daily routine. However, in this area, it is possible to toggle their selection. The configuration will be stored for each user.

It is also possible to create new workouts. Adding a new workout consists of providing a title, description, and an image.

These mockups are not dictating the final look of the application. They just assist us to define what to do first and how to place the elements. During the process, the final positioning and look will probably change a lot. Nevertheless, we have our strict guideline, and this is the most important outcome for this stage of the project management and development.

Logo

You have probably noticed that all the screens contain a nice logo. This logo was designed by a very good friend of mine, a great graphic designer called Carina. I have already mentioned this logo in the *Learning Vue.js 2* book, but I would love to mention it again. Here it is:

The ProFitOro logotype designed by my friend Carina

Isn't it nice? Doesn't it reflect what our application will allow us to do — use the Pomodoro technique combined with small workouts? We even defined ProFitOro's motto:

Take breaks during work. Exercise during breaks.

Summary

In this chapter, we applied the very basic principles of designing an application's user interface. We brainstormed, defined our personas and wrote user stories, retrieved nouns and verbs from these stories, and ended up with some nice mockups for our application.

In the next chapter, we will start implementing our ProFitOro. We will use Vue.js to scaffold the application and split it into important components. Thus, in the next chapter we will do the following:

- Scaffold the ProFitOro application using vue-cli with the `webpack` template
- Split the application into the components and create all the necessary components for the application
- Implement a basic Pomodoro timer using Vue.js and Bootstrap

4
Let It Pomodoro!

The previous chapter ended with a nice set of mockups for the *ProFitOro* application. We have previously defined what the application should do; we have also determined an average user profile, and we are ready to implement it. In this chapter, we will finally start coding. So, in this chapter, we will do the following:

- Scaffold *ProFitOro* using vue-cli with the `webpack` template
- Define all the needed application's components
- Create placeholders for all the components
- Implement a component that will be responsible for rendering the Pomodoro timer using Vue.js and Bootstrap
- Revisit the basics of trigonometric functions (you were not expecting that, right?)

Scaffolding the application

Before everything, let's make sure that we are on the same page, at least regarding the node version. The version of Node.js I'm using is *6.11.1*.

Let's start by creating a skeleton for our application. We will use vue-cli with the `webpack` template. If you don't remember what **vue-cli** is about and where it comes from, check the official Vue documentation in this regard at `https://github.com/vuejs/vue-cli`. If for some reason you still haven't installed it, proceed with its installation:

```
npm install -g vue-cli
```

Now, let's bootstrap our application. I'm sure you remember that, in order to initialize the application with `vue-cli`, you must run the `vue init` command followed by the name of the template to be used and the name of the project itself. We are going to use the `webpack` template, and our application's name is `profitoro`. So, let's initialize it:

```
vue init webpack profitoro
```

During the initialization process you will be asked some questions. Just keep hitting *Enter* to answer the default `Yes` to all of them; `Yes` because for this application we will need everything: linters, vue-router, unit testing, end-to-end testing, everything. This is gonna be huge!

Your console output should look nearly the same as mine:

Console output on application's initialization

Now, run `npm install` inside the newly created `profitoro` directory:

```
cd profitoro
npm install
```

Let's install the `sass` loader because we are going to use the `sass` preprocessor to style our application:

```
npm install sass-loader node-sass --save-dev
```

Finally, we are ready to run it:

```
npm run dev
```

Your new Vue application is ready to be worked on. In order to have a clean playground for our ProFitOro, remove everything related to the `Hello` component that are installed, along with the default installation process. As an alternative, just open the code files of *Chapter 4, Let it Pomodoro!* and get the boilerplate code from the `chapter4/1/profitoro` folder.

Defining ProFitOro components

Our application consists of two main screens.

One of the screens is the so-called *Landing page*; this page consists of the following parts:

- A logo
- A tagline
- An authentication section
- A link to the application to be used without being registered

Schematically, this is how our components are positioned on the screen:

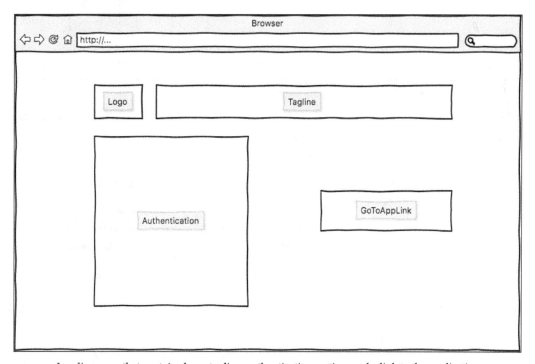

Landing page that contains logo, tagline, authentication section, and a link to the application

The second screen is the main application screen. This screen contains three parts:

- A header
- A footer
- The content

The content part contains the Pomodoro timer. If the user is authenticated, it will contain settings, workouts, and statistics as well:

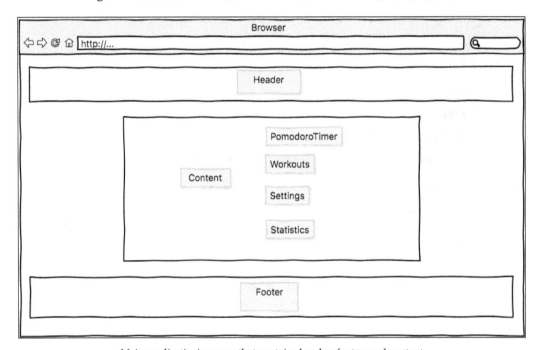

Main application's screen that contains header, footer, and content

Let's create a folder called components and subfolders called main, landing, and common for the corresponding sub-components.

Components for the landing and main pages will reside in the components folder; the remaining 11 components will be distributed between the respective subfolders.

For each defined component file, add the template, script, and style sections. Add the lang="sass" attribute to the style tag because, as I already mentioned, we are going to use the sass preprocessor to style our components. So, for example, HeaderComponent.vue will look as follows:

```
//HeaderComponent.vue
<template>
  <div>Header</div>
```

```
</template>
<script>
  export default {


  }
</script>
<style scoped lang="sass">

</style>
```

As a result, we have 13 placeholders for our components ready to be filled with the necessary data. These components are going to be used and reused. This is because Vue components are *re-usable components*, and that is why they are so powerful. During the development process, we will inevitably add more components and subcomponents, but here is our base:

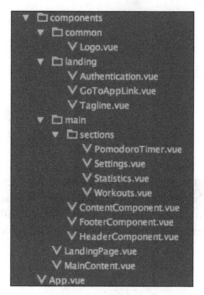

13 base components for ProFitOro

Check our bootstrapped components in the `chapter4/2/profitoro` folder.

Let's also prepare our `LandingPage` and `MainContent` components by filling them with the needed subcomponents. Before that, add an `index.js` file to every subfolder and export the corresponding subfolder's content in it. This will enable an easier import afterwards. Thus, start with the folder `common` and add `index.js` file with the following content:

```
//common/index.js
export {default as Logo} from './Logo'
```

Repeat the same operation for the folders `sections`, `main`, and `landing`.

Now we can compose our landing page and main content components. Let's start with `LandingPage.vue`. This component consists of a logo, an authentication section, a link to the app, and a tagline. Import all these components, export them to the `components` object, and use them in the `template`! The fact that we have exported these components in the `index.js` file allows us to import them as follows:

```
//LandingPage.vue
import {Authentication, GoToAppLink, Tagline} from './landing'
import {Logo} from './common'
```

Now we can use these imported components in the `components` object of the `LandingPage` component. By the way, have you ever seen so many words *component* in the same phrase? "Component, component, component" and the exported object looks as the following:

```
//LandingPage.vue
export default {
  components: {
    Logo,
    Authentication,
    GoToAppLink,
    Tagline
  }
}
```

After being exported within the `components` object, all these components can be used inside the template. Note that everything that is **CamelCased** will become **KebabCased** inside the template. So, our `GoToAppLink` will look like `go-to-app-link`. Thus, our components inside the template will look as follows:

```
<logo></logo>
<tagline></tagline>
<authentication></authentication>
<go-to-app-link></go-to-app-link>
```

Hence, our whole `LandingPage` component will have the following code for now:

```
//LandingPage.vue
<template>
  <div>
    <logo></logo>
    <tagline></tagline>
```

```
      <authentication></authentication>
      <go-to-app-link></go-to-app-link>
    </div>
  </template>
  <script>
    import {Authentication, GoToAppLink, Tagline} from './landing'
    import {Logo} from './common'
    export default {
      components: {
        Logo,
        Authentication,
        GoToAppLink,
        Tagline
      }
    }
  </script>
  <style scoped lang="sass">

  </style>
```

Let's tell App.vue to render this component:

```
//App.vue
<template>
  <div id="app">
    <h1>Welcome to Profitoro</h1>
    <landing-page></landing-page>
  </div>
</template>

<script>
  import LandingPage from './components/LandingPage'
  export default {
    name: 'app',
    components: {
      LandingPage
    }
  }
</script>
```

Check the page. Can you see your components? I'm sure, you can:

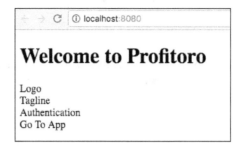

LandingPage component

Now, we *only* have to implement the corresponding components and our landing page is ready!

Exercise

Do the same for the MainContent component—import and export all necessary subcomponents and add them to the template. After that, call the MainContent component in the App.vue, just like we just did with the LandingPage component. If in doubt, check the code in the chapter4/3/profitoro folder.

Implementing the Pomodoro timer

One of the most important components of our application is, without any doubt, the Pomodoro timer. It performs the main functionality of the application. So, it might be a good idea to implement it in the first place.

I am thinking of some kind of a circular timer. Something like this:

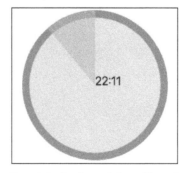

Circular timer to be implemented as a Pomodoro timer

As time passes, the highlighted sector will move counterclockwise and the time will count down as well. To implement this kind of structure, I am thinking of three components:

- *SvgCircleSector*: This component will just receive an angle as a property and color the corresponding sector of the SVG circle.

- *CountDownTimer*: This component will receive the number of seconds to countdown, implement the timer and calculate the angle to pass to the `SvgCircularComponent` on each timer update.

- *PomodoroTimer*: We have already bootstrapped this component. This component will be responsible to call the `CountDownTimer` component with the initial time and update it to the corresponding number of seconds depending on the current working Pomodoro or break interval.

SVG and trigonometry

Let's start by defining our `SvgCircleSector` component. This component will receive `angle` and `text` as properties and draw an SVG circle with a highlighted sector of a given angle. Create a folder called `timer` inside the `components/main/sections` folder and then create an `SvgCircleSector.vue` file in it. Define the needed sections for `template`, `script`, and `style`. You can also export `props` with the `angle` and `text` properties that this component will receive from its parent:

```
//SvgCircleSector.vue
<template>
  <div>
  </div>
</template>
<script>
  export default {
    props: ['angle', 'text']
  }
</script>
<style scoped lang="scss">
</style>
```

So, how do we draw a circle using the SVG and by highlighting its sector? First of all, let's draw two circles: one inside the other. Let's make the bigger one of 100px radius and the smaller one of 90px radius. Essentially, we have to provide the center, *x* and *y* coordinates, the radius (r), and the fill attributes. Check the documentation regarding the circles in SVG at https://developer.mozilla.org/en-US/docs/Web/SVG/Element/circle. We will end up with something like this:

```
<svg width="200" height="200" xmlns="http://www.w3.org/2000/svg">
    <circle r="100" cx="100" cy="100" fill="gray"></circle>
    <circle r="90" cx="100" cy="100" fill="lightgray"></circle>
</svg>
```

Thus, we've obtained our two circles, one inside the other:

Two circles drawn with the SVG circle element

Now, in order to draw a circle's highlighted sector, we will use the *path* SVG element (https://developer.mozilla.org/en-US/docs/Web/SVG/Element/path).

With the SVG path element, you are able to draw whatever you want. Its main attribute, called d, is basically a way to program your path using, let's say, the SVG domain-specific language. For example, this is how to draw a triangle inside our circles:

```
<path d="M100,100 V0 L0,100 H0 z"></path>
```

What do these codes stand for? M means *move*, L means *line*, V means *vertical line*, H means *horizontal line*, and z means *stop the path here*. So, we tell our path to first move to 100,100 (the circle center), then to draw a vertical line until it reaches the 0 point of the *y* axis, then to draw a line to the 0, 100 *x,y* coordinates, then to draw a horizontal line until it reaches the 100 *x* coordinate, and then to stop. Our two-dimension coordinates area is composed of the *x* and *y* axes, where *x* starts at 0 and goes up until 200 from the left to the right and *y* starts at 0 and goes up until 200 from top to bottom.

This is how the (x, y) coordinates look for the center and extreme points of our small circle coordinate system:

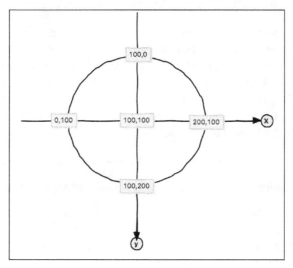

Marked points represent the (x,y) coordinates of our SVG circle with the center at (100,100)

Thus, if we start at (100,100), draw a vertical line to (100,0), and then draw a line to (0, 100) and then draw a horizontal line until (100,100), we end up with a right triangle drawn in the upper-left quadrant of our circle:

Path draws a triangle inside the circle

This was just a small introduction into the path SVG element and what is achievable with it. However, we still need to draw a circle sector and not just a triangle.
In order to draw a sector using path, we can use a command A inside a d attribute.
A means *arc*. It's probably the most complicated command of the path. It receives the following information: *rx, ry, x-axis-rotation, large-arc-flag, sweep-flag, x, y*.

The first four attributes in our case can always be `100, 100, 0, 0`. If you want to understand why, check the w3c documentation regarding arc path attributes at `https://www.w3.org/TR/SVG/paths.html#PathDataEllipticalArcCommands`.

For us, the most important attributes are the last three ones. The *sweep-flag* means the orientation of the *arc*; it can be either `0` or `1` for clockwise and counterclockwise orientation. In our case, it will always be *0* because this is how we want our arc to be drawn (counterclockwise). As for the last *x* and *y* values, these are the values that determine where the arc will stop. So, for example, if we want to draw the upper-left sector at *90* degrees, we would stop the arc at the (`0, 100`) coordinates — *x* is `0` and *y* is `100` — thus our d attribute will look as follows:

```
d="M100,100 L100,0 A100,100 0 0,0 0,100 z"
```

The whole SVG element containing two circles and the sector would look like this:

```
<svg width="200" height="200" xmlns="http://www.w3.org/2000/svg">
  <circle r="100" cx="100" cy="100" fill="gray"></circle>
  <circle r="90" cx="100" cy="100" fill="lightgray"></circle>
  <path id="sector" fill="darkgray" opacity="0.6" d="M100,100
  L100,0 A100,100 0 0,0 0, 100 z"></path>
</svg>
```

This code produces the following result:

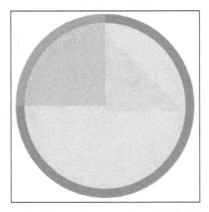

Sector of 90 degrees drawn with path SVG element

We must actually define this d attribute as a dynamic attribute on which the computed value will depend. To express this, we must use v-bind with an attribute following the semicolon: v-bind:d, or just simply, :d. Let's name the corresponding property path and add it to the exported object computed of our component:

```
//SvgCircleSector.vue
<template>
  <div>
    <svg class="timer" width="200" height="200"
    xmlns="http://www.w3.org/2000/svg">
      <...>
      <path class="segment" :d="path"></path>
    </svg>
  </div>
</template>
<script>
  function calcPath (angle) {
    let d
    d = "M100,100 L100,0 A100,100 0 0,0 0, 100 z"
    return d
  }
  export default {
    props: ['angle', 'text'],
    computed: {
      path () {
        return calcPath(this.angle)
      }
    }
  }
</script>
```

I introduced a function called calcPath that will determine our path string. For now, it returns the path that will highlight the *90* degree area.

We are almost done. We can actually draw a segment, but what is missing is the ability to draw a segment for any angle. Our SvgCircleSector component will receive an angle as a property. This angle will not always equal *90* degrees. We should come up with a formula that will calculate the end *x* and *y* coordinates, given the angle. If you are not interested in revisiting basic trigonometry, just skip this part and proceed to the end of this section.

This is how I calculate the *x, y* coordinates for the angles that are less than *180* degrees:

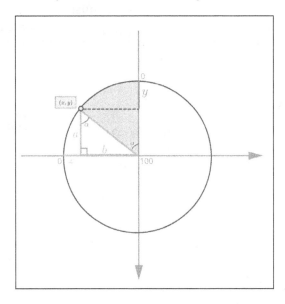

To calculate (x,y) for angle α, we need to calculate the a and b sides of the right triangle

From the figure, we can see that:

```
x = 100 - b
y = 100 - a
```

Thus, we just need to calculate a and b. This is an easy task. We can calculate the legs of the right triangle knowing the angle and the hypotenuse. The hypotenuse c is equal to the circle's radius (100 in our case). The leg a, which is adjacent to the angle, is equal to c * cosα and the leg b, which is the opposite to the angle's leg, is equal to c * sinα. Thus:

```
x = 100 - 100 * sinα
y = 100 - 100 * cosα
```

For the angle that is greater than *180* degrees, we have the following scheme:

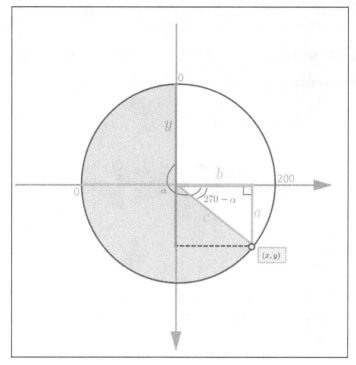

For the angle greater than 180°, we also have to calculate the sides of the right triangle

Can I tell you a secret? I am really bad at drawing these kind of schemes. I tried everything from sketches on paper to drawing using Gimp. Everything was looking really ugly. Fortunately, I have my brother *Illia* who created these graphics in five minutes using Sketch. Thank you very much, *Ilushka*!

Back to our case. In this case, the angle of the right triangle equals 270° - α. Our x equals 100 + b and y equals 100 + a. Here are the simple calculations:

```
a = c * sin (270 - α)
a = c * sin (180 + (90 - α))
a = -c * sin (90 - α)
a = -c * cosα
b = c * cos (270 - α)
b = c * cos (180 + (90 - α))
b = -c * cos (90 - α)
b = -c * sinα
```

Therefore:

```
x = 100 + (-100 * sinα) = 100 - 100*sinα
y = 100 + (-100 * cosα) = 100 - 100*cosα
```

This is exactly the same as for the angles that are less than *180* degrees!

This is what the JavaScript code for the calculations of the *x*, *y* coordinates will look like:

```
function calcEndPoint (angle) {
  let x, y

  x = 100 - 100 * Math.sin(Math.PI * angle / 180)
  y = 100 - 100 * Math.cos(Math.PI * angle / 180)

  return {
    x, y
  }
}
```

Now, we can finally define a function that will determine a d string attribute for the path element depending on the angle. This function will call the `calcEndPoint` function and will return a `string` containing a final d attribute:

```
function calcPath (angle) {
  let d
  let {x, y} = calcEndPoint(angle)
  if (angle <= 180) {
    d = `M100,100 L100, 0 A100,100 0 0,0 ${x}, ${y} z`
  } else {
    d = `M100,100 L100, 0 A100,100 0 0,0 100, 200 A100,100 0 0,
    0 ${x}, ${y} z`
  }
  return d
}
```

To finalize our component, let's introduce a text SVG element that will just render a text property passed to the component. It should also be possible to draw a circle without any text; therefore, let's make this element conditional. We achieve it using the `v-if` directive:

```
//SvgCircleSector.vue
<template>
  <div>
    <svg class="timer" width="200" height="200"
    xmlns="http://www.w3.org/2000/svg">
      <...>
```

```
    <text v-if="text != ''" class="text" x="100" y="100">
      {{text}}
    </text>
  </svg>
</div>
</template>
```

Let's also extract the styling for the big and small circles, and for the path and text to the style section. Let's define meaningful classes so that our template will look as follows:

```
//SvgCircleSector.vue
<template>
  <div>
    <svg class="timer" width="200" height="200"
    xmlns="http://www.w3.org/2000/svg">
      <circle class="bigCircle" r="100" cx="100"
      cy="100"></circle>
      <circle class="smallCircle" r="90" cx="100"
      cy="100"></circle>
      <path class="segment" :d="path"></path>
      <text v-if="text != ''" class="text" x="100" y="100">
        {{text}}
      </text>
    </svg>
  </div>
</template>
```

Inside the style tags, let's define variables for colors and use them for our circles. Extracting colors to the variables will help us to change them easily in the future, if we decide to change the color scheme of our application. Thus, the styling for our SVG component will look like the following:

```
//SvgCircleSector.vue
<style scoped lang="scss">
  $big-circle-color: gray;
  $small-circle-color: lightgray;
  $segment-color: darkgray;
  $text-color: black;

  .bigCircle {
    fill: $big-circle-color;
  }
  .smallCircle {
    fill: $small-circle-color;
  }
  .segment {
    fill: $segment-color;opacity: 0.6;
  }
```

```
      .text {
        font-size: 1em;
        stroke-width: 0;
        opacity: .9;
        fill: $text-color;
      }
  </style>
```

Exercise

Until now, we were using an absolute size for our circle; it always had a radius of `100` pixels. Use the `viewBox` and `preserveAspectRatio` attributes applied to the `svg` element to make our circle responsive. Play with it; invoke this component in the `PomodoroTimer` component with different angle property to see how it works. I was able to come up with this kind of crazy page:

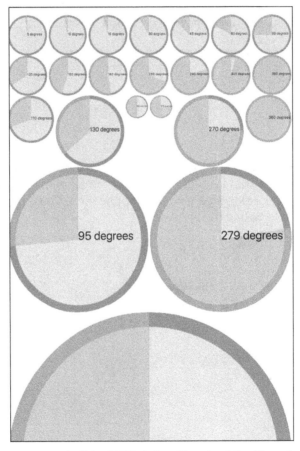

Crazy page composed of lots of SVG circles with sector defined by a given angle

Check the code in the `chapter4/4/profitoro` folder. Particularly, pay attention to the `SvgCircleSector.vue` component that resides inside the `components/sections/timer` folder and to the `PomodoroTimer.vue` component where the circle component is being called plenty of times with different angle properties.

Implementing the countdown timer component

Now that we have a fully functional component that renders a circle with a highlighted area given an angle, we will implement the `CountDownTimer` component. This component will receive a number of seconds to count down as a property. It will contain the controls element: a set of buttons that will allow you to *start*, *pause* and *stop* the timer. Once the timer is started, the seconds will be counted down and the angle will be recalculated accordingly. This recalculated angle is passed to the `SvgCircleSector` component as well as the calculated text. The text will contain the number of minutes and seconds that are left on the timer to end.

To start, create a `CountDownTimer.vue` file inside the `components/main/sections/timer` folder. Let's invoke the `SvgCircleSector` component from this component with some arbitrary values for the `angle` and `text` properties:

```
//CountDownTimer.vue
<template>
  <div class="container">
    <div>
      <svg-circle-sector :angle="30" :text="'Hello'"></svg-circle-
      sector>
    </div>
  </div>
</template>
<script>
  import SvgCircleSector from './SvgCircleSector'
  export default {
    components: {
      SvgCircleSector
    }
  }
</script>
<style scoped lang="scss">

</style>
```

Open the page. It's a bit huge. It doesn't even fit on my screen:

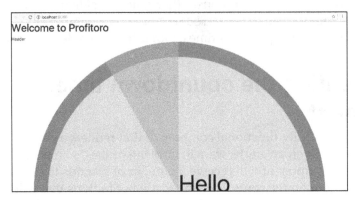

Our component doesn't fit on my screen

However, if I open it on a mobile, it renders without any problem and actually looks nice:

Our component actually fits quite well on the mobile screen

It happens because our circle is responsive. If you try to resize your browser, you will see that the circle resizes accordingly. Its width is always *100%* of the browser. When the height of the page is bigger than the width (which is the case of the mobile browser) it looks nice, but when the width is greater than the height (as in the case of the desktop screen), it looks really big and ugly. So, our circle is responsive but not really adaptive. But we are using Bootstrap! Bootstrap is a big friend when it comes to responsiveness and adaptiveness.

Responsiveness and adaptiveness of the countdown timer using Bootstrap

In order to achieve adaptiveness to any device, we will build our layout using the Bootstrap grid system at `https://v4-alpha.getbootstrap.com/layout/grid/`.

 Mind that this URL is for the alpha version, and the next version will be available on the official website.

This system is based on a twelve-column row layout. The `row` and `col` classes include different tiers, one for each media query. Thus, the same element can have different relative sizes based on the device size. The names of these classes are self-explanatory. The wrapping row class name is `row`. Then, each column may have a class called `col`. This is, for example, a simple row with four columns of equal size:

```
<div class="row">
  <div class="col">Column 1</div>
  <div class="col">Column 2</div>
  <div class="col">Column 3</div>
  <div class="col">Column 4</div>
</div>
```

This code will produce the following result:

Column 1	Column 2	Column 3	Column 4

Bootstrap row with four equal-sized columns

The class `col` can be combined with the size that you want to give to your column:

```
<div class="col-*">Column 1</div>
```

Here, `*` can be anything from 1 to 12 since each row can contain up to twelve columns. Here's the example of a row with four columns of different sizes:

```
<div class="row">
  <div class="col-6">Column 1</div>
  <div class="col-3">Column 2</div>
  <div class="col-2">Column 3</div>
  <div class="col-1">Column 4</div>
</div>
```

So, the first column will occupy half of the row, the second will be the fourth part of the row, the third one is 1/6th part of the row, and the last on is 1/12th part of the row. Here's what it looks like:

Column 1	Column 2	Column 3	Column 4

Bootstrap row with different-sized columns

Don't mind the black borders; I've added them so the column width becomes more obvious. Bootstrap will draw your layout without any borders, unless you tell it to include them.

Bootstrap also provides a technique for offsetting columns for a given number of columns at `https://v4-alpha.getbootstrap.com/layout/grid/#offsetting-columns`.

 Mind that this URL is for the alpha version, and the next version will be available on the official website.

This is how, for example, we make two columns, one of which is of the size 6 and the other is of the size 2 with an offset of 4:

```
<div class="row">
  <div class="col-6">Column 1</div>
  <div class="col-2 offset-4">Column 2</div>
</div>
```

Here's what it looks like:

Column 1	Column 2

Row with two columns, one of which is displayed with an offset of size 4

You can even play with the columns and change their order by playing with `push-*` and `pull-*` classes. For more information, visit `https://v4-alpha.getbootstrap.com/layout/grid/#push-and-pull`.

 Mind that this URL is for the alpha version, and the next version will be available on the official website

These classes play almost the same role as the `offset-*` classes; they allow more flexibility for your columns. For example, if we want to render a column of size 3 and a column of size 9 and change their order, we will need to push the column of size 3 for 9 positions and pull column of size 9 for 3 positions:

```
<div class="row">
  <div class="col-3 push-9">Column 1</div>
  <div class="col-9 pull-3">Column 2</div>
</div>
```

This code will produce the following layout:

Column 2	Column 1

Changed columns order using push-* and pull-* classes

Try all these examples and check that, however you resize your page, the proportions of your layout will always be the same. This is a powerful feature of Bootstrap's layouts; you don't even have to bother making your layout responsive. What about the different devices that I mentioned in the first paragraph of this section? Until now, we were exploring classes called `col-*`, `offset-*`, `push-*`, and `pull-*`. Bootstrap also provides this set of classes for each kind of media query.

There are five types of devices in Bootstrap:

xs	Extra small devices	Portrait phones (<544px)
sm	Small devices	Landscape phones (≥544px - <768px)
md	Medium devices	Tablets (≥768px - <992px)
lg	Large devices	Desktops (≥992px - <1200px)
xl	Extra-large devices	Desktops (≥1200px)

In order to indicate the desired behavior on a given device, you just pass the device designation between the class name and its size. So, for example, if you want two columns of size 8 and 4, respectively, to transform into two stacked columns on mobile, you could do something like the following:

```
<div class="row">
  <div class="col-sm-12 col-md-8">Column 1</div>
  <div class="col-sm-12 col-md-4">Column 2</div>
</div>
```

If you open this code in the browser and try to resize the page, you will see that once the size is less than 544 pixels, the columns will stack:

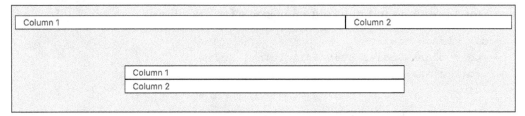

Two-column layout becomes a stacked equal-sized column layout on a small screen

So what should we do with our timer? I would say that it can occupy the whole width (*100%*) on small devices, 2/3 of the width on medium-width devices, become half of the width on large devices, and 1/3 of the width of extra-large devices. So, it will require the following classes:

- **col-sm-12** for small devices
- **col-md-8** for medium-width devices
- **col-lg-6** for large devices
- **col-xl-4** for extra-large devices

I also want my circle to appear in the center of the screen. For this, I will use the `justify-content-center` class, applied to the row:

```
<div class="row justify-content-center">
  <svg-circle-sector class="col-sm-12 col-md-8 col-lg-6 col-xl-4"
  :angle="30" :text="'Hello'"></svg-circle-sector>
</div>
```

Open the page and try to resize it and simulate different devices, testing the portrait and landscape view. Our circle resizes accordingly. Check the code in the `chapter4/5/profitoro` folder; particularly, pay attention to the `components/CountDownTimer.vue` component.

Countdown timer component – let's count down time!

We have already achieved the responsiveness of the countdown timer component. Let's finally make it a real countdown timer component. Let's start by adding controls: start, pause, and stop buttons. For now, I will make them look like links. For this, I will use the `btn-link` class of Bootstrap at `https://v4-alpha.getbootstrap.com/components/buttons/`.

Mind that this URL is for the alpha version, and the next version will be available on the official website.

I will also use the Vue's `v-on` directive to bind a method on each button click at `https://vuejs.org/v2/api/#v-on`:

```
<button v-on:click="start">Start</button>
```

Alternatively, we could simply use:

```
<button @click="start">Start</button>
```

Hence, the code for buttons will look like the following:

```
<div class="controls">
  <div class="btn-group" role="group">
    <button @click="start" type="button"
    class="btn btn-link">Start</button>
    <button @click="pause" type="button"
    class="btn btn-link">Pause</button>
    <button @click="stop" type="button"
    class="btn btn-link">Stop</button>
  </div>
</div>
```

Add the `text-center` class to the wrapping container `div`, so the buttons are centrally aligned. Now, with the control buttons, our timer looks like this:

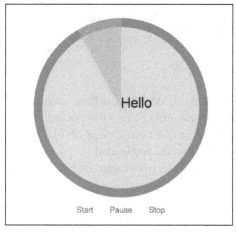

Countdown timer with control buttons

When we started discussing this component, we said that it will receive the time in seconds to countdown from its parent. Let's add a property called `time` and let's pass this property from the parent component:

```
//CountDownTimer.vue
<script>
  <...>
  export default {
    props: ['time']
    <...>
  }
</script>
```

For now, let's export this property as a computed hard-coded property in the `PomodorTimer` component and bind it to the `CountDownTimer` component. Let's hardcode it to 25 minutes, or 25 * 60 seconds:

```
//PomodoroTimer.vue
<template>
  <div>
    <count-down-timer :time="time"></count-down-timer>
  </div>
</template>
<script>
  import CountDownTimer from './timer/CountDownTimer'
  export default {
    computed: {
      time () {
        return 25 * 60
      }
    },
    components: {
      CountDownTimer
    }
  }
</script>
```

Ok, so our countdown component receives the time in seconds. How will it update the `angle` and the `text`? Since we cannot change the parent's property (`time`), we need to introduce a value belonging to this component and then we will be able to change it inside the component and compute angle and text values based on this value. Let's introduce this new value and call it `timestamp`. Put it inside the data function of the countdown component:

```
//CountDownTimer.vue
data () {
  return {
    timestamp: this.time
  }
},
```

Let's now add a computed value for the `angle`. How do we calculate the angle based on the timestamp in seconds? If we knew the value in degrees for each second, then we would just multiply this value by the number of needed seconds:

```
angle = DegreesPerSecond * this.timestamp
```

Knowing the initial time in seconds, it's easy to calculate the number of degrees for each second. Since the whole circumference has *360 degrees*, we just need to divide *360* by the *initial time*:

```
DegreesPerSecond = 360/this.time
```

Last, but not least, since our timer is a counterclockwise timer, we need to pass the inverse angle to the `SvgCircleSector` component, so our final computed value for the angle will look like this:

```
computed: {
  angle () {
    return 360 - (360 / this.time * this.timestamp)
  }
}
```

Replace the hardcoded angle binding in the template by the value of the angle:

```
<svg-circle-sector :angle="angle"></svg-circle-sector>
```

Play with the value of `timestamp`; try to set it from `0 * 60` to `25 * 60`. You will see how the highlighted area changes accordingly:

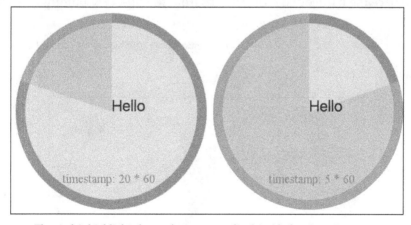

The circle's highlighted area changes accordingly with the given timestamp

I'm not sure about you, but I am tired of seeing this Hello. Let's do something about it. The text of the timer should display the number of minutes and seconds remaining until the end of the countdown time; it corresponds to the un-highlighted area of the timer circle. This is a pretty easy calculation. If we divide our timestamp by 60 and obtain the whole part of the division, we will get the current number of minutes. If we obtain the rest of this division, we will obtain the current number of seconds. The text should display minutes and seconds divided by the colon (:). So, let's add these three computed values:

```
//CountDownTimer.vue
computed: {
  angle () {
    return 360 - (360 / this.time * this.timestamp)
  },
  minutes () {
    return Math.floor(this.timestamp / 60)
  },
  seconds () {
    return this.timestamp % 60
  },
  text () {
    return `${this.minutes}:${this.seconds}`
  }
},
```

Note that we are using ES6 templates for computing our text (https://developer.mozilla.org/en/docs/Web/JavaScript/Reference/Template_literals).

Finally, replace the hardcoded string Hello from the property binding with the text value:

```
<svg-circle-sector :angle="angle" :text="text"></svg-circle-sector>
```

Isn't it much better now?

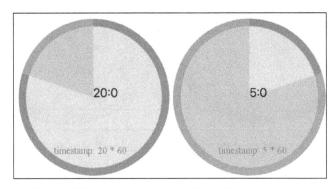

The text of the timer changes according to the remaining time

Well, the only missing thing now is to actually start the timer and make it countdown. We already invoked the `start`, `pause`, and `stop` methods on each of the corresponding button clicks. Let's create these methods:

```
//CountDownTimer.vue
methods: {
  start () {
  },
  pause () {
  },
  stop () {

  }
},
```

What should happen inside these methods? The `start` method should set an interval that each second will decrease the timer by one second. The `pause` method should pause this interval and the `stop` method should clear this interval and reset the timestamp. Introduce a new variable called `interval` in the data function of the component and add the needed methods:

```
//CountDownTimer.vue
data () {
  return {
    timestamp: this.time,
    interval: null
  }
},
<...>
methods: {
  start () {
    this.interval = setInterval(() => {
      this.timestamp--
      if (this.timestamp === 0) {
        this.timestamp = this.time
      }
    }, 1000)
  },
  pause () {
    clearInterval(this.interval)
  },
  stop () {
    clearInterval(this.interval)
    this.timestamp = this.time
  }
}
```

And... we are done! Open the page, click on the control buttons, play with different values for the initial time, and check how nicely it works! Check the code for the `CountDownTimer` component in the `chapter4/6/profitoro` folder.

Exercise

Our countdown timer looks really nice, but it still has some problems. First of all, the text doesn't look that nice. When the number of minutes or seconds is less than 9, it displays the corresponding text without the trailing 0, for example, **5:5** for *5 minutes and 5 seconds*. This doesn't look exactly like time. Introduce a method, let's call it `leftpad`, that will add an extra 0 for this kind of cases. And please, try to not to break the internet! (`https://www.theregister.co.uk/2016/03/23/npm_left_pad_chaos/`)

Another problem with our timer is that we can click on any button at any time. If you click a lot on the start button, the result will be unexpectedly ugly. Introduce three data variables — `isStarted`, `isPaused`, and `isStopped` — that will be toggled on each method accordingly. Bind the `disabled` class to the control buttons. This class should be activated based on the mentioned variable's values. So, the behaviour should be the following:

- The start button should be disabled if the timer is already started and is not paused.
- The pause and stop buttons should be disabled if the timer is not started. They should also be disabled if the timer is already paused or stopped.

To bind the class conditionally, use `v-bind:className={expression}`, or simply the `:className={expression}` notation. For example:

```
<button :class="{disabled: isStarted}">Start</button>
```

To check it for yourself, have a look at the `chapter4/7/profitoro` directory, particularly at the `components/CountDownTimer.vue` component.

Pomodoro timer

So, we already have a fully functional countdown timer. We are more than close to the final purpose of our application with the countdown timer that is able to countdown any given amount of time. We just have to implement a Pomodoro timer based on it. Our Pomodoro timer has to initialize the countdown component with the working Pomodoro time and reset it to the resting time once Pomodoro is done. After the break is over, it has to reset it again to the working Pomodoro time. and so on. Don't forget that the break after three regular pomodoros is slightly bigger than the usual one.

Let's create a `config` file with these values so we can easily change it whenever we need to test the application with different timings. So, we need to specify the `workingPomodoro`, `shortBreak`, and `longBreak` values. Let's also specify the number of working *pomodoros* until the long break. By default, it will be three, but in case you are a workaholic, you can specify a longer Pomodoro break only after *23485* regular Pomodoros (don't do that, I still need you!). So, our config file is a regular `.js` file and its content looks like the following:

```
//src/config.js
export default {
   workingPomodoro: 25,
   shortBreak: 5,
   longBreak: 10,
   pomodorosTillLongBreak: 3
}
```

Import this file in the `PomodoroTimer` component. Let's also define the essential data for this component. So, the Pomodoro timer has three main states; it is either in its working state, or it's on a short break, or it's on a long break. It should also count the amount of Pomodoros until the long break. So, our data for the `PomodoroTimer` component will look like the following:

```
//PomodoroTimer.vue
data () {
   return {
     isWorking: true,
     isShortBreak: false,
     isLongBreak: false,
     pomodoros: 0
   }
}
```

Now, we can compute the value of `time` based on the current state of the Pomodoro timer. For this, we just need to multiply the number of minutes corresponding to the current interval by `60`. We need to define which interval in minutes is the correct one and base our decision on the current state of the application. Here it comes, our nice `if-else` construction for the computed value:

```
//PomodoroTimer.vue
computed: {
   time () {
     let minutes

     if (this.isWorking) {
       minutes = config.workingPomodoro
```

```
    } else if (this.isShortBreak) {
      minutes = config.shortBreak
    } else if (this.isLongBreak) {
      minutes = config.longBreak
    }

    return minutes * 60
  }
}
```

This is more than clear, right? Now, we must write the code that will toggle between working Pomodoro, short break, and long break. Let's call this method togglePomodoro. What should this method do? First of all, the isWorking state should be set to true or false depending on the previous value (this.isWorking = !this.isWorking). Then, we should reset both isShortBreak and isLongBreak values. Then we have to check whether the state of isWorking is false, which means that we are currently on a break. If yes, we have to increase the number of pomodoros performed until that moment. And then we need to set one of the breaking states to true depending on the number of pomodoros. Here's the method:

```
//PomodoroTimer.vue
methods: {
  togglePomodoro () {
    // toggle the working state
    this.isWorking = !this.isWorking

    // reset break states
    this.isShortBreak = this.isLongBreak = false

    // we have switched to the working state, just return
    if (this.isWorking) {
      return
    }

    // we have switched to the break state, increase the number of
    // pomodoros and choose between long and short break
    this.pomodoros ++
    this.isLongBreak = this.pomodoros %
    config.pomodorosTillLongBreak === 0
    this.isShortBreak = !this.isLongBreak
  }
}
```

Now, we just have to find a way to call this method. When should it be called? It's clear that this method should be called each time that the countdown timer reaches its zero, but how can we be aware of that? Somehow, the countdown timer component has to communicate to its parent that it has stopped at zero. Luckily for us, with Vue.js, components can emit events using the `this.$emit` method. So, we will trigger this event from the countdown component and bind its handler to the component invoked from the `PomodoroTimer`. Let's call this event `finished`. Open the `CountDownTimer.vue` component and find a place where we check that the decreased timestamp has reached its zero value. At this point, we have to shout *Hey, parent! I have finished my task! Give me another one*. This is a simple code:

```
// CountDownTimer.vue
<...>
if (this.timestamp <= 0) {
    this.$emit('finished')
    this.timestamp = this.time
}
```

Binding this event is more than simple. It's like any other event; just use @ followed by the event name attached to the component inside the template of `PomodoroTimer`:

```
<count-down-timer @finished="togglePomodoro" :time="time"></count-
down-timer>
```

Check the application's page now. Try to play with the timing values in the config file. Check that everything works.

Exercise

Have you already started to use your fresh Pomodoro timer for your daily routine? If yes, I am sure that while the timer is doing its job, you are very happily navigating other tabs and doing other things. Have you noticed that the time is taking longer than it should? Our browsers are really clever; in order to not screw up with your CPU, they stay pretty idle in the inactive tabs. This actually makes perfect sense. Why should inactive tabs perform complex calculations or run some crazy animations based on `setIntervals` and `setTimeout` functions if you are not looking at them? While it makes perfect sense in terms of performance, it doesn't make much sense for our application.

It should countdown 25 minutes no matter what. For this exercise, improve our countdown timer so that it always counts down the exact number of seconds passed to it, even if it is open in the hidden or inactive browser tab. Google it; you will see a whole internet of *Stackoverflow* results:

The internet full of the results googling the strange behaviour of setInerval in the inactive tabs

Another thing that I would like you to do for this exercise is to add a watcher for the time property in the CountDownTimer component that will restart the timer. This will allow us to be more precise with the timer resets whenever the time is changed in the PomodoroTimer component. Check the Vue documentation in this regard, at https://vuejs.org/v2/guide/computed.html#Watchers.

For both tasks, take a look at the `chapter4/8/profitoro` application's folder to check for yourself. The only component where the changes are applied is the `CountDownTimer.vue` component. Pay attention to the `setInterval` function and how the `timestamp` is updated.

Introducing workouts

I have been so enthusiastic writing this chapter, calculating sine, cosine, drawing SVG, implementing a timer, and taking care of the inactive tabs and stuff that I almost forgot to do my workout! I like planks and pushups, what about you? By the way, haven't you also forgotten that workouts are a part of our application? During the breaks, we are supposed to do simple exercises and not just check our social networks!

We will implement full-fledged workouts and their management in the next chapters; for now, let's just leave a nice placeholder for the workout and hard code one exercise in this placeholder (I vote for pushups since the book is mine, but you can add the workout or exercise of your own preference). Open the `PomodoroTimer.vue` component and wrap up a countdown component into a `div` with a class `row`. We will make this row contain two columns, one of which will be the countdown timer, and the other is a conditionally rendered element containing a workout. Why conditionally? Because we only need this element displayed during the Pomodoro breaks. We will use the `v-show` directive so that the containing element will always be present, and only the `display` property will change. The markup will thus look like the following:

```
//PomodoroTimer.vue
<div class="container">
  <div class="row">
    <div v-show="!isWorking" class="col-sm-4">
      WORKOUT TIME!
    </div>
    <count-down-timer class="col-sm-8" @finished="togglePomodoro"
    :time="time"></count-down-timer>
  </div>
</div>
```

Note `col-sm-4` and `col-sm-8`. Again, I want the columns to look different on bigger devices and stacked on small ones!

What element should we use to display our workout? For some reason, I like Bootstrap's `jumbotrons` (`https://v4-alpha.getbootstrap.com/components/jumbotron/`) very much, so I will use a `jumbotron` containing a header element for the workout's title, the lead element for the workout's description, and an image element to display the workout's image.

 Mind that the URL of Bootstrap's Jumbotron component is for the alpha version, and the next version will be available on the official website

So, my markup structure for displaying the workout looks like the following:

```
//PomodoroTimer.vue
<div class="jumbotron">
  <div class="container">
    <img class="img-fluid rounded" src="IMAGE_SOURCE" alt="">
    <h2>Push-ups</h2>
    <lead>
      Description: lorem ipsum
    </lead>
  </div>
</div>
```

Feel free to add another nice workout for you in this section, so you are able to exercise until you finish reading the book. Check the code for this section in the `section4/9/profitoro` folder.

This is how my Pomodoro looks on my laptop's screen:

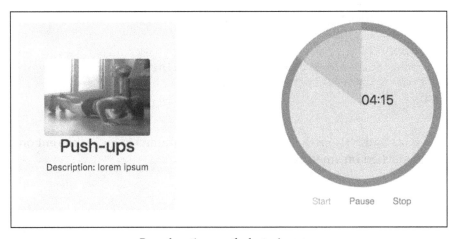

Pomodoro timer on the laptop's screen

This is how it looks on the mobile screen:

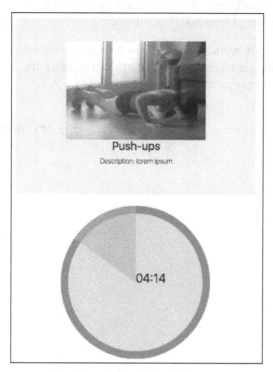

Pomodoro timer on the mobile screen

It's not that beautiful, of course, but it's responsive and adaptive, and we haven't done any CSS black magic for it!

Summary

In this chapter, we have done a lot of things. We have implemented the main functionality of our Pomodoro timer, and now it is fully functional, configurable, usable, and responsive. We bootstrapped our ProFitOro application, separated it into components, created a skeleton for each of the defined components, and fully implemented one of them. We even revisited some trigonometry, because math is everywhere. We implemented our timer and we made it work, even on the hidden and inactive tabs. We made the application responsive and adaptive to different device sizes using the powerful Bootstrap layout classes. Our application is functional, but it is far from beautiful. Don't mind these shades of gray though; let's stick to them for now. In the end of the book, you will get your beautiful ProFitOro styles, I promise you!

We are ready to continue our journey in the world of technology. In the next chapter, we will learn how to configure our Pomodoro and how to store the configuration and usage statistics using Firebase. Thus, in the next chapter we will:

- Get back to Vuex centralized state management architecture and combine it with the Google Firebase storage system to store the application's critical data, such as configuration and statistics
- Implement the configuration of ProFitOro
- Implement the storing, retrieval, and displaying of ProFitOro usage statistics data

5
Configuring Your Pomodoro

In the previous chapter, we implemented the main feature of our ProFitOro application – the Pomodoro timer. We even added a hardcoded workout, so we can exercise during our breaks. Actually, I already started using ProFitOro. While I'm writing these words, the Pomodoro clock counts down – *tick tick tick tick*.

In this chapter, we are going to explore the *Firebase Realtime Database's* possibilities and its API. We are going to manage storing, retrieving, and updating usage statistics and configuration of our application. We will use the Vuex store to bring the application's data from the database to the frontend application.

To bring this possibility to the UI, we will use Vue's reactivity combined with the power of Bootstrap. Thus, in this chapter we are going to implement the statistics and settings ProFitOro components using:

- Firebase Realtime Database
- Vue.js reactive data bindings and Vuex state management
- The power of Bootstrap to make things responsive

Setting up a Vuex store

Before starting with real data from the database, let's set up the Vuex store for our ProFitOro. We will use it to manage the Pomodoro timer configuration, user settings, such as the username, and a profile picture URL. We will also use it to store and retrieve the application's usage statistics.

From *Chapter 2, Hello User Explained*, you already know how the Vuex store works. We must define data that will represent the application's state and then we must provide all the needed getters to get the data and all the needed mutations to update the data. Once all this is set, we will be able to access this data from the components.

After the application's store is ready and set up, we can connect it to the real-time database and slightly adjust the getters and mutations to operate the real data.

First of all, we need to tell our application that it will use the Vuex store. To do that, let's add the npm dependency for vuex:

```
npm install vuex --save
```

Now, we need to define a basic structure of our store. Our Vuex store will contain the following:

- **State**: The initial state of the application's data.
- **Getters**: Methods that retrieve the state's attributes.
- **Mutations**: Methods that provide a way to change the state.
- **Actions**: Methods that can be dispatched to invoke mutations. The only difference between actions and mutations is that actions can be asynchronous and we might need them for our application.

Sounds pretty easy, right? Just create a folder called store and create JavaScript files for all the things that we have just indicated. Also create the index.js file that will instantiate a Vuex store with all these things. Here is your structure:

```
> tree src/store
src/store
├── actions.js
├── getters.js
├── index.js
├── mutations.js
└── state.js

0 directories, 5 files
```

The structure of the store folder

When we first mentioned the Vuex store in *Chapter 2*, *Hello User Explained*, we simplified the structure and introduced all the store's components in the same file. Now, we will follow the nice modular structure and let everything reside in its own place. We could even go further and separate the state into the modules (one for configuration, another one for settings, and so on) but it would probably be overkill for the complexity level of ProFitOro. However, if you want to check how to separate your store into logical modules, check the section about modules in this great documentation about Vuex: https://vuex.vuejs.org/en/.

Nevertheless, let's continue with our store. After having created the structure, import all of the store's components into `index.js` and create a Vuex instance, passing all of them as parameters. Do not forget to import Vuex and to tell Vue to use it! Thus, the entry point of our store will look as follows:

```js
//store/index.js
import Vue from 'vue'
import Vuex from 'vuex'
import state from './state'
import getters from './getters'
import mutations from './mutations'
import actions from './actions'

Vue.use(Vuex)

export default new Vuex.Store({
  state,
  getters,
  mutations,
  actions
})
```

The only thing that matters now, so our setup is totally complete, is to get our application to know that it is now using this store. In this way, the store will become available in all the components. The only thing that you need to do to make it possible is to import our store in the application's entry point (`main.js`) and to pass it to the Vue instance:

```js
//main.js
import Vue from 'vue'
import App from './App'
import store from './store'

new Vue({
  el: '#app',
  template: '<App/>',
  components: { App },
  store
})
```

Now we are totally ready to start our magic with the store. Have you been missing coding? Well, here you go! Let's start by replacing the `config` file that we've created as a container for the Pomodoro timing properties with the state and the getters of our store. Just copy all the configuration elements of the `config` file to our state and create a getter for it:

```
//store/state.js
const config = {
   workingPomodoro: 25,
   shortBreak: 5,
   longBreak: 10,
   pomodorosTillLongBreak: 3
}

export default {
   config
}
```

Let's now move to getters. Getters are not just regular functions. Behind the scenes, they receive the state as a parameter, so you can access the data of the application's state, without any effort of dependency injections, because it has already been managed for you by Vuex. So, just create a function that receives the state as a parameter and returns any of the state's data! If needed, inside the getter, you can perform any operations on the data. So, the getter for the `config` file could look something like this:

```
//store/getters.js
function getConfig (state) {
   return state.config
}
```

Since we are using ES6, it can be rewritten in a more succinct and elegant way:

```
//store/getters.js

var getConfig = (state) => state.config
```

Then, it can be exported:

```
//store/getters.js
export default {
   getConfig: getConfig
}
```

Alternatively, we can simply use:

```
//store/getter.js
export default {
  getConfig
}
```

The whole thing can actually be written as:

```
//store/getters.js
export default {
  getConfig: state => state.config
}
```

How amazingly simple is that? At the time I started working with JavaScript (don't ask me when, I don't like to feel old myself), I could barely imagine that such syntax would ever be possible.

You can now use your new getter inside any application's component. How? Do you remember how easy it was to access the state using the `this.$store.state` attribute? In the same way, inside the computed data function, you can access your `getters`:

```
computed: {
  config () {
    return this.$store.getters.getConfig
  }
},
```

From now on, `this.config` can be used in all the component's computed values and methods. Let's imagine now, that inside the same component, we need to use more than one getter. Imagine, for example, that we create getters for each of the config's values. So, for every value you would have to repeat this tedious code: `this.$store.getters.bla-bla-bla`. Argh! There must an easier way... and there is. Vuex is kind enough to provide us with a helper object which is called `mapGetters`. If you simply import this object into your component, you can invoke your getters using `mapGetters` with the ES6 spread operator:

```
import { mapGetters } from 'vuex'

export default {
  computed: {
    ...mapGetters([
      'getConfig'
    ])
  }
}
```

Alternatively, if you want to map your getters methods to some other names, just use an object:

```
import { mapGetters } from 'vuex'

export default {
  computed: {
    ...mapGetters({
      config: 'getConfig'
    })
  }
}
```

So, this is what we are going to do. We are going to use the mapGetters helper inside the PomodoroTimer component and we will remove the reference to the imported config file (also, do not forget to remove the file itself; we don't want dead code in our code base). We will replace all the references to config with this.config. So, our PomodoroTimer script's section will look as follows:

```
//PomodoroTimer.vue
<script>
  // ...
  import { mapGetters } from 'vuex'
  // ...
  export default {
    data () {
      // ...
    },
    computed: {
      ...mapGetters({
        config: 'getConfig'
      }),
      time () {
        let minutes
        if (this.isWorking) {
          minutes = this.config.workingPomodoro
        } else if (this.isShortBreak) {
          minutes = this.config.shortBreak
        } else if (this.isLongBreak) {
          minutes = this.config.longBreak
        }

        return minutes * 60
      }
    },
    // ...
    methods: {
      togglePomodoro () {
```

```
    // ...
    this.isLongBreak = this.pomodoros %
    this.config.pomodorosTillLongBreak === 0
  }
 }
}
</script>
```

Check your page, everything should work the same way it has been working before. What is the advantage of this new approach?—someone might ask,—we've been here for half a chapter setting up this store and its methods, getters, actions, whatever... In the end, we have the exact same behavior. What for? Well, do you remember that the whole aim of this chapter is to be able to configure and reconfigure the Pomodoro timing settings and to store them in the database? If we had to introduce the database reference and all the operations of retrieving and storing data inside our components, our life would be harder. Imagine that at some point Firebase does not suit your needs and you wish to switch to another data source, or even a different technology, let's say *Elasticsearch* or even *MongoDB*. You would have to change your component and its methods, as well as its computed values. Doesn't it sound like hell to maintain all that?

Having your data to reside inside the store and with your getters being responsible for retrieving them will enable you to only have to change your getters if you decide to change the underlying data source. Your components will always be left untouched! It's an abstraction of the data and logic layers of your application. Abstractions are a very cool thing in the software engineering field.

Let's define a basic markup for the Settings.vue component. Check our mockups.

This component will contain two main areas:

- Personal settings configuration area
- Pomodoro timer settings configuration area

Again, I will use Bootstrap grid classes to help me build a nice, responsive layout. I want it to make two stack columns on small devices, two equal-size columns on medium sized devices, and two different sized columns on large devices. Thus, I will use the row class for the wrapping div and corresponding col-*-* classes for the two main areas of our Settings component:

```
// Settings.vue
<div class="row justify-content-center">
  <div class="col-sm-12 col-md-6 col-lg-4">
    <div class="container">
      <h2>Account settings</h2>
      account settings
```

```
      </div>
    </div>
    <div class="col-sm-12 col-md-6 col-lg-8">
      <div class="container">
        <h2>Set your pomodoro timer</h2>
        pomodoro timer configuration
      </div>
    </div>
  </div>
```

Let's concentrate for now only on the Pomodoro timing settings configuration. I created a component called `SetTimer.vue`. This component just contains a number-type input and emits a method whenever its value changes. Within the Pomodoro settings container, I will render this component three times using different values from the imported `mapGetters` helper:

```
//Settings.vue
<template>
  <...>
    <div class="row justify-content-center align-items-center">
      <div class="col-md-5 col-sm-10">
        <set-timer :value="config.workingPomodoro"></set-timer>
        <div class="figure-caption">Pomodoro</div>
      </div>
      <div class="col-md-4 col-sm-10">
        <set-timer :value="config.longBreak"></set-timer>
        <div class="figure-caption">Long break</div>
      </div>
      <div class="col-md-3 col-sm-10">
        <set-timer :value="config.shortBreak"></set-timer>
        <div class="figure-caption">Short break</div>
      </div>
    </div>
  <...>
</template>
```

With some CSS magic for the SetTimer component, I am able to render three input circles like the following:

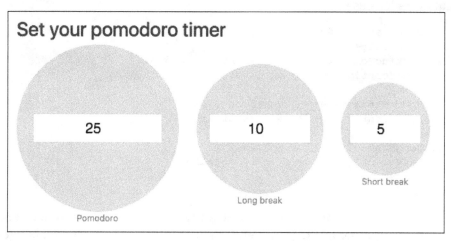

Set your pomodoro timer

| 25 | 10 | 5 |

Pomodoro

Long break

Short break

Input balls that allow us to set timers for different Pomodoro interval

You can find the corresponding code in the chapter5/1/profitoro folder. In particular, check the SetTimer.vue component inside the components/main/sections/timer folder and how it's being called with the corresponding values inside the Settings.vue component.

Defining actions and mutations

It's great that our components can now get data from the store, but it would be probably even more interesting if our components were also able to change the data in the store. On the other hand, we all know that we cannot modify the store's state directly.

The state should not be touched by any of the components. However, you also remember from our chapter about the Vuex store that there are special functions that can mutate the store. They are even called mutations. These functions can do whatever they/you want with the Vuex store data. These mutations can be called using the commit method applied to the store. Under the hood, they essentially receive two parameters – the state and the value.

I will define three mutations – one for each of the timer's definitions. These mutations will update the corresponding attribute of the `config` object with a new value. Thus, my mutations look as follows:

```
//store/mutations.js
export default {
  setWorkingPomodoro (state, workingPomodoro) {
    state.config.workingPomodoro = workingPomodoro
  },
  setShortBreak (state, shortBreak) {
    state.config.shortBreak = shortBreak
  },
  setLongBreak (state, longBreak) {
    state.config.longBreak = longBreak
  }
}
```

Now we can define actions. Actions will basically call our mutations, so it can be considered as duplicate work. However, keep in mind that the difference between actions and mutations is that actions can actually be asynchronous, so it might come in handy when we connect our actions to the database. For now, let's just tell the actions to verify the received values before committing them. The `actions` method receives the store and a new value. Since the store provides us with the essential method called `commit`, which is called with the name of the needed mutation, we can define each action as follows:

```
actionName ({commit}, newValue) {
  commit('mutationName', newValue)
}
```

 We can write {commit} as a parameter and use the `commit` function right away, because we are using ES6 and object destructing just works perfectly for us (`https://developer.mozilla.org/en/docs/Web/JavaScript/Reference/Operators/Destructuring_assignment`).

Thus, my actions look like this:

```
//store/actions.js
export default {
  setWorkingPomodoro ({commit}, workingPomodoro) {
    if (workingPomodoro) {
      commit('setWorkingPomodoro', parseInt(workingPomodoro, 10))
    }
  },
  setShortBreak ({commit}, shortBreak) {
    if (shortBreak) {
```

```
      commit('setShortBreak', parseInt(shortBreak, 10))
    }
  },
  setLongBreak ({commit}, longBreak) {
    if (longBreak) {
      commit('setLongBreak', parseInt(longBreak, 10))
    }
  }
}
```

Now, let's go back to the `Settings.vue` component. This component should import actions and call them when needed, right? How do we import actions? Do you remember the `mapGetters` helper? There is a similar helper for actions called `mapActions`. So, we can just import it along with the `mapGetters` helper and use it with a spread operator (...) inside the `methods` object:

```
//Settings.vue
<script>
  import {mapGetters, mapActions} from 'vuex'
  <...>
  export default {
    <...>
    methods: {
      ...mapActions(['setWorkingPomodoro', 'setShortBreak',
      'setLongBreak'])
    }
  }
</script>
```

Now, we have to invoke the needed actions whenever the values of the `set-timer` inputs change. In the previous paragraph, we discussed that the `SetTimer` component emits the `changeValue` event. So, the only thing we have to do now is to bind this event to all three `set-timer` components and call the corresponding methods:

```
<div class="col-md-5 col-sm-10">
  <set-timer :value="config.workingPomodoro"
  @valueChanged="setWorkingPomodoro"></set-timer>
  <div class="figure-caption">Pomodoro</div>
</div>
<div class="col-md-4 col-sm-10">
  <set-timer :value="config.longBreak"
  @valueChanged="setLongBreak"></set-timer>
  <div class="figure-caption">Long break</div>
</div>
```

```
<div class="col-md-3 col-sm-10">
  <set-timer :value="config.shortBreak"
  @valueChanged="setShortBreak"></set-timer>
  <div class="figure-caption">Short break</div>
</div>
```

Open the page and try to change the values of each timer setting.

If you are using the Chrome browser and still haven't installed Vue developer tools, please do it. You will see how handy and lovely it is! Just follow this link: `https://goo.gl/22khXD`.

Having installed the Vue devtools extension, you will immediately see how the values are being changed in the Vuex store:

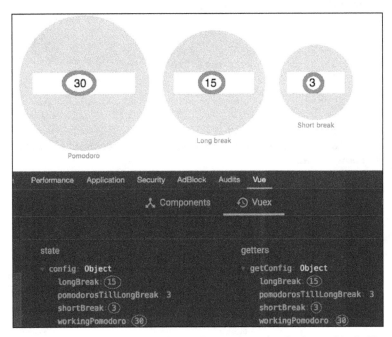

Once the values are changed in the input boxes, they are immediately changed in the Vuex store

Check the final code for this section in the `chapter5/2/profitoro` folder. Pay attention to the `actions.js` and `mutations.js` files inside the store folder and to the `Settings.vue` component.

Setting up a Firebase project

I hope that you still remember how to set up Firebase projects from the first chapters of this book. Open your Firebase console at `https://console.firebase.google.com`, click on the **Add project** button, name it, and choose your country. The Firebase project is ready. Wasn't that easy? Let's now prepare our database. The following data will be stored in it:

- **Configuration**: The configuration of our Pomodoro timer values
- **Statistics**: Statistical data of the Pomodoro usage

Each of these objects will be accessible via a special key that will correspond to a user's ID; this is because, in the next chapter, we are going to implement an authentication mechanism.

The configuration object will contain values – `workingPomodoro`, `longBreak` and `shortBreak` – that are already familiar to us.

Let's add a configuration object to our database with some fake data:

```
{
  "configuration": {
    "test": {
      "workingPomodoro": 25,
      "shortBreak": 5,
      "longBreak": 10
    }
  }
}
```

You can even create this as a simple JSON file and import it to your database:

Import JSON file to your real-time Firebase database

Congratulations, your real-time database is ready! Keep in mind that, by default, the security rules will not allow you to access your data from the exterior unless you are authenticated. Let's, for now, remove these rules. We will add them later, once we have implemented our authentication mechanism. Click on the **RULES** tab and replace the existing ones with this object:

```
{
  "rules": {
    ".read": true,
    ".write": true
  }
}
```

Now we are ready to access our real-time database from our Vue application.

Connecting the Vuex store to the Firebase database

So, now we have to connect our Vuex store to the Firebase database. We could use the native Firebase API for binding the state data to the database data, but why would we deal with promises and stuff if someone already did that for us? This someone is called Eduardo and he has created Vuexfire – Firebase bindings for Vuex (https://github.com/posva/vuexfire). If you were at the *vueconf2017 conference* in *Wroclaw*, you probably remember this guy:

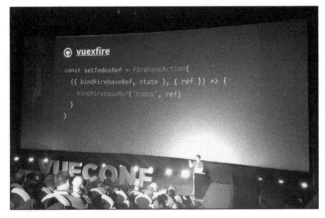

Eduardo talking about Vue and Firebase during the Vue conference

Vuexfire comes with Firebase mutations and actions that will do all the behind the scenes jobs for you, while you just export them within your mutations and actions objects. So, to start with, install both `firebase` and `vuexfire`:

```
npm install vue firebase vuexfire -save
```

Import `firebase` and `firebaseMutations` in your store's `index.js` entry point:

```
//store/index.js
import firebase from 'firebase'
import { firebaseMutations } from 'vuexfire'
```

Now, we need to obtain the reference to the Firebase application. Firebase comes with an initialization method, `initializeApp`, which receives an object composed of lots of application settings data – app ID, authentication domain, and so on. For now, we have to at least provide the database URL. In order to get your database URL, just go to your Firebase project settings and click on the **Add Firebase to your web app** button:

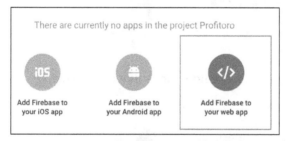

Click on the Add Firebase to your web app button

Copy the database URL, or even the whole configuration object, and paste it to your store's `index.js` file:

```
//store/index.js
let app = firebase.initializeApp({
  databaseURL: 'https://profitoro-ad0f0.firebaseio.com'
})
```

You are now ready to obtain the reference to the configuration object. Once we implement the authentication mechanism, we will use the authenticated user's ID to get the current user's configuration from the database. For now, let's use our hardcoded ID `test`:

```
let configRef = app.database().ref('/configuration/test')
```

I will export the `configRef` reference using the spread operator in the state object. So, this reference becomes accessible by the actions:

```
//store/index.js
export default new Vuex.Store({
  state: {
    ...state,
    configRef
  }
})
```

In order to make the whole Vuexfire magic work, we have to also export `firebaseMutations` within the `mutations` object:

```
//store/index.js
export default new Vuex.Store({
  mutations: {
    ...mutations,
    ...firebaseMutations
  },
  actions
})
```

So, our whole `store/index.js` now looks like the following:

```
//store/index.js
import Vue from 'vue'
import Vuex from 'vuex'
import state from './state'
import getters from './getters'
import mutations from './mutations'
import actions from './actions'
import firebase from 'firebase'
import { firebaseMutations } from 'vuexfire'
Vue.use(Vuex)

// Initialize Firebase
let config = {
  databaseURL: 'https://profitoro-ad0f0.firebaseio.com'
}
let app = firebase.initializeApp(config)
let configRef = app.database().ref('/configuration/test')

export default new Vuex.Store({
  state: {
    ...state,
```

```
      configRef
    },
    getters,
    mutations: {
      ...mutations,
      ...firebaseMutations
    },
    actions
  })
```

Let's go to our actions now. It is very important that before doing anything else, we bind our database reference to the corresponding state's attribute. In our case, we must bind the state's `config` object to its corresponding reference `configRef`. For that, our friend Eduardo provides us with the actions enhancer called `firebaseAction` that implements the `bindFirebaseRef` method. Just call this method and you don't have to worry about promises and their callbacks.

Open `action.js` and import `firebaseAction` enhancer:

```
//store/actions.js
import { firebaseAction } from 'vuexfire'
```

Let's now create an action called `bindConfig`, where we will actually bind two things together using the `bindFirebaseRef` method:

```
//store/actions.js
bindConfig: firebaseAction(({bindFirebaseRef, state}) => {
  bindFirebaseRef('config', state.configRef)
})
```

When should this action be dispatched? Probably on the `Settings.vue` component creation, since this component is responsible for rendering the `config` state. Thus, inside the `Settings.vue` we bind the state of the `created` component and inside of it, we just call the `bindConfig` action:

```
//Settings.vue
export default {
  //...
  methods: {
    ...mapActions(['setWorkingPomodoro', 'setShortBreak',
'setLongBreak', 'bindConfig'])
  },
  created () {
    this.bindConfig()
  }
}
```

If you open the page now, you will see that everything remains the same. The only difference is that, now, we are using the data coming from our real-time database and not from the hardcoded `config` object. You can check it by completely deleting the content of the `config` object inside the state store's object and ensuring that everything is still be working.

If you try to change the input values and then refresh the page, you will see that the applied changes are not saved. This happens because we did not update the database reference. So let's update it! The good thing about it is that we don't need to change *anything* inside our components; we just have to slightly change our *actions*. We will use the `update` method called on the reference. Please check the Firebase real-time database documentation on reading and writing data: `https://firebase.google.com/docs/database/web/read-and-write`.

So, we will pass the `state` object to each of the actions and call the `update` method on `state.configRef`, passing to it the corresponding changed attribute. So, it might look as simple as the following code snippet:

```
//store/actions.js
setWorkingPomodoro ({commit, state}, workingPomodoro) {
  state.configRef.update({workingPomodoro})
},
```

Do not forget to perform the needed checks, parse the updated attribute to an integer, and also check if `configRef` is available. If it's not available, just call the `commit` method with the corresponding mutation's name. Check the final code for this section in the `chapter5/3/profitoro` folder. Pay special attention to the `store/index.js` and `store/actions.js` files and to the `Settings.vue` component.

If you open your page and change the Pomodoro timer values and keep looking at your Firebase console database tab you will see the differences immediately!

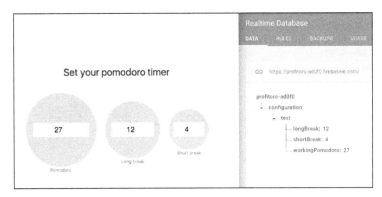

The changes applied to the Pomodoro timer configuration boxes are propagated immediately to the real-time database

If you change values directly in the database, you will also see that the changes are immediately propagated to your view.

Exercise

You have learned how to connect the real-time Firebase database to your Vue application and used this knowledge to update the configurations for Pomodoro timers. Now, apply your knowledge to the statistics area. For the sake of simplicity, just display the total amount of Pomodoros executed since the user started using the application. For that you will need to do the following:

1. Add another object called `statistics` containing the `totalPomodoros` attribute that initially equals 0 in your Firebase database.

2. Create an entry in the store's `state` to hold the statistics data.

3. Map `totalPomodoros` of the statistics state's object to the Firebase reference using the `firebaseAction` enhancer and the `bindFirebaseRef` method.

4. Create an action that will update the `totalPomodoros` reference.

5. Call this action whenever it has to be called inside the `PomodoroTimer` component.

6. Display this value inside the `Statistics.vue` component.

Try to do it yourself. It shouldn't be difficult. Follow the same logic we applied in the `Settings.vue` component. If in doubt, check the `chapter5/4/profitoro` folder, particularly the store's files – `index.js`, `state.js` and `actions.js`. Then check how the corresponding actions have been used inside the `PomodoroTimer` component and how it is rendered in the `Statistics` component. Good luck!

Summary

In this chapter, you learned how to use the real-time Firebase database with the Vue application. You learned how to use Vuexfire and its methods to correctly bind our Vuex store state to the database reference. We were not only able to read and render the data from the database but we were also able to update it. So, in this chapter, we saw Vuex, Firebase, and Vuexfire in action. I guess we should be proud of ourselves.

However, let's not forget that we have used a hardcoded user ID in order to get the user's data. Also, we had to expose our database to the world by changing the security rules, which doesn't seem right either. It seems that it's time to enable the authentication mechanism!

And we will do it in the next chapter! In the next chapter, we are going to learn how to set up the authentication mechanism using the Firebase authentication framework. We will learn how to use it in our application using Vuefire (Firebase bindings for Vue: `https://github.com/vuejs/vuefire`). We will also implement the very initial view of our application responsible for providing a way of registering and performing the login. We will use Bootstrap form elements in order to make this screen responsive and adaptive to all screen sizes. So, let's move on to the next chapter! Do not forget to do some pushups first!

6
Please Authenticate!

In the previous chapter, we connected our ProFitOro application to the real-time database. Whenever a user updates the Pomodoro timer settings, these are stored in the database and immediately propagated between the components that use them. Since we had no authentication mechanism, we had to use a fake user in order to be able to test our changes. In this chapter, we are going to have real users!

We will use the Firebase authentication API in this regard. So in this chapter, we are going to do the following:

- Discuss the meaning of AAA and the difference between authentication and authorization
- Explore the Firebase authentication API
- Create a page for sign-in and login, and connect it with the Firebase authentication API
- Connect the user's settings with the user's authentication

AAA explained

Triple-A, or **AAA**, stands for **Authentication, Authorization, and Accounting**. Initially, this term was invented as a term to describe the security network protocol; however, it can be easily applied to any system, web resource, or site.

So, what does AAA mean and why should we bother?

Authentication is the process of uniquely identifying the users of a system. An authenticated user is a user whose access to a system is granted. Usually, the authentication is done via some username and password. When you have to provide your username and password to open your Facebook page, you are authenticating yourself.

Your passport is a way of authenticating yourself at the airport. The passport control agent will look at your face and then check your passport. So anything that allows you to *pass* is a part of your authentication. It can be a special word (password) that is only known by you and the system or it can be something that you port (passport) with you that can help the system to uniquely identify you.

Authorization is a way to control what resources each user has rights (permissions) to access. If you are developing Facebook applications, you have access to the developer's page, whereas usual users don't have access to this page.

Accounting measures resources allocated for each user. If you have a Dropbox business standard account, you can use up to 2 TB of storage space, whereas having a normal free Dropbox account gives you only 2 GB of space.

For our application, we should be concerned with the first two As of Triple-A – *Authentication* and *Authorization*. In computer science, we often use term **auth**, referring rather to authentication or authorization or even to both of them at the same time. So we will implement auth, where auth refers to both authentication and authorization. What is the difference between these two terms in the context of our ProFitOro application? Well, authentication will allow users to log in to the system, so this is easy. What about authorization?

Do you remember that we decided that only authenticated users will have access to the configuration of Pomodoro settings and statistical data? This is authorization. Later on, we might go further and implement a special role – fitness trainer. The users with this role will have access to the workouts area and be able to add new workouts.

In this chapter, we will use the Firebase authentication mechanism to add the possibility of signing in and logging in to our application and to control what users have access to.

How does authentication work with Firebase?

In the previous chapter, you learned how to use the Firebase API to create a Firebase application instance and use it through your application. We were able to access the database, read it, and store data in it.

The way you work with the Firebase authentication API is very similar. You create a Firebase instance, providing a `config` object to it, and you use the `firebase.auth()` method to access different methods related with the authentication. Check your Firebase console's **Authentication** tab:

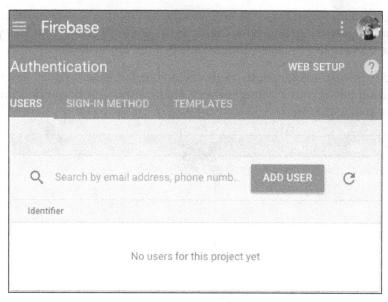

There are no users yet but we will fix it in a minute!

The Firebase SDK provides several ways for users to authenticate:

- **Email and password based authentication**: The classic way for authenticating users. Firebase provides a way to sign in users with email/password and log them in. It also provides methods to reset the user password.

- **Federated entity provider authentication**: The way of authenticating users with an external entity provider, such as Google, Facebook, Twitter, or GitHub.

- **Phone number authentication**: The way of authenticating users by sending them an SMS with a code that they will have to input to confirm their identity.

- **Custom auth system integration**: The way of integrating an already existing auth solution with the Firebase authentication API.

- **Anonymous user authentication**: The way of providing Firebase features (such as access to the Firebase database) without being authenticated. We can, for example, use this anonymous account to provide access to the default configuration stored in the database.

For our application, we will use the first and the last methods, so we will allow users to sign in and log in using their email and password combination and we will allow anonymous users to use the basic functionality of the application.

You should explicitly activate both methods in your Firebase console. Just open the **Authentication** tab of your Firebase project, click on the sign-in method link, and enable these two methods:

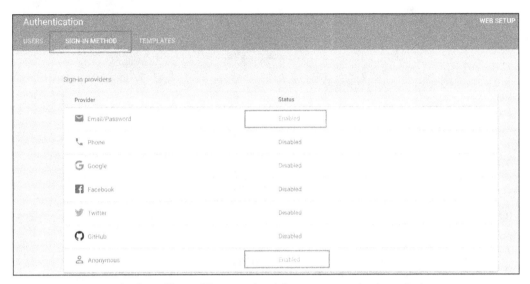

Explicitly enable email/password and the anonymous sign-in methods

The workflow of using the Firebase authentication API is the following:

1. Create all the necessary methods for the sign-in and login.
2. Implement all the necessary UI for your authentication.
3. Connect changes in the UI to the authentication methods.

Did you spot something nice in step 3? *Connect changes in the UI to the authentication methods.* You remember that we are dealing with a reactive data binding framework, don't you? So this is going to be fun!

How to connect the Firebase authentication API to a web application

In order to connect your application to the Firebase authentication API, you should start by creating a Firebase application instance:

```
let config = {
  apiKey: 'YourAPIKey',
  databaseURL: 'YourDBURL',
  authDomain: 'YourAuthDomain'
}
let app = firebase.initializeApp(config)
```

You can find the necessary keys and URLs in the popup that opens if you click on the **Web Setup** button:

The setup config to use Firebase in a web application

Now you can use the app instance to access the `auth()` object and its methods. Check out the official Firebase documentation regarding the authentication API: `https://firebase.google.com/docs/auth/users`.

The most important part of the API for us is the methods to create and sign in a user, and the method that listens to the changes in the authentication state:

```
app.auth().createUserWithEmailAndPassword(email, password)
```

Or:

```
app.auth().signInWithEmailAndPassword(email, password)
```

The method that listens to the changes in the authentication state of the application is called onAuthStateChanged. You can set the important properties inside of this method considering the state your application needs to have depending on the user being logged in or not:

```
app.auth().onAuthStateChanged((user) => {
  if (user) {
    // user is logged in
  } else {
    // user is logged out
  }
})
```

That is all! In our application, we just have to provide a visual way to pass the username and the password to the API.

Authenticating to the ProFitOro application

Let us now make signing in and logging in to our ProFitOro application possible! First, we have to set up the Firebase instance and figure out where we should put all the methods related to authentication. The Firebase application initialization has already been done inside the store/index.js file. Just add the apiKey and authDomain configuration entries if you still do not have them included in the config:

```
// store/index.js
let config = {
  apiKey: 'YourAPIKey',
  databaseURL: 'https://profitoro-ad0f0.firebaseio.com',
  authDomain: 'profitoro-ad0f0.firebaseapp.com'
}
let firebaseApp = firebase.initializeApp(config)
```

I will also export firebaseApp within the store's state property using the spread ... operator:

```
//store/index.js
export default new Vuex.Store({
  state: {
    ...state,
    firebaseApp
  },
  <...>
})
```

```
// store/state.js
export default {
  config,
  statistics,
  user,
  isAnonymous: false
}
```

Let us also create a small mutation that will reset the value of the `user` object to the given value:

```
// store/mutations.js
export default {
  <...>
  setUser (state, value) {
    state.user = value
  }
}
```

Now we are totally ready to create the needed actions. I will create four actions that are indispensable for our application:

- `createUser`: This action will call the Firebase auth `createUserWithEmailAndPassword` with the given email and password
- `authenticate`: This action will call the Firebase auth `signInWithEmailAndPassword` method to sign in the user with the given email and password
- `logout`: This action will call the Firebase auth `signOut` method
- `bindAuth`: This action will just set up the `onAuthStateChanged` callback and commit the `setUser` mutation

To start with, let us implement these actions in a very easy way, without any callbacks attached. So they will look like this:

```
// store/actions.js
createUser ({state}, {email, password}) {
  state.firebaseApp.auth().createUserWithEmailAndPassword(email,
  password).catch(error => {
    console.log(error.code, error.message)
  })
},
authenticate ({state}, {email, password}) {
```

```
      state.firebaseApp.auth().signInWithEmailAndPassword(email,
      password)
   },
   logout ({state}) {
      state.firebaseApp.auth().signOut()
   },
   bindAuth ({commit, state}) {
      state.firebaseApp.auth().onAuthStateChanged((user) => {
         commit('setUser', user)
      })
   },
```

Great! Now let's attach the bindAuth action to the created method of the main App. vue component:

```
// App.vue
methods: {
   ...mapActions(['bindStatistics', 'bindConfig', 'bindAuth'])
},
created () {
   this.bindAuth()
   this.bindConfig()
   this.bindStatistics()
}
```

Now, once the application is created, the listener to the authentication state will be bound immediately. What can we do with it? Right now, the only component that the App.vue component shows immediately is the main content component. However, if the user is not logged in, we should actually show the landing page component to offer the possibility to the user to sign in or log in. We can do it easily using the v-if directive bound to the user property. If the user is defined, let's show the main content component; otherwise, let's show the landing page component. How easy is that? Our App.vue component's template will look like this:

```
// App.vue
<template>
   <div id="app">
      <landing-page v-if="!user"></landing-page>
      <main-content v-if="user"></main-content>
   </div>
</template>
```

If you open the page now, you will see that the landing page is displayed:

When the application is started, the landing page is displayed because the user is not logged in

All the relevant code up to this part is in the `chapter6/1/profitoro` folder. Pay special attention to the store's files (`index.js`, `actions.js`, `mutations.js`, `state.js`) and to the `App.vue` component.

Now we are stuck on the landing page that just displays some placeholder text and there is no way to proceed to the application because we cannot log in!

Well, this is quite easy to solve: let's create a simple form to sign up and log in in the `Authentication.vue` component and connect it with our actions.

So I will add the component's data that will hold the email for registering, email for login, and the corresponding passwords:

```
// Authentication.vue
export default {
  data () {
    return {
      registerEmail: '',
      registerPassword: '',
      loginEmail: '',
      loginPassword: ''
    }
  }
}
```

I will also add a very simple markup that will display the inputs for the corresponding data:

```
<template>
  <div>
    <h1>Register</h1>
    <input v-model="registerEmail" type="text" placeholder="email">
    <input v-model="registerPassword" type="password"
    placeholder="password">
    <button>Register!</button>
    <h1>Login</h1>
```

```
        <input v-model="loginEmail" type="text" placeholder="email">
        <input v-model="loginPassword" type="password"
        placeholder="password">
        <button>Log in!</button>
    </div>
</template>
```

Let's now import the necessary actions (`authenticate` and `createUser`) and create methods that will call these actions:

```
// Authentication.vue
<script>
  import {mapActions} from 'vuex'

  export default {
    <...>
    methods: {
      ...mapActions(['createUser', 'authenticate']),
      onRegisterClick () {
        this.createUser({email: this.registerEmail, password:
        this.registerPassword})
      },
      onLoginClick () {
        this.authenticate({email: this.loginEmail, password:
        this.loginPassword})
      }
    }
  }
</script>
```

Now we just have to attach the event binding the `v-on:click` directive to the corresponding buttons:

```
// Authentication.vue
<template>
  <div>
    <h1>Register</h1>
    <input v-model="registerEmail" type="text"
    placeholder="email">
    <input v-model="registerPassword" type="password"
    placeholder="password">
```

```
    <button @click="onRegisterClick">Register!</button>
    <h1>Login</h1>
    <input v-model="loginEmail" type="text" placeholder="email">
    <input v-model="loginPassword" type="password"
    placeholder="password">
    <button @click="onLoginClick">Log in!</button>
  </div>
</template>
```

Let's also add a button to our `HeaderComponent.vue` component. This button should allow the user to log out. This is very easy; we don't even have to create any method, we just have to bind the event to the actual action. So the whole markup and the needed script will look as simple as this:

```
// HeaderComponent.vue
<template>
  <div>
    <button @click="logout">Logout</button>
  </div>
</template>
<script>
  import {mapActions} from 'vuex'

  export default {
    methods: {
      ...mapActions(['logout'])
    }
  }
</script>
```

And…that's it! Open the page and try to register in your application! It works! Once you are logged in, not only you will see the Pomodoro timer but you will also be able to see the logout button. Click on it and check that you are actually thrown out of the application to the landing page. Try to log in again. Everything works like a charm.

Do not forget to open your Firebase console and check the **Authentication** tab. You should see all your registered users there:

Monitor your registered users through the Firebase console's Authentication tab

Congratulations! You just used the Firebase authentication API to implement a full authentication mechanism for your application. You can find the corresponding code in the `chapter6/2/profitoro` folder. Pay special attention to the `Authentication.vue` and `HeaderComponent.vue` components.

Making the authentication UI great again

We have just implemented the authentication mechanism for our ProFitOro application. That's great, but the UI of our authentication page looks as if we've used a time machine and gone back 20 years to the early days of the internet. Let's fix it using our powerful friend – Bootstrap.

First of all, I would like to make my landing page layout a two-column grid layout, so the whole sign-in/login belongs to the left column and the button that leads the user to the application without being registered stays on the right side. However, I would like these two columns to be stacked on mobile devices.

This is nothing new for you; I suppose that you remember how to use Bootstrap's grid layout in order to achieve this behavior: `https://v4-alpha.getbootstrap.com/layout/grid/`. So, in our `LandingPage` component, I will just wrap the authentication and `go-to-app-link` components into the `div` with the `row` class and add the corresponding `col-*` classes to these components:

```
// LandingPage.vue
<template>
  <div>
    <...>
    <div class="container row justify-content-center">
      <div class="col-sm-12 col-md-6 col-lg-6">
        <authentication></authentication>
      </div>
      <div class="col-sm-12 col-md-6 col-lg-6">
        <go-to-app-link></go-to-app-link>
      </div>
    </div>
  </div>
</template>
```

That's it! Now you have a nice two-column layout, which transforms into the single-column layout on small-sized devices:

This is how our layout looks on the desktop device

As you can see, on the desktop device, we have a nice two-column layout. If you resize your browser to the size of a mobile device, the right column jumps behind the left column:

This is how our layout looks on the mobile device

Now let's have a look at our `Authentication.vue` component. In order to make it nicer than a 20-year-old web page, let's apply Bootstrap's magic to it. To do so, we will use the classes of Bootstrap's forms: `https://v4-alpha.getbootstrap.com/components/forms/`.

We will wrap the whole form into the `<form>` tag and each of the inputs into the `div` with the `form-group` class. We will also add the class `form-control` to each of the inputs. So the input for email, for example, will look as follows:

```
<div class="form-group">
  <input class="form-control" v-model="email" type="email"
  placeholder="email">
</div>
```

As a small exercise, do the following:

- Make it only one form that has a button to switch between the login and sign-up forms

- Make it only one method that would call one of the actions depending on which state the form is in at the moment

- Explore Bootstrap's utilities classes to remove all the borders except the bottom border and to remove the round corners from them: `https://v4-alpha.getbootstrap.com/utilities/borders/`

In the end, your form should look like the following:

Already a member? Log in here!	Don't have an account? Sign up here!
email	email
password	password
LOGIN	SIGN UP
Don't have an account? Sign up here!	Already a member? Log in here!

This is how both forms should be looking at the end. They should be toggled with a bottom button

Try to achieve it by yourself. To check your work, have a look at the `chapter6/3/profitoro` folder. In particular, check the code of the `Authentication.vue` component. It is very different!

Managing the anonymous user

ProFitOro allows unregistered users to use the application as well. The only difference is that these unregistered users are not allowed to configure their settings as well, as they do not have access to their statistical data. They also cannot manage workouts. So, this is where we meet the second A of the triple-A definition – *authorization*. How can we manage these users? How can they actually enter the application if we only allow our users to sign up and log in? Well, for some reason, we have prepared the part that says **Go to App**. Let me remind you how it looks in the mockups:

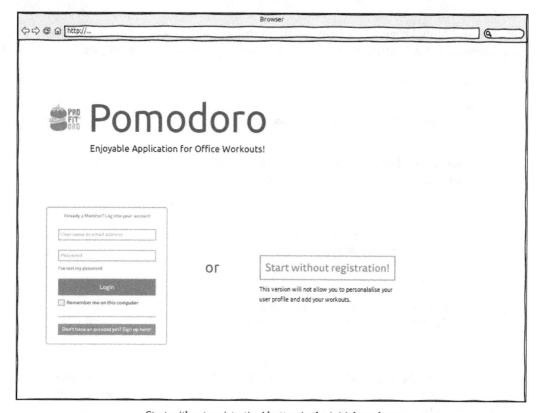

Start without registration! button in the initial mockups

Luckily for us, the Firebase authentication API provides a method to sign in the anonymous user. The returned user object contains the isAnonymous attribute, which will allow us to manage the resources that can or can't be accessible to this anonymous user. So let's add the action called authenticateAnonymous and call the corresponding Firebase auth method within it:

```js
// store/actions.js
authenticateAnonymous ({state}) {
  state.firebaseApp.auth().signInAnonymously().catch(error => {
    console.log(error.code, error.message)
  })
},
```

Here we are! Now let's just slightly modify a mutation that sets the user and the **isAnonymous** state's attribute to the corresponding one in the user object:

```js
// store/mutations.js
setUser (state, value) {
  state.user = value
  state.isAnonymous = value.isAnonymous
}
```

Let's also modify the binding configuration and statistics actions and execute the actual binding only if the user is set and only if the user is not anonymous:

```js
// state/actions.js
bindConfig: firebaseAction(({bindFirebaseRef, state}) => {
  if (state.user && !state.isAnonymous) {
    bindFirebaseRef('config', state.configRef)
  }
}),
bindStatistics: firebaseAction(({bindFirebaseRef, state}) => {
  if (state.user && !state.isAnonymous) {
    bindFirebaseRef('statistics', state.statisticsRef)
  }
})
```

We are done with the backend! Now let's implement this button! There are only three steps to achieve it. Open the GoToAppLink.vue component, import the mapActions helper, add the button, and use the v-on:click directive to bind the event listener to it that will call the corresponding action:

```html
// GoToAppLink.vue
<template>
  <div>
    <button @click="authenticateAnonymous">
      START WITHOUT REGISTRATION
    </button>
  </div>
```

```
  </template>
  <script>
    import {mapActions} from 'vuex'

    export default {
      methods: {
        ...mapActions(['authenticateAnonymous'])
      }
    }
  </script>
```

How easy is that? Now, as a small exercise, with the help of Bootstrap, try to make things look like the following:

Already a member? Log in here!

email

password

OR

LOGIN

START WITHOUT REGISTRATION

This version will not allow you to personalise your profile or add new workouts

Don't have an account? Sign up here!

Use the corresponding Bootstrap classes to make our buttons look like this and to align the columns vertically

Check Bootstrap's classes for alignment: `https://v4-alpha.getbootstrap.com/layout/grid/#alignment`. Check as well the helper classes to get rid of rounded corners. Check yourself by having a look at the code in the `chapter6/4/profitoro` folder. Pay special attention to the `GoToAppLink.vue` component and to the store's components, such as `action.js` and `mutations.js`.

Personalizing the Pomodoro timer

Well, now that we can already sign in new users and log in the existing ones, probably we should think about taking advantage of our authentication mechanism because right now we are actually not doing anything with it. We just sign up and we just log in. Yes, we also can hide or show some content based on the user's authentication, but this is not enough. The whole point of all this effort was to be able to store and retrieve the user's custom configuration for the Pomodoro timer and the user's statistical data.

Until now, we have been using a hardcoded database object with the key test in order to access the user's data, but now, since we already have our real users, it's time to populate the database with real users' data and use it in our application. Actually, the only thing we have to do is to replace this hardcoded value with the actual user's ID. So, for example, our code to bind the config reference was looking like this:

```
// store/actions.js
bindConfig: firebaseAction(({bindFirebaseRef, state}) => {
  if (state.user && !state.isAnonymous) {
    bindFirebaseRef('config', state.configRef)
  }
}),
```

Here, the reference state.configRef has been defined in the store's entry point index.js:

```
// store/actions.js
let firebaseApp = firebase.initializeApp(config)
let db = firebaseApp.database()
let configRef = db.ref('/configuration/test')
```

Now, we cannot actually instantiate our database references within the store's entry point, because at this point (no pun intended), we still don't know whether or not our user is authenticated. So the best thing to do is to pass this code to the actual bindConfig function and to replace this test with the real user's *uid*:

```
// store/action.js
bindConfig: firebaseAction(({bindFirebaseRef, state}) => {
  if (state.user && !state.isAnonymous) {
    let db = firebaseApp.database()
    bindFirebaseRef('config',
    db.ref(`/configuration/${state.user.uid}`))
  }
}),
```

Now, my dear attentive user, I know that you are exclaiming "but how the hell is the configuration with the user's *uid* stored?" Very well noticed: it's not. We still have to store it on our user's first sign-up. We actually have to store both configuration and statistics.

The Firebase database provides a method to write new data to the database that is called set. So you basically obtain the reference (just like in the case of reading data) and set the data you need to write:

```
firebaseApp.database().ref(`/configuration/${state.user.uid}`).set(
  state.config
);
```

This will create a new entry with a given user ID in our configuration table and set the default state's `config` data. So we will have to call this method on the new user creation. We will still have to bind the database references to our state objects. In order to reduce the amount of code, I created a method, `bindFirebaseReference`, that receives the reference and the string that represents the key of the state to which it should be bound. This method will analyze whether or not the entry for the given reference already exists in the database and will create it if needed. For that, Firebase provides a nice method that can be applied to nearly everything – this method is called `once` and it receives a callback with a snapshot to whatever it has been applied to. So, inside this callback, we can analyze whether or not this snapshot has a child with a given name, or even if it has a value or it's `null`. If the value is already set, we will bind our state to it. If not, we will create a new entry. Check out the official Firebase documentation in this regard: `https://firebase.google.com/docs/database/web/read-and-write`. This is what the `once` method and its callback looks like:

```
var userId = firebase.auth().currentUser.uid;
return firebase.database().ref('/users/' + userId).once('value').then(function(snapshot) {
  var username = snapshot.val().username;
  // ...
});
```

How to use the once method to check whether the data exists in the database

Disregarding the existence or not of data, our binding reference method should call the Firebase bindings. So it will look as the following:

```
// store/actions.js
bindFirebaseReference: firebaseAction(({bindFirebaseRef, state},
{reference, toBind}) => {
  return reference.once('value').then(snapshot => {
    if (!snapshot.val()) {
      reference.set(state[toBind])
    }
    bindFirebaseRef(toBind, reference)
  })
}),
```

I also replaced both methods that were binding `config` and `statistics` by only one:

```
// store/actions.js
bindFirebaseReferences: firebaseAction(({bindFirebaseRef, state,
commit, dispatch}, user) => {
  let db = state.firebaseApp.database()
  let configRef = db.ref(`/configuration/${user.uid}`)
  let statisticsRef = db.ref(`/statistics/${user.uid}`)
```

```
    dispatch('bindFirebaseReference', {reference: configRef, toBind:
'config'}).then(() => {
        commit('setConfigRef', configRef)
    })
    dispatch('bindFirebaseReference', {reference: statisticsRef, toBind:
'statistics'}).then(() => {
        commit('setStatisticsRef', statisticsRef)
    })
}),
```

This method is being called from the `bindAuth` method. So now we can remove the calls to the actions to bind `config` and `statistics` from the `created` method of our `App.vue`. We also don't need the instantiation of references in the `store/index.js` since both references are instantiated within this new method. And we have to add two mutations that will set the references to the state so we don't need to change our Pomodoro configuration settings actions since they are using both references to update the data.

Check what the code looks like in the `chapter6/5/profitoro` folder. Check out the slight changes in the `App.vue` component, and check what the store's files are looking like now (`index.js`, `mutations.js`, `state.js`, and especially `actions.js`).

Play with your application. Sign up, log in, change the Pomodoro timer configuration, log out, and check that it works. Check your Firebase console – the **Realtime Database** tab and **Authentication** tab. Check that whatever you change, you have your data consistent everywhere – in your database, in your **Authentication** tab, and, most importantly, in your application (because the application is what your users are going to see, right?):

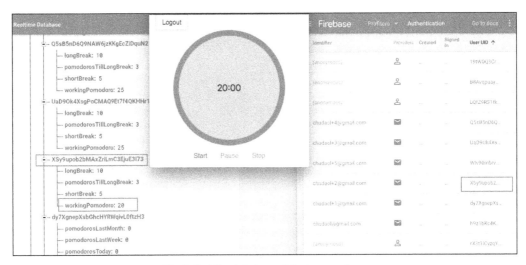

Check that the data is consistent everywhere

So now we can sign up a new user, log in as an existing user, and log in as an anonymous user. We provide a nice value to the authenticated users – to be able to configure their Pomodoro timer and to check their statistical data. Of course, our application is still far from being perfect – we don't validate the input, we accept any values in the Pomodoro configuration area, which is not right, and we don't display the possibility of changing passwords on the startup page. BUT we have our solid skeleton, which enables us to build a solid and nice application on its base. So let us move on!

Updating a user's profile

Wouldn't it be funny if we could welcome our user by displaying a welcome message saying something like **Welcome Olga**? But our users do not have names; they only have emails and passwords – two essential authentication components that are passed during the sign-up process. So, how can we do that? Well, if you have read with some attention the Firebase documentation regarding authentication (https://firebase.google.com/docs/auth/web/manage-users), you might have spotted these nice methods:

Update a user's profile

You can update a user's basic profile information—the user's display name and profile photo URL—with the `updateProfile` method. For example:

```
var user = firebase.auth().currentUser;

user.updateProfile({
  displayName: "Jane Q. User",
  photoURL: "https://example.com/jane-q-user/profile.jpg"
}).then(function() {
  // Update successful.
}, function(error) {
  // An error happened.
});
```

Set a user's email address

You can set a user's email address with the `updateEmail` method. For example:

```
var user = firebase.auth().currentUser;

user.updateEmail("user@example.com").then(function() {
  // Update successful.
}, function(error) {
  // An error happened.
});
```

Firebase methods for updating a user's profile and email address

Let's use these methods to update our user's profile and user's profile picture!

We will define three new actions – one that will update the user's display name by calling the Firebase `updateProfile` method, one that will update the user's profile picture's URL by calling the same method, and another one that will call the `updateEmail` method. Then we will create the necessary markup in the `Settings. vue` component that will bind those actions on the corresponding input's update. Sounds easy, right? Believe me, it's as easy to implement as it actually sounds.

So, let's define our actions. They will look like the following:

```javascript
// store/actions.js
updateUserName ({state, commit}, displayName) {
  state.user.updateProfile({
    displayName
  })
},
updatePhotoURL ({state}, photoURL) {
  state.user.updateProfile({
    photoURL
  })
},
updateUserEmail ({state}, email) {
  state.user.updateEmail(email).then(() => {
    // Update successful.
  }, error => {
    console.log(error)
  })
},
```

Great! Now let's switch to our `Settings.vue` component, which will be responsible for rendering the needed data to change the account settings and for updating this data by calling the needed actions when needed. So first of all, I will add three entries to the data function that will be set to the current user object's corresponding attributes once the component is `created`:

```javascript
// Settings.vue
data () {
  return {
    displayName: '',
    email: '',
    photoURL: 'static/tomato.png'
  }
},
computed: {
  ...mapGetters({user: 'getUser'})
},
```

```
created () {
  this.displayName = this.user.displayName
  this.email = this.user.email
  this.photoURL = this.user.photoURL ? this.user.photoURL : this.
photoURL
}
```

Now this data can be used within the corresponding actions. So, let's import the needed actions and create the corresponding methods:

```
// Settings.vue
methods: {
  ...mapActions(['updateUserName', 'updateUserEmail',
'updatePhotoURL']),
  onChangeUserName () {
    this.updateUserName(this.displayName)
  },
  onChangeUserEmail () {
    this.updateUserEmail(this.email)
  },
  onProfilePicChanged () {
    this.updatePhotoURL(this.photoURL)
  }
}
```

Now we can add the needed markup full of the inputs to which we will bind the data using the v-model data binding directive! We will also call the corresponding methods on each input's update:

```
// Settings.vue
<form>
  <div class="form-group">
    <figure class="figure">
      <img :src="photoURL" alt="Avatar">
      <input type="text" v-model="photoURL" @
change="onProfilePicChanged">
    </figure>
  </div>
  <div class="form-group">
    <input @change="onChangeUserName" v-model="displayName"
type="text" placeholder="Change your username">
  </div>
  <div class="form-group">
    <input @change="onChangeUserEmail" v-model="email" type="text"
placeholder="Change your username">
  </div>
</form>
```

And…we are done!

As a small exercise, do the following: add a figure caption behind our image that says **Change profile picture**. The input element for the new picture URL should only be visible when the user clicks on this figure caption. Once the URL's updating is done, the input should become invisible again.

The result should look like the following:

This is how it looks before the user clicks the Change profile picture caption

Initially, it contains the default user picture.

After the user clicks on the caption, the input for changing the picture's URL appears:

After the user clicks on the figure caption, the input appears

After the user changes the profile picture URL, the input is hidden again:

After the user changes the URL for the profile picture, the input disappears

My advice: add an additional property to the Settings.vue component's data, set it to `true` when the user clicks on the caption, and reset it to `false` when the value inside the input is changed.

Also, don't forget about our initial aim for this section – add a welcoming message inside the Header.vue component. This welcoming message should contain the user's display name. It should look something like this:

Welcoming message mentioning the user's name

Note that if you decide to change your email, you will have to log out and log in again; otherwise, you will get some Firebase security errors in your console.

The final code for this chapter can be found in the chapter6/6/profitoro folder. Note that I split both the account settings and the Pomodoro settings with two individual components (AccountSettings.vue and PomodoroTimerSettings.vue). It makes things easier to maintain. Pay attention to the store's components as well. Check the Header.vue component and how it actually displays the welcoming message.

Summary

In this chapter, we have learned how to combine the Firebase real-time database and authentication API to update a user's settings. We have built a user interface that allows a user to update their profile settings. In just a few minutes, we have built the full authentication and authorization part of our application. I don't know about you, but I feel totally amazed about it.

In the next chapter, we will finally get rid of this huge page that contains all the parts of our application – the Pomodoro timer itself, statistics data, and the settings configuration view. We will explore one really nice and important feature of Vue – `vue-router`. We will combine it with Bootstrap's navigation system in order to achieve a nice and smooth navigation. We will also explore such a hot topic as code splitting in order to achieve lazy loading for our application. So, let's go!

7
Adding a Menu and Routing Functionality Using vue-router and Nuxt.js

In the previous chapter, we added a very important feature to our application – *authentication*. Now, our users are able to register, log in to the application, and manage their resources once they are logged in. So, now they can manage the configuration of the Pomodoro timer and their account's settings. They also have access to their statistics data once they are logged in. We have learned how to use Firebase's authentication API and connect the Vue application to it. I must say, the previous chapter has been extensive in learning and a very backend oriented chapter. I enjoyed it a lot and I hope you enjoyed it as well.

Despite having this complex feature of authentication and authorization, our application still lacks navigation. For simplicity reasons, we are currently displaying all the application's parts on the main page. This is... ugly:

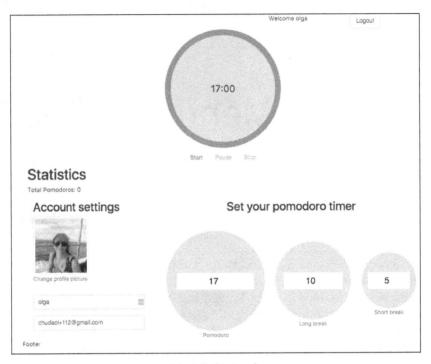

Admit it, this is ugly

In this chapter, we are not going to make things beautiful. What we are going to do is make things navigable so that all parts of the application are accessible through navigation. We are going to apply the `vue-router` mechanism in order to achieve the natural browser's navigation and we are going to use Bootstrap's `navbar` in order to have the corresponding buttons to navigate to each section easily. Thus, in this chapter we are going to:

- Explore `vue-router` again to achieve the navigation of the ProFitOro application
- Use Bootstrap's `navbar` to render the navigation bar
- Explore code splitting techniques to load each part of the application only when it's needed
- And, finally, we are going to explore the Nuxt.js template, rebuild our application using it, and achieve routing in an unobtrusive and enjoyable way

Adding navigation using vue-router

I hope you still remember from the second chapter what `vue-router` is, what it does, and how it works. Just to remind you:

> *Vue-router is the official router for Vue.js. It deeply integrates with Vue.js core to make building Single Page Applications with Vue.js a breeze.*

-(From the official documentation of vue-router)

The `vue-router` is very easy to use, and we don't need to install anything – it already comes with the default scaffolding of Vue applications with a webpack template. In a nutshell, if we have Vue components that should represent the routes, this is what we have to do:

- Tell Vue to use `vue-router`
- Create a router instance and map each component to its path
- Pass this instance to the options of a Vue instance or component
- Render it using the `router-view` component

 Check the official `vue-router` documentation: `https://router.vuejs.org`

When you create your router, you should pass the array of routes to it. Each array item represents the mapping of a given component to some path:

```
{
  name: 'home',
  component: HomeComponent,
  path: '/'
}
```

ProFitOro only has four possible routes – the Pomodoro timer itself, which we can consider as the home page, views with settings and statistics, and the view with collaborative workouts. Thus, our router looks very simple and easy to understand:

```
// router/index.js
import Vue from 'vue'
import Router from 'vue-router'
import {PomodoroTimer, Settings, Statistics, Workouts} from '@/
components/main/sections'

Vue.use(Router)
```

```
export default new Router({
  mode: 'history',
  routes: [
    {
      name: 'home',
      component: PomodoroTimer,
      path: '/'
    },
    {
      name: 'settings',
      component: Settings,
      path: '/settings'
    },
    {
      name: 'statistics',
      component: Statistics,
      path: '/statistics'
    },
    {
      name: 'workouts',
      component: Workouts,
      path: '/workouts'
    }
  ]
})
```

Now, if you import the created router in the ContentComponent view, pass it to the options of the component and render the router-view component, you will be able to see the Vue routing in action! You can also delete all the component imports, because the only thing that ContentComponent should actually import now is the router which will be responsible for everything else. So, ContentComponent will look as follows:

```
// ContentComponent.vue
<template>
  <div class="container">
    <router-view></router-view>
  </div>
</template>
<script>
  import router from '@/router'

  export default {
    router
  }
</script>
```

Open the page, type `localhost:8080/settings`, `localhost:8080/statistics`, `localhost:8080/workouts` in the browser's address bar and you will see how the views appear according to what you are actually trying to access. You must admit that this was really easy.

Now let's add the links, because we want to navigate by clicking some buttons and not by introducing the navigation URL in the browser address bar, right?

Adding navigation links with `vue-router` is fairly easy. Use the provided `router-link` component with the attribute `to` that points the link to the desired path:

```
<router-link to="/">Home</router-link>
```

Let's add these links in our `Header` component. This is the component that should be responsible for the navigation representation. So, in the `template` section of our `HeaderComponent.vue`, add the following:

```
// HeaderComponent.vue
<template>
  <router-link to="/">Home </router-link>
  <router-link to="statistics">Statistics </router-link>
  <router-link to="workouts">Workouts </router-link>
  <router-link to="settings">Settings </router-link>
</template>
```

Don't forget to import the router and export it in the component's options:

```
// HeaderComponent.vue
<script>
//...
  import router from '@/router'

  export default {
    //

    router
  }
</script>
```

With a bit of playing around with Bootstrap classes, we get something like this:

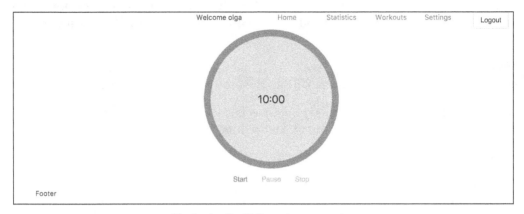

Navigating ProFitOro using vue-router

This is, in a nutshell, the basics covering routing and navigation using `vue-router` and its components. You can find the final code for this part in the `chapter7/1/profitoro` folder. Pay special attention to the router itself (`router/index.js`), `ContentComponent.vue` and the `HeaderComponent.vue` files.

Exercise - restrict the navigation according to the authentication

Don't forget that we have to restrict the navigation links according to the authentication state of the user. If the user is authenticated anonymously, we shouldn't show the navigation links at all. However, there should be a button that enables users to go back to the main page. So, this button should invoke a logout functionality and just display a different text, let's say, **Go to the start page**. You already know how to conditionally render Vue components. Our router links are no more than just regular components, so apply the conditional rendering mechanism to them based on the value of the user and its property as `isAnonymous`.

Check the solution for this exercise in the `chapter7/2/profitoro` folder. Pay attention to the `HeaderComponent` component.

Using Bootstrap navbar for navigation links

Our current navigation bar is great – it's functional, but not responsive. Luckily for us, Bootstrap has a `navbar` component that implements responsiveness and adaptiveness for us. We just have to wrap our navigation elements with some Bootstrap classes and then sit back and check our beautiful navigation bar that collapses on mobile devices and expands on desktop devices. Check Bootstrap's documentation regarding the `navbar` component: `https://v4-alpha.getbootstrap.com/components/navbar/`.

 Keep in mind that this URL is for the alpha version. The next stable version 4 will be available on the official website.

These are the classes we are going to use to transform our simple navigation bar into a Bootstrap-managed responsive navigation bar:

- `navbar`: This wraps the whole navigation bar element

- `navbar-toggleable-*`: This should also wrap the whole navigation bar element and will tell it when to toggle between expanded/collapsed state (for example, `navbar-toggleable-md` would make navigation bar collapse on medium-size devices)

- `navbar-toggler`: This is a class for the button that will be clicked to open the collapsed menu on small devices

- `navbar-toggler-*`: This tells the `toggler` element where to be positioned, for example, `navbar-toggler-right`

- `navbar-brand`: This is a class for the navigation bar element that will represent a brand (can be logo and/or text)

- `collapse navbar-collapse`: These are classes that will wrap the navigation bar elements that should be collapsed on small devices

- `nav-item`: This is a class for each of the navigation bar items

- `nav-link`: This is a class for the nested element of the `nav-item` items; this will finally be an anchor that will lead you to the given link

There are lots of other classes to define a color scheme for your navigation bar, as well as its positioning, alignment, and so on. Check the documentation and try them all. I will just change the markup of the `Header` component. So, it will look like the following:

```
// HeaderComponent.vue
<template>
  <div>
    <nav class="navbar navbar-toggleable-md navbar-light">
      <button class="navbar-toggler navbar-toggler-right"
type="button" data-toggle="collapse" data-target="#navbarHeader"
aria-controls="navbarHeader" aria-expanded="false" aria-label="Toggle
navigation">
        <span class="navbar-toggler-icon"></span>
      </button>
      <div class="navbar-brand">
        <logo></logo>
      </div>
      <div class="collapse navbar-collapse" id="navbarHeader">
        <ul class="navbar-nav ml-auto">
          <li class="nav-item">
            <router-link class="nav-link" to="/">Home
            </router-link>
          </li>
          <li class="nav-item">
            <router-link class="nav-link" to="settings">Settings
            </router-link>
          </li>
          <li class="nav-item">
            <router-link class="nav-link" to="statistics">
            Statistics </router-link>
          </li>
          <li class="nav-item">
            <router-link class="nav-link" to="workouts">Workouts
            </router-link>
          </li>
        </ul>
        <form class="form-inline my-2 my-lg-0">
          <button class="btn btn-secondary" @click="onLogout">
          Logout</button>
        </form>
      </div>
    </nav>
  </div>
</template>
```

You have probably noticed that I used our `router-link` elements with `nav-link` classes inside the navigation items. It turns out that they play really nicely together. So, we mixed the Vue routing mechanism with Bootstrap's navigation bar and achieved an elegant solution for responsive routing in our Vue application. Now, our header looks as great as this:

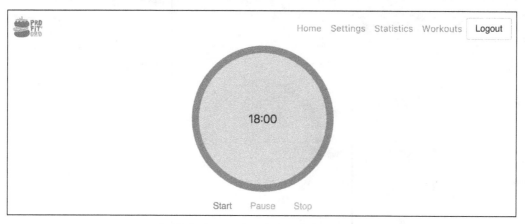

ProFitOro's navigation bar on desktop device

If we open our ProFitOro on a mobile device, we will see a nice toggle button instead of the menu:

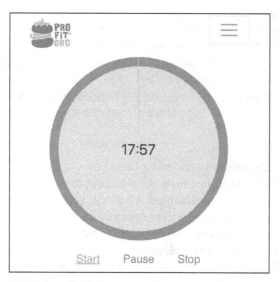

This is how ProFitOro's menu looks on a mobile device

If we click on the toggle button on the mobile device, the menu will expand vertically:

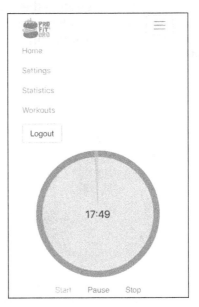

This is how an expanded ProFitOro menu looks on a mobile device

This works nicely with alpha version of Bootstrap 4, however, if you use Bootstrap 4 Beta you will see some inconsistencies. Some classes were dropped, some classes were added. In order to make it to look exactly the same, do the following:

- replace the `navbar-tooglable-md` class with the `navbar-expand-lg`
- replace `btn-secondary` buttons' class with `button-outline-secondary` swap the toggler button and brand element

The functionality of conditional rendering based on the authentication has been dropped. I will re-add it, but instead of hiding the elements when the user is anonymous, I will make them disabled. This will bring extra value to the application – an unregistered user will constantly be reminded that there is some nice functionality that he can use if he registers. Thus, I will bind the `disabled` Bootstrap class to the `router-link` elements. This class will be activated if the user is anonymous. So, each of our router links will look like the following:

```
// HeaderComponent.vue
<router-link class="nav-link" :class="{disabled:user.isAnonymous}"
to="settings">Settings </router-link>
```

If you open the page now and enter the application as an anonymous user you will see that the links appear as disabled:

For an unauthorized user the links appear as disabled

But, our user is smart, we all know that, right? Our user will do exactly the same thing that you are considering doing right now (if you haven't already done it) - open the developer tools console, go to the elements tab, edit the markup and remove the class disabled. *Ba-dum-tsss*, now you can click on the navigation links!

So, we need also to protect it on the router side. Fortunately for us, vue-router instance provides a hook method called beforeEach. This method receives both the next and previous routes and, inside it, you can evaluate them and invoke the next() method that will proceed to the next route or replace the path being invoked, depending on the condition.

Additionally, each route item can include the meta attribute where we can pass a condition on which this route can or cannot be invoked. Check the vue-router documentation in this regard: https://router.vuejs.org/en/advanced/meta.html.

So, let's add a meta attribute requiresAuth to each of three route items and use the beforeEach method like this:

```
// router/index.js
router.beforeEach((to, from, next) => {
  if (to.matched.some(record => record.meta.requiresAuth)) {
    if (!store.state.user || store.state.user.isAnonymous) {
      next({
        path: '/'
      })
    } else {
      next()
    }
  } else {
    next()
  }
})
```

Et voilá, from now on, even if you explicitly type one of the conditional routes URLs in the browser's address bar while being unauthorized, you will be redirected to the home page!

Check the final code for this part in the `chapter7/3/profitoro` folder. Pay special attention to the router itself (`router/index.js`) and to the `Header` component.

Code splitting or lazy loading

When we build our application to deploy for production, all the JavaScript is bundled into a unique JavaScript file. It's very handy, because once the browser loads this file, the whole application is already on the client side and no one is worried about loading more things. Of course, this is only valid for SPAs.

Our ProFitOro application (at least at this stage) benefits from such bundling behavior – it's small, it's a single request, everything is in place and we don't need to request anything from the server for any of the JavaScript files.

However, this kind of bundling might have some downsides. I am pretty sure that you have already built or have already seen huge JavaScript applications. There'll always be some point when loading huge bundles will become unbearably slow, especially when we want these apps to run on both desktop and mobile environments.

An obvious solution for this problem would be to split the code in such a way that different chunks of code are loaded only when they are needed. This is quite a challenge for single page applications and this is why we have a huge community working on web development nowadays.

Right now, some simple techniques already exist in the web development world that can be used to split the code in webpack applications. Check the official webpack documentation to find out more about it: `https://webpack.js.org/guides/code-splitting/`.

In order to use code splitting in a Vue.js application, you don't need to do anything complex. There is no need to reconfigure your webpack configuration files and there is no need to rewrite your components. Check this documentation entry regarding lazy loading routes: `https://router.vuejs.org/en/advanced/lazy-loading.html`.

TL;DR: in order to lazy load your routes, you just need to change the way you are importing them. So, consider the following code: `import PomodoroTimer from '@/components/main/sections/PomodoroTimer'` To lazy load your routes, you would write the following instead: `const PomodoroTimer = () => import('@/components/main/sections/PomodoroTimer')`

The rest of the code remains totally unchanged!

Thus, we just change the way that we import components in our router:

```
// router/index.js
const PomodoroTimer = () => import('@/components/main/sections/
PomodoroTimer')
const Settings = () => import('@/components/main/sections/Settings')
const Statistics = () => import('@/components/main/sections/
Statistics')
const Workouts = () => import('@/components/main/sections/Workouts')
```

That's it! Check the page and ensure that everything still works as intended. Check the network panel. You will see that now it will request different JavaScript bundles for different route views!

If you compare the network requests with the previous version, you will see that there are now actually four requests – 0.js, 1.js, 2.js, and 3.js - compared to the previous single app.js request:

Name	Status	Type	Initiator	Size	Time
jquery.js	200	script	(index)	68.0 KB	30 ms
tether.js	200	script	(index)	24.7 KB	29 ms
bootstrap.js	200	script	(index)	45.8 KB	29 ms
app.js	200	script	(index)	4.5 MB	322 ms

A single request for app.js bundle before code splitting

After the code splitting, if we navigate through the application's navigation links, we will see the following:

Name	Status	Type	Initiator	Size	Time
1.js	200	script	app.js:743	77.0 KB	4 ms
0.js	200	script	app.js:743	94.4 KB	6 ms
3.js	200	script	app.js:743	14.3 KB	6 ms
2.js	200	script	app.js:743	13.1 KB	6 ms

Considerably smaller JavaScript chunk is being requested for every route

Pay attention to the chunk sizes. Don't you agree that for big projects the code splitting technique might actually increase the application's performance? Check the router's code in the chapter7/3.1/profitoro folder.

Server-side rendering

Server-side rendering (SSR) recently became yet another popular abbreviation in the web development world. Used in addition to code splitting techniques, it helps you to boost the performance of your web application. It also positively affects your SEO, since all the content comes at once, and crawlers are able to see it immediately, contrary to cases where the content is being built in the browser after the initial request.

I found a great article about SSR that compares server and client side rendering (although it's from 2012). Check it out: `http://openmymind.net/2012/5/30/ Client-Side-vs-Server-Side-Rendering/`.

It's fairly easy to bring server-side rendering to your Vue application – check the official documentation in this regard: `https://ssr.vuejs.org`.

It is important that our applications are performant; it is also important that SEO works. However, it is also important not to abuse the tools and not to introduce implementation overhead and overkill. Do we need SSR for the ProFitOro application? To answer this question let's think about our content. If there is a lot of content which is being brought to the page and is being used as a base for the initial rendering then the answer is probably yes. Well, this is not the case for our application. We have a simple login page, our ProFitOro timer, and a couple of configuration settings. The only view where it might make sense in the future is the one that contains workouts. But for now, let's not complicate things. You can try out server-side rendering techniques for Vue applications with our ProFitOro, but keep in mind that it's not something that should be used all the time. Learn the differences between server-side rendering and pre-rendering as well (`https://github.com/ chrisvfritz/prerender-spa-plugin`) and check how our application could actually benefit from both of these techniques.

Nuxt.js

While we were busy defining our router object, router links, code splitting and learning things about the server-side rendering, someone implemented a way of developing Vue.js applications without being worried about all these things at all. Just write your code. All the things like routing, code splitting and even server-side rendering will be handled behind the scenes for you! If you are wondering what the hell it is, let me introduce you to Nuxt.js: `https://nuxtjs.org`.

So, what is Nuxt.js?

Nuxt.js is a framework for creating Universal Vue.js Applications.

Its main scope is UI rendering while abstracting away the client/server distribution.

What's so great about it? Nuxt.js introduces the concept of pages – basically, pages are also Vue components, but each one of the pages represents a *route*. Once you define your components inside the `pages` folder they become routes without any additional configuration.

In this chapter, we will totally migrate our ProFitOro to the Nuxt architecture. So, brace yourself; we are going to make lots of changes! At the end of the chapter, our efforts will be rewarded with a piece of nice, elegant code.

The Nuxt application has a single `config` file, where you can define the necessary webpack configuration, as well as `meta`, `links` and additional `scripts` for your `index.html` file. This is because Nuxt will generate your `index.html` automatically during the build process, so you don't have to have it in your application's root directory. In this config file, you can also define a transition that should happen on each route change.

The way to create a Nuxt application is very similar to creating any Vue application – all Nuxt.js functionality is built in the `nuxt-starter` template: `https://github.com/nuxt-community/starter-template`. So, creating the Vue.js application with a Nuxt template is just:

```
vue init nuxt/starter <project-name>
```

Let's create a `profitoro-nuxt` project and see how it works. Run the following command:

```
vue init nuxt/starter profitoro-nuxt
```

Click Enter to answer to the questions.

Enter the generated folder, install the dependencies, and run the application:

```
cd profitoro-nuxt
npm install
npm run dev
```

Open the page on `localhost:3000` and make sure that you see this:

The initial default page of the Nuxt application

Let's explore the folders' structure and the code. There's a folder called `pages` where you can find the `index.vue` page. There's also a folder called `components` – here we will store our components. There is a `nuxt.config.js` file where all the basic configuration is stored. In a nutshell, that's it.

Let's work on the `pages` folder. What components of our ProFitOro application can we define as `pages`? It's fairly easy to identify them, since we already have our defined routes. So, I would say that we can identify the following pages:

- `index.vue`: This will check if the user is logged in and render either the login page or the Pomodoro timer page
- `login.vue`: This page is identical to our current `LandingComponent.vue`
- `pomodoro.vue`: This will be the page that contains the Pomodoro timer component
- `settings.vue`: This page will represent our `Settings.vue` component
- `statistics.vue`: This page will be responsible for rendering the `Statistics.vue` component
- `workouts.vue`: This page will be responsible for managing the workouts

Let's create placeholders for all these pages. This is what my directory structure inside the `pages` folder looks like:

```
├── pages
│   ├── index.vue
│   ├── login.vue
│   ├── pomodoro.vue
│   ├── settings.vue
│   ├── statistics.vue
│   └── workouts.vue
```

This is the initial content of the `login.vue` page:

```
//login.vue
<template>
  <div>
     login
  </div>
</template>
<script>

</script>
<style scoped>

</style>
```

All the other pages are very similar to this one, except the `index.vue` page:

```
//index.vue
<template>
  <div>
     <pomodoro></pomodoro>
     <login></login>
  </div>
</template>
<script>
  import login from './login'
  import pomodoro from './pomodoro'

  export default {
    components: {login, pomodoro}
  }
</script>
<style>
</style>
```

If you open this application in your browser and try to type different paths (`localhost:3000/pomodoro`, `localhost:3000/settings`, and so on) in the browser's address bar, you will see how it actually renders the corresponding pages. How nice is that? We didn't have to define any routes or any additional configuration in order to achieve this behavior! Check the code for this part in the `chapter7/4/profitoro-nuxt` folder.

Adding links with nuxt-link

Just like `vue-router` provides a component called `router-link`, Nuxt provides a very similar component called `nuxt-link`. Let's change our `HeaderComponent` using nuxt-links instead of router-links and let's include this component inside our pages.

Before doing that, let's install `sass-loader`, because, if you remember, we are using the sass pre-processor for our CSS and our `HeaderComponent` is actually heavily relying on that. So, go ahead and run the following:

```
npm install --save-dev node-sass sass-loader
```

I've also re-included Bootstrap styles, using its *sass* styles instead of plain CSS. Check out the `assets/styles` folder in the `chapter7/5/profitoro-nuxt` folder. Run `npm install` inside this folder and use this as your working directory for this part.

Let's now copy our `HeaderComponent.vue` and `Logo.vue` to the `components/common` folder. Our logo's markup will change. Before it was wrapped inside the `router-link` component and pointing to the home page. Instead of using `router-link` we will use the `nuxt-link` component:

```
//components/common/Logo.vue
<template>
  <nuxt-link to="/">
    <img class="logo" :src="src" alt="ProFitOro">
  </nuxt-link>
</template>
```

Note that we are binding the `src` attribute to the `src` value. We will get our source from the `assets` folder. In the Nuxt application, we can use the `~` notation to indicate the root directory of the application. Using this notation actually facilitates the usage of the relative paths. Thus, the source data attribute for the logo will look like the following:

```
// components/common/Logo.vue
<script>
  export default {
    data () {
      return {
        src: require('~/assets/profitoro_logo.svg')
      }
    }
  }
</script>
```

Our logo is ready; now it's time to check the `HeaderComponent` component and replace all the router links with `nuxt-links`.

Open the just copied `HeaderComponent.vue` component and remove all the data used from the Vuex store for now and leave only the `import` of the `Logo` component:

```
//components/common/HeaderComponent.vue
<script>
  import Logo from '~/components/common/Logo'

  export default {
    components: {
      Logo
    }
  }
</script>
```

Also, remove all the references to any data inside the markup, leave only the links and replace them with `nuxt-link` components. So, our links section will look like the following:

```
//components/common/HeaderComponent.vue
<ul class="navbar-nav ml-auto">
  <li class="nav-item">
    <nuxt-link class="nav-link" to="/">Home </nuxt-link>
  </li>
  <li class="nav-item">
    <nuxt-link class="nav-link" to="settings">Settings </nuxt-link>
  </li>
  <li class="nav-item">
    <nuxt-link class="nav-link" to="statistics">Statistics
    </nuxt-link>
  </li>
  <li class="nav-item">
    <nuxt-link class="nav-link" to="workouts">Workouts </nuxt-link>
  </li>
</ul>
<form class="form-inline my-2 my-lg-0">
  <button class="btn btn-secondary" >Logout</button>
</form>
```

Import `HeaderComponent` to our pages (`settings`, `statistics`, `pomodoro` and `workouts`):

```
//pages/pomodoro.vue
<template>
  <div class="container">
    <header-component></header-component>
    pomodoro
  </div>
</template>
<script>
  import HeaderComponent from '~/components/common/HeaderComponent'
  export default {
    components: {
      HeaderComponent
    }
  }
</script>
<style scoped lang="scss">
  @import "../assets/styles/main";
</style>
```

Open the page. Check that our links haven't changed at all:

Our links look absolutely the same!

Check that even our responsiveness is still there. If you resize your page, you will see the Bootstrap's menu button:

Menu button is still there as well

The most important part, of course, is that the routing works! Click on the links and check that the pages change.

Have you also noticed a nice transition happening when you change from one page to another?

The transition happens automatically, we haven't written any extra code for it to happen!

You can find the final code up to this point in the `chapter7/6/profitoro-nuxt` folder.

Exercise – making the menu button work

As we have already checked, our responsive menu button is still there. However, if you click on it, nothing happens! This is because this button's behavior is defined in the `bootstrap.js` dependency and we still haven't included it. Use `nuxt.config.js` to include the necessary JavaScript files to make the menu button great again.

After you're done, check my solution in the `chapter7/7/profitoro-nuxt` folder. In particular, check the `head` section of the `nuxt.config.js` file.

Nuxt.js and Vuex store

Well, there will not be anything new in this section – the Vuex store can be used in the exact same way it has been used before. Ah, wait. Inside the Nuxt application, we have to export the function that returns Vuex store and not an instance itself. Check the official documentation in this regard: `https://nuxtjs.org/guide/vuex-store`. So, basically, we will not use the following code:

```
export default new Vuex.Store({
  state,
  getters,
  mutations: {
    ...
  },
  actions
})
```

Instead, we have to do the following:

```
export default () => Vuex.Store({
  state,
  getters,
```

```
    mutations: {
        ...
    },
    actions
})
```

Let's also use this opportunity to initialise the Firebase application in a separate file and use it as a singleton for our application. So, move the `firebaseApp` initialization to its individual `firebase/index.js` file and replace all the occurrences of the `state.firebaseApp` with the imported `firebaseApp` instance.

Last, but not least, don't forget to install the required `vuexfire` and `firebase` dependencies:

npm install --save vuexfire firebase

Check the code for this part in the `chapter7/8/profitoro-nuxt` folder. In particular, pay special attention to the `store` and `firebase` folders.

Nuxt.js middleware

Do you remember how we had to introduce the `beforeEach` method to the vue router instance in order to prevent some routes from being rendered if the user is not authenticated? There is a very similar mechanism for Nuxt.js. You just have to define a so-called `middleware` where you can redirect the request based on some conditions (for example, on the value of the `isAuthenticated` attribute from the Vuex store) and then tell the pages that they have to rely on the authentication middleware. Then, every time that an attempted routing to the given page occurs, the middleware's function will run and do whatever it demands to do.

Let's add this kind of middleware to our ProFitOro Nuxt application. Create a file `authentication.js` inside the folder `middleware` and add the following content:

```
//middleware/authenticated.js
export default function ({ store, redirect }) {
  if (!store.getters.isAuthenticated) {
    return redirect('/')
  }
}
```

This piece of code is responsible for checking the `isAuthenticated` property and redirecting the user to the home page in case it's either false or undefined.

Now, add the property middleware to the settings, statistics, and workouts pages:

```
<template>
  <...>
</template>
<script>
  //...
  export default {
    middleware: 'authenticated',
    //...
  }
</script>
```

Open the page and try to click on the corresponding links for the pages to which we just added the middleware. It will not work! Try to remove the middleware code for some of the pages and check that the routing then works. Isn't it fantastic?

Check the code for this part in the `chapter7/9/profitoro-nuxt` folder. Check the `middleware/index.js` file and Vue pages inside the `pages` folder.

Exercise – finish 'em all!

Well, we've done a lot in order to make our ProFitOro into a Nuxt.js application, but our functionality is still not totally there. We still have to copy lots of components. So, please do it. Right now, it's just a matter of a good copy-paste. So, please do it and make sure that our ProFitOro works fine.

If in doubt, check the `chapter7/10/profitoro-nuxt` folder. You will probably run into the issue of trying to login with an *Enter* key and finding yourself being an anonymous user. This is a minor issue that will be fixed in the next chapters. For now, please, every time you try to login with your valid credentials, just don't forget to click the **LOGIN** button!

Summary

In this chapter we have added basic routing to our application using different tools. First, we learned how to use vue-router to achieve routing functionality and then we used the Nuxt.js template to build a brand new application using old components and styles. We have used the concept of pages offered by Nuxt vue in order to achieve the same routing functionality as with `vue-router` and have transformed our ProFitOro application into a Nuxt application in an easy and unobtrusive way. We have significantly reduced the amount of code and learned something new. Total winners!

In this chapter we have also used Bootstrap's `navbar` to display our navigation routes in a nice and responsive way, and learned that even with the most drastic refactoring, the functionality and responsiveness stays with us when we use the Bootstrap approach. Once again – great success!

Our application is almost fully functional, however, it still lacks its main functionality – workouts. For now, during the Pomodoro intervals we are showing a hardcoded pushups workout.

Are you using the ProFitOro application while reading this book? If yes, I guess I will recognize you on the street – you will have huge muscles after doing so many pushups.

It's time to add more workouts to our application, don't you think? If you remember the requirements, workouts are the subject of collaborative work. So, we will add this functionality in the next chapter. We will use Firebase's data storage mechanism in order to store the workouts' images, the real-time database to store the workouts' objects, Bootstrap's cards layout to display different workouts and the Bootstrap-powered form in order to add new workouts to our application.

8

Let's Collaborate – Adding New Workouts Using Firebase Data Storage and Vue.js

In the previous chapter, we learned how to add some basic navigation to the Vue application using both `vue-router` and `Nuxt.js`. We have redesigned our ProFitOro application, transforming it into a Nuxt-based application. Now our application is functional, it has an authentication mechanism, and it is navigable. However, it still lacks one of the most important features – workouts. In this chapter, we are going to implement the workout management page. Do you still remember its requirements from *Chapter 2, Under the Hood – Tutorial Explained*?

This page should allow users to see the existing workouts in the database, select or deselect them to be shown up during the Pomodoro breaks, rate them, and even add new workouts. We are not going to implement all these features. However, we are going to implement enough for you to continue this application and finish its implementation with great success! So, in this chapter we are going to do the following:

- Define a responsive layout for the workout management page, which will consist of two essential parts – a searchable list of all the workouts as well as the possibility of adding a new workout to the list

- Store new workouts using the Firebase database and data storage mechanism to store workout images

- Use a Bootstrap modal to display every individual workout
- Make our footer nicer using responsive layout and the fixed-bottom class

Creating layouts using Bootstrap classes

Before we start implementing a layout for our workouts page, let me remind you what the mockup looks like:

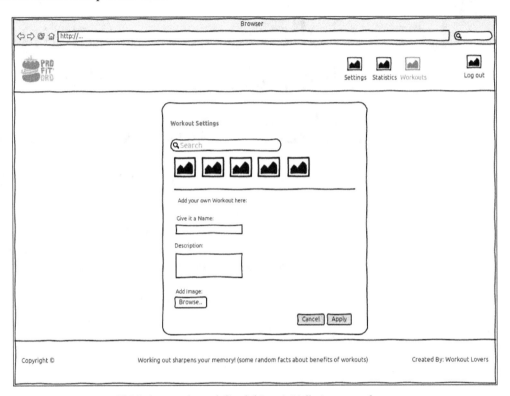

This is how we have defined things initially in our mockups

We will do some things slightly differently - something similar to what we have done in the settings page. Let's create the two-column layout that will stack on mobile devices. So, this mockup will be valid for mobile screens but it will display two columns on desktop devices.

Let's add two components – WorkoutsComponent.vue and NewWorkoutComponent.vue – inside the components/workouts folder. Add some dummy text to the templates of these new components and let's define our two-column layout in the workouts.vue page. You certainly remember that in order to have stack columns on small devices and different-sized columns on other devices, we have to use the col-*-<number> notation, where * represents the size of the device (sm for small, md for medium, lg for large, and so on) and the number represents the size of the column, which might ranges from 1 to 12. Since we want our layout to stack on small devices (this means that the size of the column should be 12) and be two equal-sized columns on medium and large devices, I came up with the following layout definition:

```
// pages/workouts.vue
<template>
  <div class="container">
    <header-component></header-component>
    <div class="row justify-content-center">
      <div class="col-sm-12 col-md-6 col-lg-6">
        <workouts-component></workouts-component>
      </div>
      <div class="col-sm-12 col-md-6 col-lg-6">
        <new-workout-component></new-workout-component>
      </div>
    </div>
    <footer-component></footer-component>
  </div>
</template>
```

Don't forget to import both the WorkoutsComponent.vue and NewWorkoutComponent.vue components to the workouts.vue page:

```
// pages/workouts.vue
<script>
  //...
  import { NewWorkoutComponent, WorkoutComponent, WorkoutsComponent }
  from '~/components/workouts'
  export default {
    components: {
    /...
      NewWorkoutComponent,
      WorkoutsComponent
    }
  }
</script>
```

Now we have a two-column responsive layout:

Two-column responsive layout for the workout management page

Check the code for this implementation in the `chapter8/1/profitoro` folder. In particular, pay attention to the content of `components/workouts` folder and to the `workouts.vue` page.

Making the footer nice

Aren't you tired of this hardcoded word "**Footer**" always lying around beneath our content?

The ugly flying hardcoded Footer always glued to our content

Let's do something with it! If you check our mockups, we have three columns there:

- One column for the copyright information
- Another one for the fact of the day
- And the last for the author information

You already know what to do, right? Again, we want these columns to be equally distributed on mediumand large-sized devices, and stack on mobile devices. Thus, our code will look like this:

```
// components/common/FooterComponent.vue
<template>
  <div class="footer">
    <div class="container row">
      <div class="copyright col-lg-4 col-md-4 col-sm-
      12">Copyright</div>
      <div class="fact col-lg-4 col-md-4 col-sm-12">Working out
      sharpens your memory</div>
      <div class="author col-lg-4 col-md-4 col-sm-12"><span
      class="bold">Workout Lovers</span></div>
    </div>
  </div>
</template>
```

Let's keep the fact of the day section hardcoded for now. Well, now our footer looks a bit nicer. At least it's not just the word "Footer" lying around:

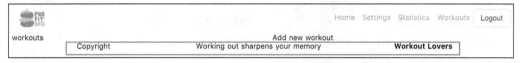

Our footer is not just the word Footer anymore but it's still glued to the main content

However, it's still stuck to the main content, which is not really nice. It would be great if our footer was fixed to the viewport's bottom. It's a common problem, and you will find a lot of articles on the internet asking for this question and providing solutions: `https://stackoverflow.com/questions/18915550/fix-footer-to-bottom-of-page`. Fortunately for us, we are using Bootstrap and it comes with a series of utility classes for sticky top, fixed bottom, and so on.

 In order to make your footer fixed with Bootstrap, just add this class to it: `fixed-bottom`

Once you add this class to your footer, you will see how it becomes stuck to the bottom of the viewport. Try to resize the viewport, moving the bottom of the page up and down, and you will see that our footer goes along the bottom.

Check the code for this section in the `chapter8/2/profitoro` folder. The only change was in the `HeaderComponent.vue` component, which is located in the `components/common` folder.

Storing new workouts using the Firebase real-time database

Before starting this section, check the code in the `chapter8/3/profitoro` folder. Both the `Workouts` and `NewWorkout` components are filled with a markup.

 Don't forget to run `npm install` and `npm run dev`!

It doesn't work yet, but it displays something:

Workout management page with some content

In this section, we are going to add workout objects to our workouts resource in the Firebase database. After that, we can finally learn how to store images using the Firebase data storage mechanism.

First, let's add Firebase bindings just like we've done for statistics and configuration objects. Open the action.js file and find the bindFirebaseReferences method. Here, we should add the binding for the workouts resource. So, this method now contains three bindings:

```js
// state/actions.js
bindFirebaseReferences: firebaseAction(({state, commit, dispatch},
user) => {
  let db = firebaseApp.database()
  let configRef = db.ref(`/configuration/${user.uid}`)
  let statisticsRef = db.ref(`/statistics/${user.uid}`)
  let workoutsRef = db.ref('/workouts')

  dispatch('bindFirebaseReference', {reference: configRef, toBind:
'config'}).then(() => {
    commit('setConfigRef', configRef)
  })
  dispatch('bindFirebaseReference', {reference: statisticsRef,
  toBind: 'statistics'}).then(() => {
    commit('setStatisticsRef', statisticsRef)
  })
  dispatch('bindFirebaseReference', {reference: workoutsRef, toBind:
  'workouts'}).then(() => {
    commit('setWorkoutsRef', workoutsRef)
  })
})
```

We should also unbind them once the application is unloaded:

```
//state/actions.js
unbindFirebaseReferences: firebaseAction(({unbindFirebaseRef, commit})
=> {
    commit('setConfigRef', null)
    commit('setStatisticsRef', null)
    commit('setWorkoutsRef', null)
    try {
      unbindFirebaseRef('config')
      unbindFirebaseRef('statistics')
      unbindFirebaseRef('workouts')
    } catch (error) {
      return
    }
})
```

Let's also add `workoutsRef` and `workouts` attributes to our state. Last but not least, don't forget to implement the mutation called `setWorkoutsRef`:

```
// state/mutations.js
setWorkoutsRef (state, value) {
  state.workoutsRef = value
}
```

Now, having the `workoutsRef` stored in our state, we can implement the action that will update it with newly created workouts. After this, we will be able to use this action inside the `NewWorkout` component and populate our workout database.

Check the Firebase documentation regarding reading and writing into the real-time database: `https://firebase.google.com/docs/database/web/read-and-write`. Scroll down until you find the *"new post creation"* example:

```
function writeNewPost(uid, username, picture, title, body) {
  // A post entry.
  var postData = {
    author: username,
    uid: uid,
    body: body,
    title: title,
    starCount: 0,
    authorPic: picture
  };

  // Get a key for a new Post.
  var newPostKey = firebase.database().ref().child('posts').push().key;

  // Write the new post's data simultaneously in the posts list and the user's post list.
  var updates = {};
  updates['/posts/' + newPostKey] = postData;
  updates['/user-posts/' + uid + '/' + newPostKey] = postData;

  return firebase.database().ref().update(updates);
}
```

New post creation example in Firebase database documentation

Don't you find this case extremely similar to ours? Each workout added by the user has its name, description, and a picture (or maybe even more than one picture). Workouts also belong to the users that created them. So, maybe we can do something very similar to this. It will also be useful to have a resource for `user-workouts` that contains workouts for each user. It might come in handy if we decide to implement the possibility for each user to delete their workouts. Before copying this code, let's just agree on the workout object data structure. What should it contain? Since it's coming from the `NewWorkout` component, it will already bring the workout's name, description, and image URLs. Should we enrich it with anything else inside the action? Probably, we should add the name and UID of the user who added it, the date when it was created, and the rating attribute. This should be more than enough for now. So, our workout data structure will look like this:

```
{
    name: 'string',
    description: 'string',
    pictures: ['string'],
    username: 'string',
    uid: 'string',
    rate: 'number',
    date: 'timestamp'
}
```

The `name`, `description`, `username`, and `uid` attributes are strings. The `pictures` attribute should be an array of URL strings, `rating` should be a number and let's store our `date` attribute in the form of a timestamp.

 It's good that we are implementing both the frontend and the backend parts, so we agree on a data schema between ourselves. If you ever work in a team that has frontend and backend developers, don't forget to agree on a data schema before any implementation takes place!

So, we know that the description, name, and picture URL should be populated inside the `NewWorkout` component. Thus, let's populate everything else inside our `action` method. In the end, it will look really similar to the Firebase example:

```
// store/actions.js
createNewWorkout ({commit, state}, workout) {
    if (!workout) {
        return
    }
```

```
    workout.username = state.user.displayName
    workout.uid = state.user.uid
    workout.date = Date.now()
    workout.rate = 0
    // Get a key for a new Workout.
    let newWorkoutKey = state.workoutsRef.push().key

    // Write the new post's data simultaneously in the posts list and
the user's post list.
    let updates = {}
    updates['/workouts/' + newWorkoutKey] = workout
    updates['/user-workouts/' + state.user.uid + '/' + newWorkoutKey] =
workout

    return firebaseApp.database().ref().update(updates)
  },
```

Note again that we are introducing a new resource called user-workouts.
We can bind this resource to our state the exact same way we have done with
the statistics and configuration user data. If we decide to implement the deletion
of user resources, it might become handy.

Now, let's move to our NewWorkout component. Here, we just need to bind some
Vue models to the corresponding inputs and the click event to the **Submit** button.
The click event on the **Apply** button should be bound to the createNewWorkout
action, invoking it along with the corresponding data. Don't worry about the
pictures yet, we will deal with them in the next section.

At this point, we can replace the hardcoded array of workouts in the Workouts
component with the state workouts object:

```
//Components/Workouts.vue
// ...
<script>
  import {mapState} from 'vuex'
  export default {
    computed: {
      ...mapState(['workouts'])
    }
  }
</script>
//...
```

Check how your newly created workouts immediately appear in the workouts section!

Check the final code for this section in the `chapter8/4/profitoro` folder. Pay attention to the store files (`actions.js`, `mutations.js`) and to the `NewWorkoutComponent` and `WorkoutsComponent` components inside the `components/workouts` folder.

Storing images using the Firebase data storage

Firebase cloud storage allows you to upload and retrieve different content (files, videos, images, and so on). In a very similar way, Firebase provides a way of accessing and managing your database, where you can access and manage your storage buckets. You can upload Blobs, strings in Base64, file objects, and so on.

First of all, you should tell your Firebase application that you are going to use Google cloud storage. Thus, you need to add a `storageBucket` attribute to your application configuration object. Check your application's settings on the Google Firebase console and copy the `storageBucket` reference to the `firebase/index.js` file:

```
// Initialize Firebase
import firebase from 'firebase'
//...
let config = {
  apiKey: 'YOUR_API_KEY',
  databaseURL: 'https://profitoro-ad0f0.firebaseio.com',
  authDomain: 'profitoro-ad0f0.firebaseapp.com',
  storageBucket: 'gs://profitoro-ad0f0.appspot.com'
}
//...
```

Now your firebase application knows what storage bucket to use. Let's also open the data storage tab of the Firebase console and add a folder for our workout images. Let's call it...workouts:

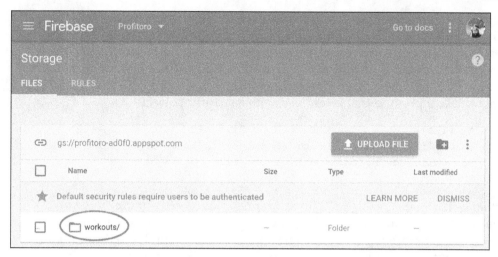

Creating a folder called "workouts" in the Firebase data storage tab

Everything is now ready to start using our cloud storage bucket.

First of all, we have to obtain the reference to our workouts folder so we can modify it. Check the Firebase API documentation regarding bucket reference creation: `https://firebase.google.com/docs/storage/web/create-reference`. In our case, the reference will look like this:

```
firebaseApp.storage().ref().child('workouts')
```

Where should we use it? Somehow, before storing workouts, we should store the picture files, obtain their cloud URLs, and assign these URLs to the workouts' `pictures` property. So, here is our plan:

- Create a method that uploads files and returns those files' download URLs
- Use this method before dispatching the `createNewWorkout` action to assign the URLs to the picture's property of the workout object

Let's create a method that will upload a file and return its `downloadURL`. Check the Firebase documentation to learn how to use its API to upload files: `https://firebase.google.com/docs/storage/web/upload-files`. Have a look at the **Upload from a Blob or File** section. You will see that we should use the method "`put`" on a cloud storage reference, providing it with a file object. This will be a promise that is resolved with a snapshot object:

```
var file = ... // use the Blob or File API
ref.put(file).then(function(snapshot) {
  console.log('Uploaded a blob or file!');
});
```

What is this `snapshot` object? This is a representation of your file stored on the cloud. It contains a lot of information, but the most important for us is its `downloadURL` attribute. So, our promise will look quite similar to the example promise but it will return `snapshot.downloadURL`. So, open the `actions.js` file and create a new method called `uploadImage`. This method will receive a file object, create a child reference on our `workout` cloud folder reference with this file's name, and then `put` a file and resolve with the `downloadURL`. So, it will look like this:

```
function _uploadImage (file) {
  let ref = firebaseApp.storage().ref().child('workouts')
  return ref.child(file.name).put(file).then(snapshot => {
    return snapshot.downloadURL
  })
}
```

Don't you see a little problem here? What will happen if two different users submit different pictures under the same name? Then these pictures will just override each other. As a small exercise, think of a way to avoid this problem.

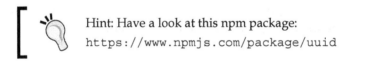

Hint: Have a look at this npm package: `https://www.npmjs.com/package/uuid`

So, we have our promise that uploads the file and returns its `downloadURL`. However, this is not yet our final action. Our final `action` method should upload an *array* of files, because that is what we get from our multiple file input – an array of file objects. Thus, our final promise will just return the result of all the promises and it will look as simple as the following:

```
uploadImages ({state}, files) {
  return Promise.all(files.map(_uploadImage))
}
```

This action can now be used inside the `NewWorkout` component before calling the `createNewWorkout` action.

First of all, we need to bind the `pictures` property to the file input element. The obvious choice would be to bind the property `pictures` to the input using the `v-model` directive:

```
<input v-model="pictures" type="file" multiple class="form-control-
file" id="imageFile">
```

Is it so obvious though? The `v-model` directive determines the *two-way data binding*, but how would we set data to it? The data of the file input is either `FileObject` or `FileList`. How would we set it? It seems that applying two-way data binding to this element doesn't make sense.

You can't actually bind reactive data to the file inputs, but you can set your data inside the change event:
https://forum.vuejs.org/t/vuejs2-file-input/633/2

Thus, we have to listen to the `change` event and set our data on each change. Let's bind this event to the `filesChange` method:

```
// NewWorkoutComponent.vue

<input @change="filesChange($event.target.files)" type="file" multiple
class="form-control-file" id="imageFile">
```

Now let's create this method and just assign `this.pictures` to the parameter we receive. Well, not *just assign*, because we receive a `FileList` object which is not exactly an array which you can iterate over. Thus, we need to transform it into a simple array of `File` objects.

We can use the ES6 spread operator for this:
`filesArray = [...fileListObject]`

Thus, our `filesChange` method will look as follows:

```
// NewWorkoutComponent.vue
export default {
  methods: {
    //...
    filesChange (files) {
      this.pictures = [...files]
```

```
    }
  //...
    }
}
```

Now we can finally update our `onCreateNew` method. First, it should dispatch the `uploadImages` action and on promise resolution dispatch the `createNewWorkout` action, assigning the result of the promise to the `pictures` array. Now this method will look as follows:

```
// NewWorkoutComponent.vue
onCreateNew (ev) {
  ev.preventDefault()
  ev.stopPropagation()
  this.uploadImages(this.pictures).then(picUrls => {
    this.createNewWorkout({
      name: this.name,
      description: this.description,
      pictures: picUrls
    })
    this.reset()
  })
}
```

Don't forget to import the `uploadImages` action. Also, create a `reset` method that will reset all the data to its initial state.

Create some workouts with images and enjoy the result!

Let's search!

So now we can create workouts and see them being displayed in the list of workouts. However, we have this nice search input, and it's doing nothing: (. Nevertheless, we are using Vue.js so it's really easy to implement this search. We just have to create a `searchTerm` data attribute and bind it to the search input and then filter the workouts array by this `searchTerm`. So, I will add the computed property, let's call it `workoutsToDisplay`, and this property will represent a filtered workouts property (the one that we import from the Vuex store's state) by its name, description, and username properties. So, it will give us the possibility of searching by all these terms:

```
// WorkoutsComponent.vue
<script>
  //...
  export default {
    //...
```

```
      computed: {
        ...mapState(['workouts']),
        workoutsToDisplay () {
          return this.workouts.filter(workout => {
            let name = workout.name.toLowerCase()
            let description = workout.description.toLowerCase()
            let username = workout.username.toLowerCase()
            let term = this.searchTerm.toLowerCase()
            return name.indexOf(term) >= 0 || description.indexOf(term)
            >= 0 || username.indexOf(term) >= 0
          })
        }
      }
    //...
    }
</script>
```

Don't forget to add the `searchTerm` property to the component's data and bind it to
the search input element:

```
<template>
  <div>
    <div class="form-group">
      <input v-model="searchTerm" class="input" type="search"
      placeholder="Search for workouts">
    </div>
  </div>
</template>
<script>
  //...
  export default {
    data () {
      return {
        name: '',
        username: '',
        datecreated: '',
        description: '',
        pictures: [],
        rate: 0,
        searchTerm: ''
      }
    }
  }
</script>
```

And, of course, instead of iterating over the workouts array to display the workout cards, we should now iterate over the `workoutsToDisplay` array. So just edit slightly the `v-for` directive of the card `div`:

```
v-for="workout in workoutsToDisplay"
```

Open the page and try to search! If I search by the user's name, only workouts created by this user will be displayed:

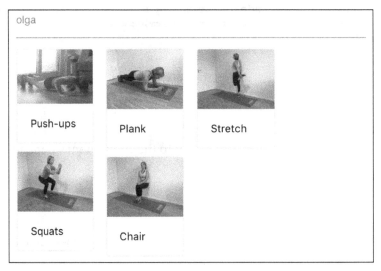

Makes sense, since I created all the existing workouts until now

If I search by the name of the workout, let's say, push-up, only this workout will appear in the list:

Searching by the workout's name

We're almost done! The only thing we have to do now is to show a randomly chosen workout from the list of workouts instead of hardcoded data during the resting periods of our Pomodoro. Try to do it yourself in the `pomodoro.vue` page.

You can now create new workouts and they will immediately appear in the workouts section. They also appear in our main page during the Pomodoro breaks.

Great job! Check the code for this part in the `chapter8/5/profitoro` folder. Pay special attention to the new actions inside the `store/actions.js` file and to the `Workouts` and `NewWorkout` components inside the `components/workouts` folder. Check how the random workout is being selected and displayed in the `pomodoro.vue` page.

Using a Bootstrap modal to show each workout

Now we can see all the existing workouts on the page, which is great. However, our users would really like to have a look at each of the workouts in detail – see the workouts' descriptions, rate them, see who has created them and when, and so on. It's unthinkable to put all this information in the tiny `card` element, so we need to have a way of magnifying each element in order to be able to see its detailed information. A Bootstrap modal is a great tool that provides this functionality. Check the Bootstrap documentation regarding the modal API: `https://v4-alpha.getbootstrap.com/components/modal/`.

> Note that Bootstrap 4, at the time of writing, is in its alpha stage and that's why at some point this link might not work anymore, so just search for the relevant information on the official Bootstrap website.

Basically, we need to have an element that will trigger a modal and a modal markup itself. In our case, each of the small workout cards should be used as a modal trigger; `WorkoutComponent` will be our modal component. So, just add `data-toggle` and `data-target` attributes to the `card` element inside the Workouts component:

```
// WorkoutsComponent.vue
<div class="card-columns">
  <div data-toggle="modal" data-target="#workoutModal"
v-for="workout in workouts" class="card">
    <img class="card-img-top img-fluid" :src="workout.pictures &&
    workout.pictures.length && workout.pictures[0]"
    :alt="workout.name">
```

```
        <div class="card-block">
          <p class="card-text">{{ workout.name }}</p>
        </div>
      </div>
    </div>
```

Now let's work on the `WorkoutComponent` component. Let's assume that it will receive the following properties:

- name
- description
- username
- datecreated
- rate
- pictures

Thus, we can build a very simple markup for our modal, something like this:

```
<template>
  <div class="modal fade" id="workoutModal" tabindex="-1"
  role="dialog" aria-hidden="true">
    <div class="modal-dialog" role="document">
      <div class="modal-content">
        <div class="modal-header">
          <h5 class="modal-title">{{ name }}</h5>
          <button type="button" class="close" data-dismiss="modal"
          aria-label="Close">
            <span aria-hidden="true">&times;</span>
          </button>
        </div>
        <div class="modal-body">
          <div class="text-center">
            <img :src="pictures && pictures.length && pictures[0]"
            class="img-fluid" :alt="name">
          </div>
          <p>{{ description }}</p>
        </div>
        <div class="modal-footer">
          <p>Created on {{ datecreated }} by {{ username }}</p>
        </div>
      </div>
    </div>
  </template>
```

Keep in mind that this modal needs to have the exact same ID attribute by which it is being targeted from the toggling element.

Don't forget to specify the required properties under the `props` attribute:

```
// WorkoutComponent.vue
<script>
  export default {
    props: ['name', 'description', 'username', 'datecreated', 'rate',
    'pictures']
  }
</script>
```

Now this component can be imported into the Workouts component and used there:

```
// WorkoutsComponent.vue
<template>
  <div>
    <...>
    <div class="card-columns">
      <...>
    </div>
    <workout-component
      :name="name"
      :description="description"
      :username="username"
      :datecreated="datecreated"
      :pictures="pictures"
      :rate="rate">
    </workout-component>
  </div>
</template>
```

If you click on some of the small cards now, the empty modal will open:

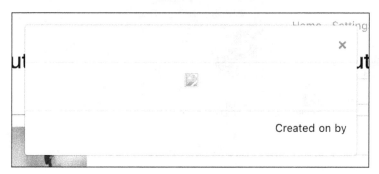

The modal works! But it's empty

We definitely should still do something, so the data of the chosen element is propagated to the component's data. Let's add a method that will do this job and bind it to the `click` event of the `card` element:

```
// WorkoutsComponent.vue

<div data-toggle="modal" data-target="#workoutModal" v-for="workout in
workouts" class="card" @click="onChosenWorkout(workout)">
```

The method will just copy the workout's data to the corresponding component's data:

```
// WorkoutsComponent.vue - methods section
onChosenWorkout (workout) {
  this.name = workout.name
  this.description = workout.description
  this.username = workout.username
  this.datecreated = workout.date
  this.rate = workout.rate
  this.pictures = workout.pictures
}
```

It looks a little bit better now!

Data binding just works!

It looks nice, all the data is here, but it's still not perfect. Think how we could improve it.

Exercise

Make the date that appears on the modal's footer human-readable. Do it in such a way that the footer appears like this:

Created on Aug 9th 17 by olga

Workout modal's footer with human-readable data

Try to use existing tools and not reinvent the wheel.

> Think of the moment.js library:
>
> https://momentjs.com/

Check for yourself and the final code until this moment in the `chapter8/6/profitoro` folder. Pay attention to the `Workouts` and `Workout` components in the `components/workout` folder.

It's time to apply some style

Our application is fully functional now; it can be used right away. Of course, it is still not perfect. It lacks validations and some functionality, several requirements have not been implemented yet, and the most important thing…it lacks beauty! It's all gray, it doesn't have style…we are humans, we love beautiful things, don't we? Everyone implements styles in their own way. I strongly recommend that if you want to use this application, please find your own style and theme for it, and please implement it and share with me. I would love to see it.

As for me, since I am not a designer, I asked my good friend Vanessa (https://www.behance.net/MeegsyWeegsy) to create a nice design for the ProFitOro application. She did a great job! Since I was busy writing this book, I had no time to implement Vanessa's design, therefore I asked my good friend, Filipe (https://github.com/fil090302), to help me with it. Filipe did a great job as well! Everything looks exactly how Vanessa implemented it. We have used `scss`, so it must be familiar to you since we've been using it already in this application as a preprocessor.

You can reuse the existing style to override some variables in order to create your own theme. Please check the final code in the `chapter8/7/profitoro` folder. All styles are located inside the `assets/styles` directory. It has the following structure:

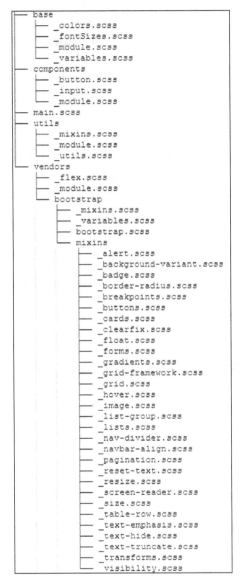

Directory structure

As for the final look, here is what it looks like.

This is the main page with the Pomodoro timer:

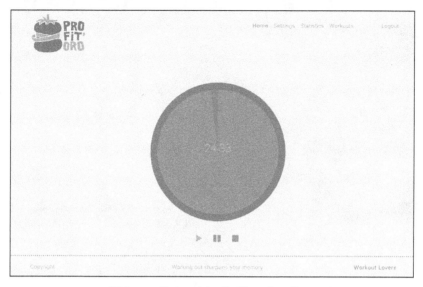

Main page that contains the Pomodoro timer

Here is what the Settings page looks like:

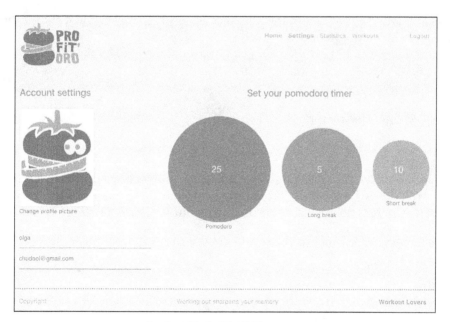

Look and feel of the Settings page

And finally, here is what the Workouts page looks like:

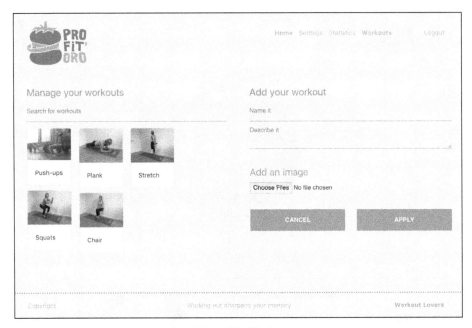

Look and feel of the Workouts page

You will still have to implement the Statistics page – right now, it just shows the total amount of completed Pomodoros:

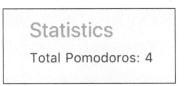

Statistics page is not fully complete, only showing the total amount of completed Pomodoros

There's still some work to do, but don't you agree that we have done great work so far? Not only do we have a fully functioning configurable Pomodoro timer, we can also already use it to do small workouts during our working day. How great is that?

Summary

In this chapter, we have finally implemented the workout management page. Now we can see all the workouts stored in the database and create our own workouts. We have learned how to use the Google Firebase data storage system and API to store static files and we were able to store newly created workouts in the Firebase real-time database. We have also learned how to use a Bootstrap modal and used it to display each workout in a nice modal popup.

In the next chapter, we will do the most important job of every software implementation process – we will test what we have done so far. We will use Jest (`https://facebook.github.io/jest/`) to test our application. After that, we will finally deploy our application and define future work. Are you ready for testing your work? Then turn the page!

9
Test Test and Test

In the previous chapter, we implemented the workout management page. We learned how to use the Google Firebase data storage mechanism to store static files and we again used the real-time database to store the workout objects. We used Bootstrap to build a responsive layout for the workout' management page and we learned how to use Bootstrap's modal component to display each individual workout in a nice popup. Now we have a totally responsible application. Thanks to Bootstrap, we had to implement nothing special to have a nice mobile representation. Here's what adding new workouts looks like on a mobile screen:

Adding a new workout on a mobile screen

And this is what our modal looks like on a mobile device:

Workout modal displayed on a mobile device

Now it's time to test our application. We are going to use Jest (`https://facebook.github.io/jest/`) to build unit tests and run snapshot testing. In this chapter, we are going to do the following:

- Learn how to configure our Vue.js application to work with Jest
- Test Vuex stores using Jest assertions

- Learn how to mock complex objects with the `jest.mock` and `jest.fn` methods
- Learn how to implement snapshot testing for Vue components

Why is testing important?

Our ProFitOro application works just fine, doesn't it? We have opened it so many times in the browser, we have checked all the implemented features, so it just works, right? Yes, that's true. Now go to your settings page and try to change the values of the timer to something strange. Try it with negative values, try it with huge values, try it with strings, and try it with empty values...do you think that can be called a nice user experience?

You wouldn't like to work during this number of minutes, would you?

Have you tried to create a strange workout? Have you tried to introduce a huge workout name at its creation and see how it displays? There are thousands of corner cases and all of them should be carefully tested. We want our application to be maintainable, reliable, and something that offers an amazing user experience.

What is Jest?

You know that Facebook guys are never tired of creating new tools. React, redux, react-native and all this reactive family was not enough for them and they created a really powerful, easy-to-use testing framework called Jest: `https://facebook.github.io/jest/`. Jest is pretty cool because it's self-contained enough for you to not to be distracted by extensive configuration or by looking for asynchronous testing plugins, mocking libraries, or fake timers to use along with your favorite framework. Jest is all in one, although pretty lightweight. Besides that, on every run, it only runs those tests that have been changed since the last test run, which is pretty elegant and nice because it's fast!

Initially created for testing React applications, Jest turned out to be suitable for other purposes, including Vue.js applications.

Check out the great talk given by Roman Kuba during the Vue.js conference in June 2017 in Poland (`https://youtu.be/pqp0PsPBO_0`), where he explains in a nutshell how to test Vue components with Jest.

Our application is not just a Vue application, it is a Nuxt application that uses Vuex stores and Firebase in it. All these dependencies make it a little bit more difficult to test because of all the things we have to mock and because of the Nuxt application particularities themselves. However, it is possible and after everything is set up, the joy of writing tests is enormous! Let's go!

Getting started with Jest

Let's start by testing a small sum function and check that it correctly sums two numbers.

The first step would be, of course, to install Jest:

```
npm install jest
```

Create a directory `test` and add a file called `sum.js` with the following content:

```
// test/sum.js
export default function sum (a, b) {
  return a + b
}
```

Now add a test spec file for this function:

```
// sum.spec.js
import sum from './sum'

describe('sum', () => {
  it('create sum of 2 numbers', () => {
    expect(sum(15, 8)).toBe(23)
  })
})
```

We need a command to run tests. Add an entry `"test"` to the `package.json` file that will call a command `jest`:

```
// package.json
"scripts": {
  //...
  "test": "jest"
}
```

Now if you run `npm test`, you will see some errors:

```
FAIL  test/sum.spec.js
 ● Test suite failed to run

   /Users/chuda/Projects/vuejs/profitoro/test/sum.spec.js:1
   ({"Object.<anonymous>":function(module,exports,require,__dirname,__filename,global,jest){import sum from './sum';
                                                                                            ^^^^^^
   SyntaxError: Unexpected token import

     at ScriptTransformer._transformAndBuildScript (node_modules/jest-runtime/build/ScriptTransformer.js:289:17)
     at process._tickCallback (internal/process/next_tick.js:109:7)
```

Errors in the test output with when we run tests with Jest

This happens because our Jest is not aware we are using *ES6*! So, we need to add the `babel-jest` dependency:

npm install babel-jest --save-dev

After *babel-jest* is installed, we have to add a `.babelrc` file with the following content:

```
// .babelrc
{
  "presets": ["es2015"]
}
```

Aren't you annoyed about your IDE warnings regarding `describe`, `it`, and other globals that are not being recognized? Just add an entry `jest: true` to your `.eslintrc.js` file:

```
// .eslintrc.js
module.exports = {
  root: true,
  parser: 'babel-eslint',
  env: {
    browser: true,
    node: true,
    jest: true
  },
  extends: 'standard',
  // required to lint *.vue files
  plugins: [
    'html'
  ],
  // add your custom rules here
  rules: {},
  globals: {}
}
```

Now if you run `npm test`, the tests are passing!

```
> ProFitOro@1.0.0 test /Users/chuda/Projects/vuejs/profitoro
> jest

 PASS  test/sum.spec.js
  sum
    ✓ create sum of 2 numbers (4ms)


Test Suites: 1 passed, 1 total
Tests:       1 passed, 1 total
Snapshots:   0 total
Time:        1.75s
Ran all test suites.
```

Congratulations! You've just set up and run your first Jest test!

Coverage

Unit tests help to guarantee that the pieces (units) of code that they are checking work for any possible and impossible input. Every written unit test covers the corresponding piece of code as a blanket, protecting this code from future failures and making ourselves comfortable with our code's functionality and maintainability. There are different types of code coverage: statement coverage, line coverage, branch coverage, and so on. The more the code is covered, the more stable it is and the more comfortable we are. That's why, while we are writing unit tests, it is very important to check the code coverage every time we run it. It's easy to check the code coverage with Jest. You don't need to install any external tool or write extra configuration. Just execute the test command with the coverage flag:

```
npm test -- --coverage
```

You will magically see this beautiful coverage output:

```
profitoro$ npm test -- --coverage

> ProFitOro@1.0.0 test /Users/chuda/Projects/vuejs/profitoro
> jest "--coverage"

 PASS  test/sum.spec.js
  sum
    ✓ create sum of 2 numbers (4ms)

Test Suites: 1 passed, 1 total
Tests:       1 passed, 1 total
Snapshots:   0 total
Time:        1.111s
Ran all test suites.
----------|----------|----------|----------|----------|-----------------|
File      | % Stmts  | % Branch | % Funcs  | % Lines  |Uncovered Lines  |
----------|----------|----------|----------|----------|-----------------|
All files |     100  |     100  |     100  |     100  |                 |
 sum.js   |     100  |     100  |     100  |     100  |                 |
----------|----------|----------|----------|----------|-----------------|
```

Running Jest tests with coverage

Works like a charm, right?

Find the code in the `chapter9/1/profitoro` directory. Don't forget to run `npm install` on it.

Testing utility functions

Let's test our code now! Let's start with utils. Create a file called `utils.spec.js` and import the `leftPad` function:

```
import { leftPad } from '~/utils/utils'
```

Have a look at this function again:

```
// utils/utils.js
export const leftPad = value => {
  if (('' + value).length > 1) {
    return value
  }

  return '0' + value
}
```

This function should return the input string if this string's length is greater than 1. If the string's length is 1, it should return the string with a preceding 0.

Seems quite easy to test it, right? We would write two test cases:

```
// test/utils.spec.js
describe('utils', () => {
  describe('leftPad', () => {
    it('should return the string itself if its length is more than 1',
() => {
      expect(leftPad('01')).toEqual('01')
    })
    it('should add a 0 from the left if the entry string is of the
length of 1', () => {
      expect(leftPad('0')).toEqual('00')
    })
  })
})
```

Argh...if you run this test, you will get an error:

```
profitoro$ npm test -- --coverage

> ProFitOro@1.0.0 test /Users/chuda/Projects/vuejs/profitoro
> jest "--coverage"

FAIL  test/utils.spec.js
 ● Test suite failed to run

   Cannot find module '~/utils/utils' from 'utils.spec.js'

     at Resolver.resolveModule (node_modules/jest-resolve/build/index.js:179:17)
     at Object.<anonymous> (test/utils.spec.js:1:116)
```

Of course, poor Jest, it is not aware of the aliases we've been using in our Nuxt application. The ~ notation for it equals nothing! Luckily for us, it is easy to fix. Just add the `jest` entry to the `package.json` file with a name mapper entry inside it:

```
// package.json
"jest": {
  "moduleNameMapper": {
    "^~(.*)$": "<rootDir>/$1"
  }
}
```

Now Jest will know that everything that starts with ~ should be mapped to the root directory. If you run `npm test -- --coverage` now, you will see that the tests are passing!

```
profitoro$ npm test -- --coverage

> ProFitOro@1.0.0 test /Users/chuda/Projects/vuejs/profitoro
> jest "--coverage"

PASS  test/sum.spec.js
PASS  test/utils.spec.js

Test Suites: 2 passed, 2 total
Tests:       3 passed, 3 total
Snapshots:   0 total
Time:        1.194s
Ran all test suites.
----------|----------|----------|----------|----------|-----------------|
File      | % Stmts  | % Branch | % Funcs  | % Lines  |Uncovered Lines  |
----------|----------|----------|----------|----------|-----------------|
All files |   53.85  |      50  |      50  |   53.85  |                 |
 test     |     100  |     100  |     100  |     100  |                 |
  sum.js  |     100  |     100  |     100  |     100  |                 |
 utils    |      50  |      50  |   33.33  |      50  |                 |
  utils.js|      50  |      50  |   33.33  |      50  |... 22,24,29,30  |
----------|----------|----------|----------|----------|-----------------|
```

After mapping the root directory alias, tests run without any problem

The code coverage, however, is really low. It's because we have another function in our utils to be tested. Check the `utils.js` file. Can you see the `numberOfSecondsFromNow` method? It also needs some test coverage. It calculates the time that has passed from the given input time until now. How should we deal with this `Date.now`? We can't predict the test result because we can't guarantee that the moment of *now* of test running will be the same as when we check it. Every millisecond matters. Easy! We should mock the `Date.now` object!

Mocking with Jest

Turns out that even something that seems impossible (stopping time) is possible with Jest. Mocking the `Date.now` object is fairly easy using the `jest.fn()` function.

Check the documentation about mocking with Jest:

```
http://facebook.github.io/jest/docs/en/snapshot-testing.html#tests-
should-be-deterministic
```

We can mock the `Date.now` function by just invoking `Date.now = jest.fn(() => 2000)`.

Now we can easily test the `'numberOfSecondsFromNow'` function:

```
// test/utils.spec.js
import { leftPad, numberOfSecondsFromNow } from '~/utils/utils'
//...
describe('numberOfSecondsFromNow', () => {
  it('should return the exact number of seconds from now', () => {
    Date.now = jest.fn(() => 2000)
    expect(numberOfSecondsFromNow(1000)).toEqual(1)
  })
})
```

The coverage is better now but it could be perfect if we could cover our funny `beep` function. What should we test in it? Let's try to test that when the `beep` function is invoked, the `Audio.play` method is called. Mocked functions have a special property called **mock** that contains all the information about this function—the number of calls that have been performed on it, the information that has been passed to them, and so on. Thus, we can mock the `Audio.prototype.play` method like this:

```
let mockAudioPlay = jest.fn()
Audio.prototype.play = mockAudioPlay
```

After invoking the beep method, we can check the number of performed calls on the mock like this:

```
expect(mockAudioPlay.mock.calls.length).toEqual(1)
```

Or we can assert that the mock has been called like this:

```
expect(mockAudioPlay).toHaveBeenCalled()
```

The whole test might look like the following:

```
describe('beep', () => {
  it('should call the Audio.play functuon', () => {
    let mockAudioPlay = jest.fn()

    Audio.prototype.play = mockAudioPlay

    beep()
    expect(mockAudioPlay.mock.calls.length).toEqual(1)
    expect(mockAudioPlay).toHaveBeenCalled()
  })
})
```

In order to avoid side effects due to mocking the native function, we might want to reset our mock after the test:

```
it('should call the Audio.play functuon', () => {
  // ...
  expect(mockAudioPlay).toHaveBeenCalled()
  mockAudioPlay.mockReset()
})
```

Check the Jest documentation in this regard: https://facebook.github.io/jest/docs/en/mock-function-api.html#mockfnmockreset.

Alternatively, you might configure your Jest settings to reset mocks automatically after each test. For this, add the clearMocks attribute to the Jest config object inside the package.json file:

```
//package.json
"jest": {
  "clearMocks": true,
  "moduleNameMapper": {
    "^~(.*)$": "<rootDir>/$1"
  }
},
```

Yay! The tests are passing. Check the coverage. It looks quite nice; however, the branch coverage is still not perfect:

```
profitoro$ npm test -- --coverage

> ProFitOro@1.0.0 test /Users/chuda/Projects/vuejs/profitoro
> jest "--coverage"

PASS  test/utils.spec.js
PASS  test/sum.spec.js

Test Suites: 2 passed, 2 total
Tests:       5 passed, 5 total
Snapshots:   0 total
Time:        1.483s
Ran all test suites.
----------|---------|----------|---------|---------|----------------|
File      | % Stmts | % Branch | % Funcs | % Lines |Uncovered Lines |
----------|---------|----------|---------|---------|----------------|
All files |   92.31 |       75 |     100 |   92.31 |                |
 test     |     100 |      100 |     100 |     100 |                |
  sum.js  |     100 |      100 |     100 |     100 |                |
 utils    |   91.67 |       75 |     100 |   91.67 |                |
  utils.js|   91.67 |       75 |     100 |   91.67 |             22 |
----------|---------|----------|---------|---------|----------------|
```

Branch coverage in for the utils.js file is only 75%

Why is this happening? First of all, check the column `Uncovered Lines`. It shows us the line that hasn't been covered by the test. It's line 22 of the `numberOfSecondsFromNow` method:

```
export const numberOfSecondsFromNow = startTime => {
  const SECOND = 1000
  if (!startTime) {
    return 0
  }
  return Math.floor((Date.now() - startTime) / SECOND)
}
```

As an alternative, you can check the `coverage` folder inside your project's directory and open the `lcov-report/index.html` file in the browser to check in a more visual way what exactly is going on:

All files / utils **utils.js**

91.67% Statements 11/12   **75%** Branches 3/4   **100%** Functions 3/3   **91.67%** Lines 11/12

```
 1        /**
 2         * Adds a trailing 0 on the left of the given value
 3         * @param {string|number} value
 4         * @returns {string}
 5         */
 6   1x   export const leftPad = value => {
 7   2x     if (('' + value).length > 1) {
 8   1x       return value
 9          }
10
11   1x     return '0' + value
12        }
13
14        /**
15         * Returns number of seconds between a given start time and now
16         * @param {timestamp} startTime
17         * @returns {number} the number of seconds
18         */
19   1x   export const numberOfSecondsFromNow = startTime => {
20   1x     const SECOND = 1000
21   1x   I if (!startTime) {
22          return 0
23        }
24   1x     return Math.floor((Date.now() - startTime) / SECOND)
25        }
26
27        // courtesy of https://stackoverflow.com/a/23395136
28   1x   export const beep = () => {
29   1x     var snd = new Audio('data:audio/wav;base64,//uQRAAAAWMSLwUIYAAsYkXgoQwAEaYLWfkWgAI0wWs/
30   1x     snd.play()
31        }
32
33
```

Code coverage HTML shows the covered and uncovered lines in a nice visual way

Here, you can clearly see that line 22 is marked as red, which means it has not been covered by tests. Well, let's cover it! Just add a new test covering the case when the `startTime` property is not passed to this method and ensure that it returns 0:

```
// test/utils.js
describe('numberOfSecondsFromNow', () => {
  it('should return 0 if no parameter is passed', () => {
    expect(numberOfSecondsFromNow()).toEqual(0)
  })
  it('should return the exact number of seconds from now', () => {
    Date.now = jest.fn(() => 2000)
    expect(numberOfSecondsFromNow(1000)).toEqual(1)
  })
})
```

Run the tests with the coverage flag now. OMG! Isn't it just fantastic?

```
profitoro$ npm test -- --coverage

> ProFitOro@1.0.0 test /Users/chuda/Projects/vuejs/profitoro
> jest "--coverage"

 PASS  test/utils.spec.js
 PASS  test/sum.spec.js

Test Suites: 2 passed, 2 total
Tests:       6 passed, 6 total
Snapshots:   0 total
Time:        1.44s
Ran all test suites.
----------|---------|----------|---------|---------|-------------------|
File      | % Stmts | % Branch | % Funcs | % Lines |Uncovered Lines |
----------|---------|----------|---------|---------|-------------------|
All files |     100 |      100 |     100 |     100 |                   |
 test     |     100 |      100 |     100 |     100 |                   |
  sum.js  |     100 |      100 |     100 |     100 |                   |
 utils    |     100 |      100 |     100 |     100 |                   |
  utils.js|     100 |      100 |     100 |     100 |                   |
----------|---------|----------|---------|---------|-------------------|
```

100% code coverage, isn't it fantastic?

The final code for this section can be found in the `chapter9/2/profitoro` folder.

Testing Vuex store with Jest

Let's now try to test our Vuex store. The most critical parts of our store to test are our actions and mutations because they can actually mutate the store's state. Let's start with the mutations. Create the `mutations.spec.js` file in the `test` folder and import `mutations.js`:

```
// test/mutations.spec.js
import mutations from '~/store/mutations'
```

We are ready to write unit tests for our mutation functions.

Testing mutations

Mutations are very simple functions that receive a state object and set some of its attribute to the given value. Thus, testing mutations is fairly easy—we have just to mock the state object and pass it to the mutation we want to test with a value we want to set. In the end, we have to check whether the value has been actually set. Let's, for example, test the mutation setWorkingPomodoro. This is what our mutation looks like:

```
// store/mutations.js
setWorkingPomodoro (state, workingPomodoro) {
  state.config.workingPomodoro = workingPomodoro
}
```

In our test, we need to create a mock for the state object. It doesn't need to represent the complete state; it needs to at least mock the workingPomodoro property of the state's config object. Then we will call the mutation, passing it our mocked state and the new value for the workingPomodoro and we will assert that this value has been applied to our mock. Thus, these are the steps:

1. Create a mock for the state object:
   ```
   let state = {config: {workingPomodoro: 1}}
   ```

2. Call the mutation with a new value:
   ```
   mutations.setWorkingPomodoro(state, 30)
   ```

3. Assert that the value has been set to the mocked object: expect(state.config).toEqual({workingPomodoro: 30})

The complete code for this test looks like the following:

```
// test/mutations.spec.js
import mutations from '~/store/mutations'

describe('mutations', () => {
  describe('setWorkingPomodoro', () => {
    it('should set the workingPomodoro property to 30', () => {
      let state = {config: {workingPomodoro: 1}}
      mutations.setWorkingPomodoro(state, 30)
      expect(state.config).toEqual({workingPomodoro: 30})
    })
  })
})
```

Test Test and Test

The exact same mechanism should be applied to test the rest of the mutations. Go ahead and finish them all!

Asynchronous testing with Jest – testing actions

Let's move on to the more complex stuff to test—our actions! Our actions are mostly asynchronous and they use complex Firebase application objects inside. This makes them quite challenging to test but we do love challenges, don't we? Let's have a look at the first action in the `actions.js` file. It's the `uploadImages` action that looks like this:

```
uploadImages ({state}, files) {
   return Promise.all(files.map(this._uploadImage))
}
```

What could we possibly test here? We could, for example, test that the `_uploadImage` function has been called the exact same number of times as the size of the array of images that was passed. For this, we must mock the `_uploadImage` method. In order to do that, let's export it as well in our `actions`:

```
// store/actions.js
function _uploadImage (file) {
  //...
}

export default {
  _uploadImage,
  uploadImages ({state}, files) {
    return Promise.all(files.map(this._uploadImage))
  }
  //...
}
```

Now we can mock this method and check the number of times the `mock` has been called. The mocking itself is pretty easy; we just need to assign the `actions._uploadImage` to the `jest.fn()`:

```
// test/actions.spec.js
it('should call method _uploadImage 3 times', () => {
  actions._uploadImage = jest.fn()
})
```

[248]

From now on, our `actions._uploadImage` has a special magical property called `mock` that we have already talked about. This object gives us the opportunity of accessing the number of calls being done on the `_uploadImage` method:

```
actions._uploadImage.mock.calls
```

So, to assert that the number of calls is three, we can just run the following assertion:

```
expect(actions._uploadImage.mock.calls.length).toEqual(3)
```

 Check the full documentation regarding mocking functions in Jest here: `https://facebook.github.io/jest/docs/mock-functions.html#content`

Very well, but where should we call this expectation? The `uploadImages` function is asynchronous; it returns a promise. Somehow, we could sneak into the future and listen to the promise resolution and call our assertion there. Shall we define some *callbacks* and invoke them once the promise is resolved? No, no need for that. Just call your function and run the assertions inside the `then` callback. Thus, our test will look as simple as follows:

```
// test/actions.spec.js
import actions from '~/store/actions'

describe('actions', () => {
  describe('uploadImages', () => {
    it('should call method _uploadImage 3 times', () => {
      actions._uploadImage = jest.fn()
      actions.uploadImages({}, [1, 2, 3]).then(() => {
        expect(actions._uploadImage.mock.calls.length).toEqual(3)
      })
    })
  })
})
```

It just works!

Let's now create a more complex mock – for our `firebaseApp`. How do we decide what and how to mock? Just look at the code and check what's being done. So let's, for example, check the `createNewWorkout` method:

```
// store/actions.js
createNewWorkout ({commit, state}, workout) {
  //...
  let newWorkoutKey = state.workoutsRef.push().key
  let updates = {}
  updates['/workouts/' + newWorkoutKey] = workout
  updates['/user-workouts/' + state.user.uid + '/' + newWorkoutKey] =
workout

  return firebaseApp.database().ref().update(updates)
}
```

What's going on here? Some new key is generated by the state's `workoutsReference` and then the object called `updates` is created. This object contains two entries – one for each of the Firebase database resources that held the workout object.

Then Firebase's database `update` method is called with this object. Thus, we have to mock the database's `update` method so we can check the data that it's being called with. We have also to inject this mock somehow into the big Firebase application mock. Create a folder to hold our mock files and call it __mocks__. Add two files to this directory – `firebaseMocks.js` and `firebaseAppMock.js`. Create an empty function for the `update` method in the `firebaseMocks` file:

```
// __mocks__/firebaseMocks.js
export default {
  update: () => {}
}
```

Create a mock for the `firebaseApp` object that will call the mocked `update` function inside its `database` method:

```
// __mocks__/firebaseAppMock.js
import firebaseMocks from './firebaseMocks'
export default {
  database: () => {
    return {
      ref: function () {
        return {
          update: firebaseMocks.update
        }
      }
    }
```

```
      }
    }
  }
```

In order to test the `createNewWorkout` method, we will use the `jest.mock` function to bind the Firebase object to its mock. Check the detailed documentation regarding the `jest.mock` function:

`http://facebook.github.io/jest/docs/en/jest-object.html#jestmockmodulename-factory-options`.

We need to bind our mock before importing the `actions.js` module. In this way, it will already use the mocked object. Thus, our import section will look like the following:

```
// test/actions.spec.js
import mockFirebaseApp from '~/__mocks__/firebaseAppMock'
jest.mock('~/firebase', () => mockFirebaseApp)

import actions from '~/store/actions'
```

Let's see what is going on with a workout object so we know what and how to mock and have a deterministic test. We have these lines:

```
// actions.js
workout.username = state.user.displayName
workout.uid = state.user.uid
```

So, our mock of the state object must contain the user object with the predefined `displayName` and `uid`. Let's create it:

```
let state = {
  user: {
    displayName: 'Olga',
    uid: 1
  }}
```

What happens next?

```
workout.date = Date.now()
workout.rate = 0
```

Once again, we need to mock the `Date.now` object. Let's do the same as we did in the `utils` test spec:

```
Date.now = jest.fn(() => 2000)
```

Let's read our method further. It contains a line that generates the `newWorkoutKey` variable based on the `workoutsRef` state's object:

```
let newWorkoutKey = state.workoutsRef.push().key
```

Let's mock the `workoutsRef` in our state mock as well:

```
let state = {
  user: {
    displayName: 'Olga',
    uid: 1
  },
  workoutsRef: {
    push: function () {
      return {
        key: 59
      }
    }
  }
}}
```

Now we know that when we call the `addNewWorkout` method, in the end it is expected to call the Firebase database `update` method with an object that will contain two entries – one with a key `/user-workouts/1/59` and another with a key `/workouts/59`, both with the same entry for the `workout` object:

```
{
  'date': 2000,
  'rate': 0,
  'uid': 1,
  'username': 'Olga'
}
```

So, first we need to create a spy. A spy is a special function that will replace the function we bind it to and spy on whatever has been happening with this function. Again, you don't need to install any external plugin or library for spies. Jest provides them out of the box.

Check out Jest spies in the official documentation:
`http://facebook.github.io/jest/docs/jest-object.html#jestspyonobject-methodname`

So, we want to spy on the `update` mock function. Let's create a spy on it:

```
const spy = jest.spyOn(firebaseMocks, 'update')
```

In the end, our assertion will look like this:

```
expect(spy).toHaveBeenCalledWith({
  '/user-workouts/1/59': {
    'date': 2000,
    'rate': 0,
    'uid': 1,
    'username': 'Olga'
  },
  '/workouts/59': {
    'date': 2000,
    'rate': 0,
    'uid': 1,
    'username': 'Olga'
  }
})
```

The whole test will look like the following:

```
describe('createNewWorkout', () => {
  it('should call update with', () => {
    const spy = jest.spyOn(firebaseMocks, 'update')
    Date.now = jest.fn(() => 2000)
    let state = {
      user: {
        displayName: 'Olga',
        uid: 1
      },
      workoutsRef: {
        push: function () {
          return {
            key: 59
          }
        }
    }}
    actions.createNewWorkout({state: state}, {})
    expect(spy).toHaveBeenCalledWith({
      '/user-workouts/1/59': {
        'date': 2000,
```

```
        'rate': 0,
        'uid': 1,
        'username': 'Olga'
      },
      '/workouts/59': {
        'date': 2000,
        'rate': 0,
        'uid': 1,
        'username': 'Olga'
      }
    })
  })
})
```

Now you know how to create mocks on different Firebase methods and how to create spies on them, you can create the rest of test specifications to test the rest of the actions. Check out the code for this section in the `chapter9/3/profitoro` folder.

Let's move forward and learn how we can actually test our Vue components with Jest!

Making Jest work with Vuex, Nuxt.js, Firebase, and Vue components

It's not the easiest task to test Vue components that rely on the Vuex store and Nuxt. js. We have to prepare several things.

First of all, we must install `jest-vue-preprocessor` in order to tell Jest that Vue components files are valid. We must also install `babel-preset-stage-2`, otherwise Jest will complain about the ES6 *spread* operator. Run the following command:

npm install --save-dev jest-vue-preprocessor babel-preset-stage-2

Once the dependencies are installed, add the `stage-2` entry to the `.babelrc` file:

```
// .babelrc
{
  "presets": ["es2015", "stage-2"]
}
```

Now we need to tell Jest that it should use the `babel-jest` transformer for the regular JavaScript files and the `jest-vue-transformer` for the Vue files. In order to do so, add the following to the jest entry in the `package.json` file:

```
// package.json
"jest": {
    "transform": {
        "^.+\\.js$": "<rootDir>/node_modules/babel-jest",
        ".*\\.(vue)$": "<rootDir>/node_modules/jest-vue-preprocessor"
    }
}
```

We use some images and styles in our components. This might result in some errors because Jest doesn't know what these SVG files are about. Let's add yet another entry to the `moduleNameMapper` Jest entry in the `package.json` file:

```
// package.json
"jest": {
  "moduleNameMapper": {
      "\\.(jpg|jpeg|png|gif|eot|otf|webp|svg|ttf|woff|woff2|mp4|webm|wav|mp3|m4a|aac|oga)$": "<rootDir>/__mocks__/fileMock.js",
  "\\.(css|scss)$": "<rootDir>/__mocks__/styleMock.js",
      // ...
  }
}
```

We are doing this because we don't really want to test pictures or CSS/SCSS files.

Add `styleMock.js` and `fileMock.js` to the `__mocks__` directory with the following content:

```
// styleMock.js
module.exports = {}

// fileMock.js
module.exports = 'test-file-stub'
```

Check out the official documentation for more details in this regard:
`https://facebook.github.io/jest/docs/webpack.html`.

Add name mappers for both Vue and Vuex files:

```
// package.json
"jest": {
  // ...
  "moduleNameMapper": {
    // ...
    "^vue$": "vue/dist/vue.common.js",
    "^vuex$": "vuex/dist/vuex.common.js",
    "^~(.*)$": "<rootDir>/$1"
  }
},
```

As a last step of configuration, we need to map the names for the Vue files. Jest is dumb and it can't understand that we are actually importing the Vue file if we are importing it without its extension. Thus, we must tell it that whatever is being imported from the `components` or `pages` folder is a Vue file. So, in the end of these configuration steps, our `moduleNamMapper` entry for jest will look as follows:

```
"jest": {
  //...
  "moduleNameMapper": {
    "\\.(jpg|jpeg|png|gif|eot|otf|webp|svg|ttf|woff|woff2|mp4|webm|wav
|mp3|m4a|aac|oga)$": "<rootDir>/__mocks__/fileMock.js",
    "\\.(css|scss)$": "<rootDir>/__mocks__/styleMock.js",
    "^vue$": "vue/dist/vue.common.js",
    "^vuex$": "vuex/dist/vuex.common.js",
    "^~/(components|pages)(.*)$": "<rootDir>/$1/$2.vue",
    "^~(.*)$": "<rootDir>/$1"
  }
}
```

We are now ready to test our components. You can find the final code with all these configuration steps in the `chapter9/4/profitoro` folder.

Testing Vue components using Jest

Let's start by testing the `Header` component. Since it depends on the Vuex store which, in its turn, highly depends on Firebase, we must do the exact same thing we just did to test our Vuex actions—mock the Firebase application before injecting the store into the tested component. Start by creating a spec file `HeaderComponent.spec.js` and paste the following to its `import` section:

```
import Vue from 'vue'
import mockFirebaseApp from '~/__mocks__/firebaseAppMock'
jest.mock('~/firebase', () => mockFirebaseApp)
import store from '~/store'
import HeaderComponent from '~/components/common/HeaderComponent'
```

Note that we first mock the Firebase application and then import our store.
Now, to be able to properly test our component with the mocked store, we need to
inject the store into it. The best way to do that is to create a `Vue` instance with the
`HeaderComponent` in it:

```
// HeaderComponent.spec.js
let $mounted

beforeEach(() => {
  $mounted = new Vue({
    template: '<header-component ref="headercomponent"></header-
component>',
    store: store(),
    components: {
      'header-component': HeaderComponent
    }
  }).$mount()
})
```

Note that we have bound the reference to the mounted component. Now we
will be able to access our header component by invoking `$mounted.$refs.
headercomponent`:

```
let $headerComponent = $mounted.$refs.headercomponent
```

What can we test in this component? It actually doesn't have so many functionalities.
It has a method `onLogout` which calls the `logout` action and pushes the / path to the
component's `$router` property. So, we could actually mock the `$router` property,
call the `onLogout` method, and check this property's value. We can also spy on the
`logout` action and check that it has been called. Thus, our test for the `onLogout`
method of the component can look like the following:

```
// HeaderComponent.spec.js
test('onLogout', () => {
  let $headerComponent = $mounted.$refs.headercomponent
  $headerComponent.$router = []
  const spy = jest.spyOn($headerComponent, 'logout')
  $headerComponent.onLogout()
  expect(spy).toHaveBeenCalled()
  expect($headerComponent.$router).toEqual(['/'])
})
```

Run the tests. You will see a lot of errors related to the Nuxt component not being properly registered:

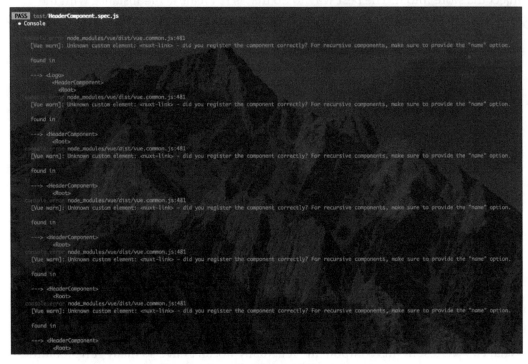

Vue errors regarding the nuxt-link component

Well, if you can live with these errors, just live with them. Otherwise, run your tests in production mode:

```
// package.json
"test": "NODE_ENV=production jest"
```

 Be aware that if you run your tests in production mode, you can actually miss some relevant errors.

Congratulations! You were able to test a Vue component that depends on Nuxt, Vuex and Firebase with Jest! Check the code for this test in the `chapter9/5/ profitoro` directory.

Snapshot testing with Jest

One of the coolest features of Jest is *snapshot testing*. What is snapshot testing? When our components are being rendered, they produce some HTML markup, right? It would be really important that once your application is stable, none of the newly added functionality breaks the already existing stable markup, don't you think? That's why snapshot testing exists. Once you generate a snapshot for some component, it will persist in the snapshot folder and on each test run, it will compare the output with the existing snapshot. Creating a snapshot is really easy. After you mount your component, you should just call the expectation toMatchSnapshot on this component's HTML:

```
let $html = $mounted.$el.outerHTML
expect($html).toMatchSnapshot()
```

I will run snapshot testing for all the pages inside one test suite file. Before doing that, I will mock the getters of our Vuex store because there are some pages that use the user object, which is not initialized, thus resulting in an error. So, create a file gettersMock inside our __mocks__ folder and add the following content:

```
// __mocks__/gettersMock.js
export default {
  getUser: () => {
    return {displayName: 'Olga'}
  },
  getConfig: () => {
    return {
      workingPomodoro: 25,
      shortBreak: 5,
      longBreak: 10,
      pomodorosTillLongBreak: 3
    }
  },
  getDisplayName: () => {
    return 'Olga'
  },
  getWorkouts: () => {
    return []
  },
  getTotalPomodoros: () => {
    return 10
  },
  isAuthenticated: () => {
    return false
  }
}
```

Let's go back to the imports. As we've already figured out, Jest is not really great in figuring out what is what in our imports, thus it will complain about relative imports (those that start from the dot, for example, in our `index.js` files inside each of the `components` folders). Let's replace all those relative import paths with their absolute equivalent:

```
// components/landing/index.js
export {default as Authentication} from '~/components/landing/
Authentication'
//...
```

I've also added one more mapping to the name mapper entry inside the `package.json` `jest` entry:

```
"jest": {
  "moduleNameMapper": {
    //...
    "^~/(components/)(common|landing|workouts)$": "<rootDir>/$1/$2"
    //...
  }
}
```

Great! Create a `pages.snapshot.spec.js` file and import all the necessary mock objects and all the pages. Don't forget to bind the corresponding mocks to Vuex `getters` functions and to the Firebase application object. Your import section should look like the following:

```
// pages.snapshot.spec.js
import Vue from 'vue'
import mockFirebaseApp from '~/__mocks__/firebaseAppMock'
import mockGetters from '~/__mocks__/getterMocks'
jest.mock('~/firebase', () => mockFirebaseApp)
jest.mock('~/store/getters', () => mockGetters)
import store from '~/store'
import IndexPage from '~/pages/index'
import AboutPage from '~/pages/about'
import LoginPage from '~/pages/login'
import PomodoroPage from '~/pages/pomodoro'
import SettingsPage from '~/pages/settings'
import StatisticsPage from '~/pages/statistics'
import WorkoutsPage from '~/pages/workouts'
```

We will create a test spec for each of the pages. We will bind each page component in the same way as we have bound the `Header` component. We will export the components that we want to test as components of a Vue instance and mount this Vue instance after being created. Thus, the index component binding will look as follows:

```
// pages.snapshot.spec.js
let $mounted = new Vue({
  template: '<index-page></index-page>',
  store: store(),
  components: {
    'index-page': IndexPage
  }
}).$mount()
```

The only thing that you have to do now is to execute the snapshot expectation. Thus, the full test spec for the index page will look as follows:

```
// pages.snapshot.spec.js
describe('pages', () => {
  test('index snapshot', () => {
    let $mounted = new Vue({
      template: '<index-page></index-page>',
      store: store(),
      components: {
        'index-page': IndexPage
      }
    }).$mount()
    let $html = $mounted.$el.outerHTML
    expect($html).toMatchSnapshot()
  })
})
```

Repeat the exact same steps for all the pages. Run the tests! Check the coverage. Now we are talking! We've actually touched almost all the components of our application! Look at this:

```
Ran all test suites.
----------------------------|----------|----------|----------|----------|-----------------|
File                        | % Stmts  | % Branch | % Funcs  | % Lines  |Uncovered Lines  |
----------------------------|----------|----------|----------|----------|-----------------|
All files                   |   48.56  |   33.33  |   52.78  |   56.42  |                 |
 components/common          |   73.91  |     50   |   85.71  |    100   |                 |
  FooterComponent.vue       |    100   |    100   |    100   |    100   |                 |
  HeaderComponent.vue       |    62.5  |     50   |     75   |    100   |            8,52 |
  Logo.vue                  |    100   |    100   |    100   |    100   |                 |
  index.js                  |    100   |    100   |    100   |    100   |                 |
 components/landing         |   60.71  |   33.33  |     70   |   77.27  |                 |
  Authentication.vue        |     50   |   33.33  |    62.5  |   68.75  | 65,68,69,70,71  |
  LogoText.vue              |    100   |    100   |    100   |    100   |                 |
  Tagline.vue               |    100   |    100   |    100   |    100   |                 |
  index.js                  |    100   |    100   |    100   |    100   |                 |
 components/settings        |     55   |   42.86  |   46.15  |   78.57  |                 |
  AccountSettings.vue       |     45   |   33.33  |    37.5  |   64.29  | 46,49,52,55,56  |
  PomodoroTimerSettings.vue |    62.5  |     50   |   66.67  |    100   |            8,38 |
  SetTimer.vue              |     75   |    100   |     50   |     75   |              19 |
 components/timer           |   51.72  |   31.25  |   64.71  |   51.72  |                 |
  CountDownTimer.vue        |   34.21  |     25   |   53.85  |   34.21  |... 105,106,111  |
  SvgCircleSector.vue       |     85   |     50   |    100   |     85   |        36,37,59 |
 components/workouts        |   34.38  |   29.41  |   41.18  |   45.83  |                 |
  NewWorkoutComponent.vue   |   19.35  |   16.67  |   22.22  |   28.57  |... 62,63,64,69  |
  WorkoutComponent.vue      |    100   |    100   |    100   |    100   |                 |
  WorkoutsComponent.vue     |   43.33  |   36.36  |   57.14  |   54.17  |... 78,79,80,81  |
  index.js                  |    100   |    100   |    100   |    100   |                 |
 pages                      |   61.29  |   37.84  |   73.68  |     76   |                 |
  about.vue                 |    100   |    100   |    100   |    100   |                 |
  index.vue                 |   66.67  |     50   |     80   |    100   |        8,25,32  |
  login.vue                 |    100   |    100   |    100   |    100   |                 |
  pomodoro.vue              |   41.46  |   26.32  |   57.14  |   48.57  |... 108,109,111  |
  settings.vue              |    100   |     75   |    100   |    100   |              18 |
  statistics.vue            |     50   |     25   |     50   |    100   |               8 |
  workouts.vue              |    100   |    100   |    100   |    100   |                 |
 store                      |   24.74  |    8.33  |    9.52  |   24.74  |                 |
  actions.js                |   17.57  |    4.55  |      0   |   17.57  |... 237,238,240  |
  getters.js                |   16.67  |     50   |   16.67  |   16.67  |     2,3,4,5,6   |
  index.js                  |    100   |    100   |    100   |    100   |                 |
  mutations.js              |    12.5  |    100   |    100   |    12.5  |... 15,18,21,24  |
  state.js                  |    100   |    100   |    100   |    100   |                 |
 test                       |    100   |    100   |    100   |    100   |                 |
  sum.js                    |    100   |    100   |    100   |    100   |                 |
 utils                      |    100   |    100   |    100   |    100   |                 |
  utils.js                  |    100   |    100   |    100   |    100   |                 |
----------------------------|----------|----------|----------|----------|-----------------|
```

Almost all the components and files of our application appear in the coverage report!

The most important thing, which is actually the whole purpose of the snapshot testing, is the generated folder called __snapshots__ inside the test folder. Here, you will find the newly generated snapshots of all the HTML markup of all your pages. These snapshots look like this:

```
// Jest Snapshot v1, https://goo.gl/fbAQLP

exports['pages about snapshot 1'] = `
"<div><header class=\\"header\\"><div class=\\"container\\"><nav class=\\"navbar navbar-toggleable-md navbar-light row\\"><button type=\\"button\\" data-toggle=\\"collapse\\" data-target>
    ProFitOro application is a time management application that combines the Pomodoro technique with office workouts.
    </p> <p class=\\"lead\\"><nuxt-link to=\\"login\\">Click here to login </nuxt-link> or just <nuxt-link to=\\"pomodoro\\">start using ProFitOro </nuxt-link>without registration.
    </p> <p class=\\"lead\\">
    Every time your Pomodoro working interval ends, you will be presented with a small workout that you have to perform during the Pomodoro resting period.
    </p> <h4 class=\\"title\\">There are some advantages to become a <nuxt-link to=\\"login\\">registered user</nuxt-link>:</h4> <p>
    As a registered user you can <nuxt-link to=\\"settings\\">configure</nuxt-link> your Pomodoro timing settings.
    </p> <p>
    You can also <nuxt-link to=\\"workouts\\">manage</nuxt-link> workouts, choosing your favourite ones, rating them and even creating your own workouts that will be displayed to everyb
    </p> <p>
    You can also <nuxt-link to=\\"statistics\\">check your statistics</nuxt-link> along the time you use ProFitOro!
    </p> <h4 class=\\"title\\">Book</h4> <p>
    This application has been developed as a part of the book <a href=\\"https://www.packtpub.com/web-development/web-development-bootstrap-and-vuejs\\">\\"Web development using Vue.js,
    </p> <h4 class=\\"title\\">Credits</h4> <p>Logo creation: <a href=\\"mailto:car.mar@gmail.com\\">Carina</a></p> <p>Mockups implementation: <a href=\\"https://github.com/Safure\\">Saf

exports['pages index snapshot 1'] = `"<div><!----> <div class=\\"landingPage\\"><div class=\\"container row justify-content-center align-items-center\\"><div class=\\"col-sm-12 col-md-12\\

exports['pages login snapshot 1'] = `"<div class=\\"landingPage\\"><div class=\\"container row justify-content-center align-items-center\\"><div class=\\"col-sm-12 col-md-12\\"><h1 class=

exports['pages pomodoro snapshot 1'] = `
"<div><header class=\\"header\\"><div class=\\"container\\"><nav class=\\"navbar navbar-toggleable-md navbar-light row\\"><button type=\\"button\\" data-toggle=\\"collapse\\" data-target>
    </p></div></div></div> <div class=\\"countdown-holder col-sm-12 col-md-12\\"><div class=\\"content\\"><div class=\\"timer-holder countdown-timer col-sm-12 col-md-10 col-lg-6\\
    25:00
    </text></svg></div></div> <div class=\\"controls\\"><div role=\\"group\\" class=\\"btn-group\\"><button type=\\"button\\" class=\\"btn btn-link\\"><img src=\\"test-file-stub\\"></bu
```

Jest snapshots of the ProFitOro pages

Every time you do something that will affect your markup, the tests will fail. If you really want to update snapshots, run the tests with the update flag:

```
npm test -- --u
```

I find snapshot testing a really fun and exciting feature!

 It is very important that you commit your snapshot files! Check the detailed documentation regarding the snapshot testing in the official Jest website:

`https://facebook.github.io/jest/docs/snapshot-testing.html`

The final code for this chapter can be found in the `chapter9/6/profitoro` folder.

Summary

In this chapter, we used very hot technology to test our Vue application. We used Jest and learned how to create mocks, test components, and run snapshot testing with it.

In the next chapter, we will finally see our application live! We will deploy it using Google Firebase Hosting and provide the necessary CI/CD tooling so our application is deployed and tested automatically each time it is pushed to the master branch. Are you ready to see your work live, up and running? Let's go!

10
Deploying Using Firebase

In the previous chapter, we set up the testing framework for our application's code, which will allow us from now on to cover it with unit tests and snapshot tests. In this chapter, we are going to make our application live! We will also set up the **Continuous Integration** (CI) and **Continuous Deployment** (CD) environments. Hence, in this chapter we are going to learn how to do the following:

- Deploy to Firebase hosting using Firebase tools locally
- Set up the CI workflow using CircleCI
- Set up both staging and production environments using Firebase and CircleCI

Deploying from your local machine

In this section, we are going to deploy our application using the Firebase command-line tools. We have already done it. Check the Google Firebase documentation for a quick start: `https://firebase.google.com/docs/hosting/quickstart`.

Basically, if you haven't yet installed Firebase tools, do it now!

```
npm install -g firebase-tools
```

Now switch inside your project's directory and initialize a Firebase project:

```
firebase init
```

From the drop-down menu that appears, choose **hosting**.

 It's not really obvious, so keep in mind that to actually choose something from the list, you have to press *Space*.

Press Space to select the Hosting feature

After that, select your ProFitOro project from the list and after that, indicate the folder dist for the build's output directory:

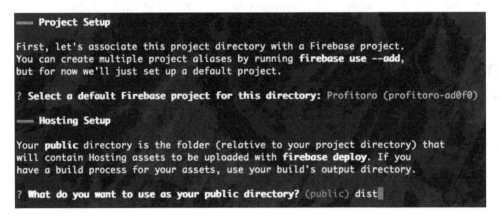

Type dist for the public directory of your assets

Answer No to the next question and you are done! Make sure that Firebase creates both firebase.json and .firebaserc files in your project's folder.

This is what the `firebase.json` file looks like:

```
// firebase.json
{
  "hosting": {
    "public": "dist"
  }
}
```

And this is what your `.firebaserc` file will look like:

```
.firebasercs
{
  "projects": {
    "default": "profitoro-ad0f0"
  }
}
```

You are done! Now if we generate our static assets with the `npm run generate` command, these assets will end up in the `dist` folder. If you run `firebase deploy` after that, your application will be immediately deployed!

So, go ahead and run the following:

```
npm run generate
firebase deploy
```

If you run into some errors or issues, please do the following:

- Make sure your Firebase CLI is up to date
- If necessary, re-authenticate with `firebase login --reauth`
- In case of error, try adding the project with `firebase use --add`

Congrats! Your application is up and running!

 You might ask why we would bother with the whole Nuxt routing and server-side rendering if, in the end, we are just generating static assets to deploy. The thing is that, unfortunately, Firebase only hosts static files. In order to be able to run a node server, we should have used another container, such as, for example, Heroku: `https://stackoverflow.com/questions/30172320/firebase-hosting-with-own-server-node-js`.

There is another thing that you should be aware of: it turns out that now it's not possible to run our application locally; if we try to do that, we will get a `webpack` error:

```
TypeError

__WEBPACK_IMPORTED_MODULE_1__firebase___default.a.auth is not
a function
```

webpack error when we try to run the application locally

For some reason, our `actions.js` file tries to import the `firebase.json` instead of the Firebase application `index.js` file located inside the `firebase` directory. This is quite simple to fix. Rename the Firebase directory `firebaseapp` – in the end, it's what's located inside. Please find the code corresponding to this section in the `chapter10/1/profitoro` folder. Pay attention to the new `firebase.json` · and `.firebaserc` files in the root directory and that all the imports of the Firebase application changed to the `firebaseapp` folder.

Setting up CI/CD using CircleCI

Right now, if we want to deploy our application, we first have to run tests locally to ensure that everything is okay and nothing is broken and then deploy it using the `firebase deploy` command. Ideally, all of this should be automated. Ideally, if we push our code to the master branch, everything should just happen without our intervention. The process of automated deployment with automated test checks is called Continuous Deployment. This term means exactly what it sounds like – your code is being deployed continuously. There are lots of tools that allow you to automatically deploy your code to production once you hit the button or just push to the master branch. Starting with the good old but reliable Jenkins, going to Codeship, CloudFlare, CircleCI, Travis…the list is endless! We will use CircleCI, because it integrates nicely with GitHub. If you want to check how to deploy with Travis, check out my previous book on Vue.js:

```
https://www.packtpub.com/web-development/learning-vuejs-2
```

First of all, you should host your project on GitHub. Please follow the GitHub documentation to learn how to initialize your repository:

```
https://help.github.com/articles/adding-an-existing-project-to-
github-using-the-command-line/
```

Or just fork mine:

```
https://github.com/chudaol/profitoro
```

Once your repository is online, create your account on CircleCI:

```
https://circleci.com
```

Using the CircleCI web interface, create a new project and select your repository from the list. After that, select the Linux operating system and Node for language:

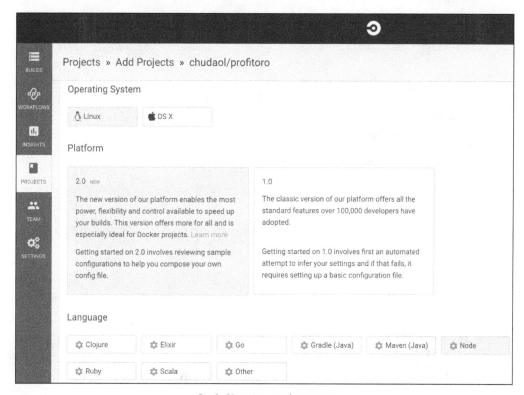

CircleCI project configuration

Now we must add a CircleCI configuration to our project so the first knows what to do once we push. Create the `.circleci` folder with a file named `config.yml` along with the following content:

```
// .circleci/config.yml
# Javascript Node CircleCI 2.0 configuration file
#
# Check https://circleci.com/docs/2.0/language-javascript/ for more
details
#
version: 2
jobs:
  build:
    docker:
```

```
        # specify the version you desire here
        - image: circleci/node:7.10

        # Specify service dependencies here if necessary
        # CircleCI maintains a library of pre-built images
        # documented at https://circleci.com/docs/2.0/circleci-
        images/
        # - image: circleci/mongo:3.4.4

    working_directory: ~/repo

    steps:
        - checkout

        # Download and cache dependencies
        - restore_cache:
            keys:
            - v1-dependencies-{{ checksum "package.json" }}
            # fallback to using the latest cache if no exact match
            is found
            - v1-dependencies-

        - run: npm install

        - save_cache:
            paths:
                - node_modules
            key: v1-dependencies-{{ checksum "package.json" }}

        # run tests!
        - run: npm test
```

Commit and push your changes to master. Go to the CircleCI interface and click on the **Start building** button:

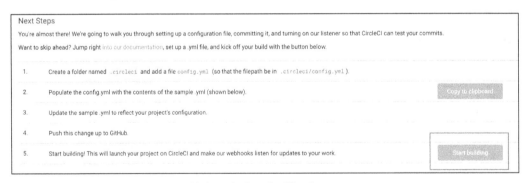

Click on the Start building button

If you are as lucky as I am, you will see the following successful output:

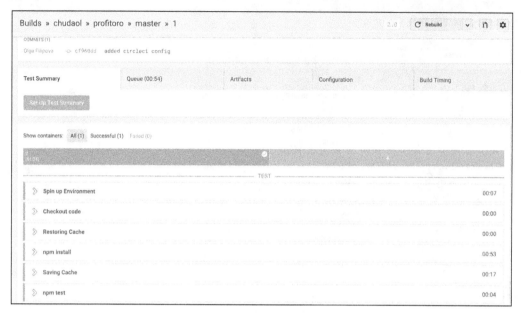

CircleCI success!

Let's add a status badge to our README.md file so it appears on GitHub. Go to your CircleCI project settings (click on the cog near the project's name):

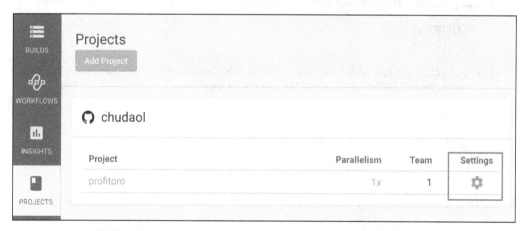

Click on the cog near the project's name to open your project's Settings tab

In the **Settings** section, select **Notifications | Status Badges**:

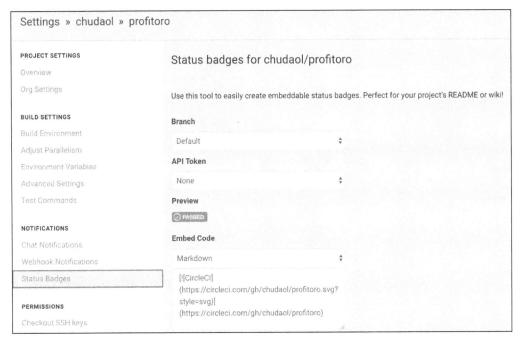

Navigate to Settings | Notifications | Status Badges

Copy and paste the markdown code to your `README.md` file so it looks as follows:

```
// README.md
# Profitoro

[![CircleCI](https://circleci.com/gh/chudaol/profitoro.svg?style=svg)]
(https://circleci.com/gh/chudaol/profitoro)

> Take breaks during work. Exercise during breaks.
```

Commit and push your changes to master!

If you now open your GitHub repository, you will see this nice badge saying **PASSED**:

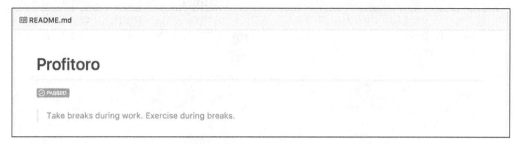

CircleCI badge shows a nice message: Passed

But our whole point is not only to see a nice green badge, it is to actually be able to deploy to the Firebase hosting container. In order to do that, we must configure CircleCI. We do that by adding the `deploy` section to the `config.yml` file. Check the documentation at `https://circleci.com/docs/2.0/configuration-reference/#deploy`. To be able to deploy to the Firebase hosting, we need to be logged in. It's obvious that CircleCI is not, in any case, logged in to our Firebase account. Luckily for us, that's easy to solve. We need to generate a CI token and then use it in our `deploy` command.

 A Firebase CI token can be generated using the `firebase login:ci` command.

Just run this command in your console:

```
firebase login:ci
```

You will get output similar to this:

```
Visit this URL on any device to log in:
https://accounts.google.com/o/oauth2/auth?client_id=563584335869-fqrhgmd4
ormprojects.readonly%20https%3A%2F%2Fwww.googleapis.com%2Fauth%2Ffirebase
ost%3A9005

Waiting for authentication...

✔ Success! Use this token to login on a CI server:

1/dF4EI ,N,0Y-N:CL        .ASyr07c

Example: firebase deploy --token "$FIREBASE_TOKEN"
```

Output of the Firebase login:ci command

Go to the web interface of your CircleCI and find the settings of your project. On the left-hand side, you will see the tab called **Build settings**. Click on the **Environment Variables** link and the **Environment Variables** section will pop up. Click on the **Add Variable** button and add the variable named FIREBASE_TOKEN with a value of YOUR_GENERATED_TOKEN:

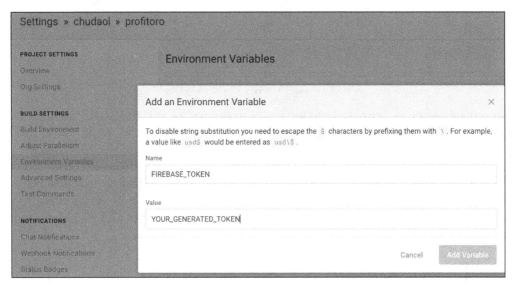

Add a new environment variable to your CircleCI project settings

Let's now add a deploy step to the config.yml file. Before doing that, remember that we have to invoke the firebase deploy command. Well, for this, we should have installed the Firebase tools globally on the CircleCI server. Instead of polluting the CircleCI server with some globally installed software, let's install it as a *dev dependency* and then invoke the command from the node_modules folder. Hence, as a first step, install firebase-tools as a dev dependency:

```
npm install --save-dev firebase-tools
```

Now we can finally add the deploy step. During this step, we must generate assets with the npm run generate command and run firebase deploy with our token (the command would be firebase deploy --token=<YOUR_FIREBASE_TOKEN>). We don't have to specify the token itself, because we've already created an environment variable for it, so the command will look like the following:

```
firebase deploy --token=$FIREBASE_TOKEN
```

The whole `deploy` entry will look as follows:

```
// .circleci/config.yml
jobs:
  build:
    #...

    steps:
      - checkout

    #...
    # deploy!
    - deploy:
        command: |
          if [ "${CIRCLE_BRANCH}" == "master" ]; then
            npm run generate
            ./node_modules/.bin/firebase deploy --
            token=$FIREBASE_TOKEN --non-interactive
          fi
```

Push the changes. Check your CircleCI console. After successful deployment, check your Firebase console on the **Hosting** tab and make sure that the last deployment has been done exactly at this moment:

Make sure that the last deployment has been done on exactly this moment!

Isn't that fantastic? Every time you push new changes to master, they will be tested first, and only if all the tests pass will they be deployed to your Firebase hosting provider! How long did it take us to set up all this? 20 minutes? Yay!

Setting up staging and production environments

You probably know that it's not very good practice to deploy to production right away. Even if the tests pass, we have to check whether everything is right first and that's why we need a *staging* environment.

Let's create a new project on the Firebase console and call it `profitoro-staging`. Let's now add a new environment to our project using the Firebase command-line tool. Just run this command in your console:

```
firebase use -add
```

Select the right project:

```
[profitoro$ firebase use --add
? Which project do you want to add?
  aasd-d22f8
  fir-demo-project
  pleaseintroduceyourself-4bb4a
  profitoro-ad0f0
> profitoro-staging
  test-404ac
```

Select a newly created profitoro-staging project

Type the alias `staging` in the next step:

```
What alias do you want to use for this project? (e.g. staging) staging
```

Check that a new entry has been added to your `.firebaserc` file:

```
// .firebaserc
{
  "projects": {
    "default": "profitoro-ad0f0",
    "staging": "profitoro-staging"
  }
}
```

If you now locally run the command `firebase use staging` and `firebase deploy` after it, your project will be deployed to our newly created staging environment. If you want to switch and deploy to your production environment, just run the command `firebase use default` followed by the `firebase deploy` command.

Now we need to reconfigure our CircleCI workflow. What we want to achieve is to deploy the assets to the staging server automatically and then run manual approval in order to deploy to production. For that, we will use the workflow configuration with manual approval. Please check the CircleCI official documentation page in this regard: `https://circleci.com/docs/2.0/workflows/#holding-a-workflow-for-a-manual-approval`.

We will end up with two very similar jobs – the first one will be called `build` and it will contain the exact same content as before, with the only difference being that the deploy step will use the alias `staging`:

```
version: 2
jobs:
  build:
    docker
    #...


      # deploy to staging!
    - deploy:
        command: |
          if [ "${CIRCLE_BRANCH}" == "master" ]; then
            npm run generate
            ./node_modules/.bin/firebase use staging
            ./node_modules/.bin/firebase deploy --
            token=$FIREBASE_TOKEN --non-interactive
          fi
```

The second job will be called `deploy`, and it will perform the exact same steps as the `staging` job (just to be totally sure that everything is okay). The only difference is that it will use the `default` alias before deploying:

```
build:
  #...
deploy:
  docker:
    # ...
    # deploy to production!
  - deploy:
      command: |
        if [ "${CIRCLE_BRANCH}" == "master" ]; then
          npm run generate
          ./node_modules/.bin/firebase use default
          ./node_modules/.bin/firebase deploy --
          token=$FIREBASE_TOKEN --non-interactive
        fi
```

After that, we will add a new entry called `workflows` that will look as follows:

```
// .circleci/config.yml
jobs:
  build:
    #...
  deploy:
    #...
workflows:
  version: 2
  build-and-approval-deploy:
    jobs:
      - build
      - hold:
          type: approval
          requires:
            - build
      - deploy:
          requires:
            - hold
```

Commit and push to master. Check your CircleCI console. After successful deployment to the staging environment, click on the **Workflow** tab and check that it's actually **ON HOLD**:

Workflow is ON HOLD

Check your staging environment website and ensure that everything is all right.

After being totally sure that everything is okay, we can promote our build to production. Click on your workflow and click on the **Approve** button:

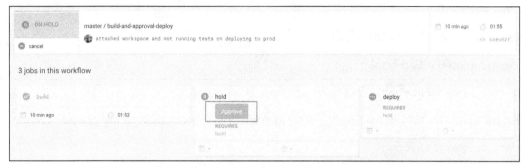

Now we can manually approve the production deployment

After a while, there will be great success! Isn't it fantastic?

Even though this is out of the scope of this book, keep in mind that you don't want to screw up your production database while running some checks on your staging environment. Therefore, for staging to be real staging and production to be real production, we should have also set up a staging database.

Check the code for this section in the `chapter10/2/profitoro` folder. The only two things you need to pay attention to are the `.firebaserc` configuration file and the configuration for the CircleCI that resides in the `.circleci/config.yml` directory.

What have we achieved?

Dear reader, we've been on a huge journey. We have built our responsive application from the very start until its deployment. We used nice technologies such as Vue.js, Bootstrap 4, and Google Firebase to build our application. Not only did we use all these technologies and learn how they play together, we actually followed the whole process of software development.

We started from the business idea, definition of requirements, definition of user stories, and creation of mockups. We continued with the actual implementation – both frontend and backend. We did thorough testing using Jest and we ended up with the deployment of our application into two different environments. Even more than just a deployment – we've implemented a CD strategy that will perform the deployment process for us automatically.

The most important thing – we've ended up with a fully functional application that will allow us to manage our time during work and stay fit!

Check it out live:

`https://profitorolife.com/`

I even created a Facebook page:

`https://www.facebook.com/profitoro/`

If you liked the ProFitOro logotype, send some love and thanks to my friend Carina:

`car.marg@gmail.com`

If you liked the way the mockups were created, you should thank my friend and colleague Safi:

`https://github.com/Safure`

If you liked the design and the illustration of ProFitOro, check out the other works of my friend Vanessa (`https://www.behance.net/MeegsyWeegsy`) and talk to her in case you feel she might help you as well.

If you liked the way the design was implemented with SCSS, give some *likes* to my friend Filipe (`https://github.com/fil090302`).

Summary

In this chapter, we used CircleCI and Firebase to guarantee continuous quality of our continuously deployed software. As I already mentioned, it's so nice to see something that you've created from scratch up and running!

However, our work is not finished yet. There are so many improvements to make. We need validations. We need to write more tests to increase our code coverage! We need more workouts and we need them to look beautiful. We probably need some back office where someone responsible can check every added workout and approve it before it actually ends up in the list of workouts visible to everyone.

We need a proper statistics page with some beautiful graphics. We need to optimize the image rendering. We need to show more than one picture for each of the workouts. We probably need to add video support for the workouts. We also need to work a bit on the workout screen that appears once the Pomodoro working timer is over. Right now, it looks like this:

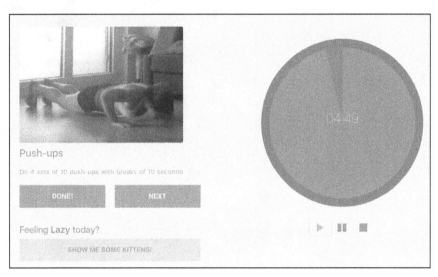

There are a lot of buttons here! None of them actually works :(

There are three buttons and none of them work.

So, as you can see, although we have finished the book and we have a functional piece of software, we still have some work to do. Actually, this makes me really happy, because it makes me feel that I don't have to say goodbye just now.

Share your ideas with me, do something amazing and share it with me, create some pull requests or issues on GitHub. I will be glad to answer you. Please email me if you have any questions, suggestions, or thoughts at `chudao1@gmail.com`.

Thank you for reading this book and… go to work…out!

Index

A

accounting 158
actions
  defining 145-148
alert component
  reference 75
anonymous user
  managing 171-173
application
  deploying 22, 23
  scaffolding 99, 100
asynchronous testing
  Jest, using 248-254
authentication
  about 157
  working, with Firebase 158
authentication API, Firebase
  reference 161, 177
authentication UI
  enhancing 168, 169, 170
authorization 158

B

Bootstrap
  about 66
  components 67-70
  functionalities 66
  layout 70, 71
  reference 66
  used, for adding form 13, 14
  used, for checking adaptiveness of
    countdown timer component 119-122
  used, for checking responsiveness of
    countdown timer component 119-122
  utilities 70
  Vue.js, combining with 71-74
Bootstrap classes
  used, for creating layouts 208, 209
Bootstrap modal
  reference 223
  used, for displaying workout 223-227
Bootstrap navbar
  using, for navigation links 189-194
Bootstrap-powered markup
  adding 10-13
Bootstrap-Vue
  reference 74
buttons, Bootstrap
  reference 68, 123

C

CamelCased 104
Card Bootstrap's component
  reference 71
cards, Bootstrap documentation
  reference 11
CI/CD
  setting up, Circle CI used 268-275
Circle CI
  reference 269, 277
  used, for setting up CI/CD 268-275
classes for alignment, Bootstrap
  reference 173
code splitting 194, 195
components
  message cards, extracting to 19-21
  of Bootstrap 67-70
  of Vue 46-51

Continuous Deployment (CD) 265
Continuous Integration (CI) 265
countdown timer component
  adaptiveness 120
  down time, counting 122-127
  responsiveness 119
custom domain
  Firebase project, connecting to 24, 25
custom templates, vue-cli
  reference 32

D

database entry
  adding, to Firebase application
    database 3, 4

E

element 29

F

file uploading
  reference 218
Firebase
  about 2, 75
  services 76
Firebase API documentation
  reference 217
Firebase application database
  database entry, adding 3, 4
Firebase authentication API
  connecting, to web application 161, 162
  workflow 160
Firebase console
  project, creating in 2, 3
  reference 2, 149
Firebase database
  Vuex store, connecting to 150-155
Firebase data storage
  used, for storing images 216-223
Firebase project
  connecting, to custom domain 24, 25
  setting up 149, 150
  Vue.js application, connecting to 6-10

Firebase real-time database
  documentation, reference 213
  used, for storing workouts 211-216
Firebase real-time database documentation
  reference 154
Firebase SDK
  anonymous user authentication 159
  custom auth system integration 159
  email based authentication 159
  federated entity provider
    authentication 159
  password based authentication 159
  phone number authentication 159
flex-box
  reference 70
footer
  customizing 210, 211
form
  adding, Bootstrap used 13, 14
forms, Bootstrap documentation
  reference 13
functionalities, Bootstrap
  references 66
functional requirements
  gathering 81, 82

G

GoDaddy
  reference 24
Google Firebase
  reference 265

H

Heroku
  reference 267
History API
  reference 53
Human-Computer Interaction (HCI) 89

I

images
  storing, Firebase data storage used 216-223

J

Jest
about 236
asynchronous testing 248-254
coverage 239
documentation, reference 243
mocking, reference 242
mocking with 242-246
reference 234, 236
used, for snapshot testing 259-263
used, for testing Vue components 256-258
used, for testing Vuex store 246
using 236, 237
working, with Firebase 254-256
working, with Nuxt.js 254-256
working, with Vue components 254-256
working, with Vuex 254-256
jest.mock function
reference 251
Jest spies
reference 252
jumbotrons
reference 134

K

KebabCased 104

L

layouts
creating, Bootstrap classes used 208, 209
lazy loading
about 194, 195
reference 194
local machine
deploying from 265-268

M

menu button
working 203
message cards
extracting, to components 19-21

mobile screen
workouts, adding 233, 234
mock 242
mocking functions
reference 249
mockups
about 88
login page 90
logo 96
Pomodoro timer, displaying 91
Settings area 93
statistics 94
workout, during break 92
workouts 95
mode* history option
reference 55
moment.js library
reference 227
mutations, Vuex store
defining 145-148
reference 62

N

navbar component
reference 189
navigation
adding, vue-router used 185-188
restricting, according to authentication 188
navigation links
Bootstrap navbar, using 189-193
nouns
retrieving 86
npm package
reference 218
Nuxt.js
about 196-199
and Vuex store 203, 204
URL 196
Nuxt.js middleware 204, 205
nuxt-link
used, for adding links 200-202
nuxt-starter template
about 197
reference 197

O

offsetting columns
  reference 120
one-way data binding 29

P

path SVG element
  reference 108
personas 82-84
please introduce yourself page
  about 1, 2
  reference 1
Pomodoro technique
  reference 80
Pomodoro timer
  about 128-132
  countdown timer component,
      implementing 117, 118
  implementing 106, 107
  main principles 81
  personalizing 173-176
  SVG and trigonometry 107-116
prerender-spa-plugin
  reference 196
problem
  stating 80
ProFitOro application
  authenticating to 162-168
  reference 268
ProFitOro components
  defining 101-106
project
  creating, in Firebase console 2, 3
pull-* class
  reference 120
push-* class
  reference 120

R

responsive application 280
router-view component
  reference 56

S

server-side rendering (SSSR)
  about 196
  reference 196
services, Firebase
  authentication 76
  database 76
  hosting 76
  storage 76
Single Page Applications (SPA) 53
snapshot testing
  Jest, using 259-263
  reference 263
staging and production environments
  setting up 276-279
style
  applying 227-230

T

template literals
  reference 126
templates, vue-cli
  browserify 32
  browserify-simple 32
  simple 32
  webpack 32
  webpack-simple 32
testing
  importance 235
two-way data binding 29

U

Unified Modeling Language (UML) 85
user profile
  updating 177-181
user stories 84, 85
utility functions
  testing 240, 242

V

verbs
  retrieving 86-88
v-on directive
  reference 123

Vue
  components 46-51
Vue application
  URL 196
vue-cli
  about 31
  reference 31, 99
Vue components
  testing, with Jest 256-258
Vue directives
  about 32
  conditional rendering 33, 34
  data, binding 38, 40, 41
  events, handling 41-46
  loops 37, 38
  text, versus HTML 34-36
Vue documentation
  reference 5
vuefire wrapper
  reference 77
Vue instance 29
Vue.js
  about 28
  combining, with Bootstrap 71-74
  functionalities, adding 14-17
  including, in script 31
  reference 29, 268
  utility functions, adding 17, 18
Vue.js application
  connecting, to Firebase project 6-10
  scaffolding 4, 5
Vue project
  about 31
  CDN version, using 31
  npm dependency, adding to package.json
    file 31
vue-router
  reference 193
  used, for adding navigation 185-188

Vue router 53-56
Vuex
  reference, for modules 138
Vuexfire
  reference 150
Vuex state management architecture 57-65
Vuex store
  actions 138
  connecting, to Firebase database 150-155
  getters 62, 138
  mutations 62, 138
  reference 203
  setting up 137-145
  state 62, 138
  testing, actions 248, 249
  testing, Jest used 246
  testing, mutations 247

W

watchers
  reference 133
web application
  Firebase authentication API, connecting
    to 161, 162
webpack documentation
  reference 194
WireframeSketcher
  reference 89
workout
  about 133, 135
  displaying, with Bootstrap modal 223-227
  storing, with Firebase real-time
    database 211-215

www.ingramcontent.com/pod-product-compliance
Lightning Source LLC
Chambersburg PA
CBHW080626060326
40690CB00021B/4828